The Essential Pinter

HAROLD PINTER

The Essential Pinter

Grove Press
New York

PLAYS

POEMS AND PROSE

FIRST EDITION

Library of Congress Cataloging-in-Publication Data

Pinter, Harold, 1930–
  [Selections. 2006]
  The essential Pinter / Harold Pinter
    p. cm.
  ISBN-10: 0-8021-4269-9
  ISBN-13: 978-0-8021-4269-6
  I. Title
PR6066.I53A6 2006
822'.914—dc22   2006043518

Grove Press
an imprint of Grove/Atlantic, Inc.
841 Broadway
New York, NY 10003

Distributed by Publishers Group West

www.groveatlantic.com

06 07 08 09 10 11 12   10 9 8 7 6 5 4 3 2 1

CONTENTS

Art, Truth, & Politics: The 2005 Nobel Lecture   1

PLAYS

The Birthday Party   15
The Caretaker   103
The Homecoming   181
Landscape   257
Old Times   277
One for the Road   319
Mountain Language   337
Celebration   351
Press Conference   387

POEMS

Paris   395
It Is Here   396
Joseph Brearley 1909–1977 (Teacher of English)   397
Message   398
American Football   399
The Bombs   400
Democracy   401
Cancer Cells   402
Death May Be Ageing   403
Death   404

The Essential Pinter

ART, TRUTH & POLITICS

—

THE NOBEL LECTURE

First aired December 7, 2005 at the
Swedish Academy, Stockholm, Sweden

In 1958 I wrote the following:

"There are no hard distinctions between what is real and what is unreal, nor between what is true and what is false. A thing is not necessarily either true or false; it can be both true and false."

I believe that these assertions still make sense and do still apply to the exploration of reality through art. So as a writer I stand by them but as a citizen I cannot. As a citizen I must ask: What is true? What is false?

Truth in drama is forever elusive. You never quite find it but the search for it is compulsive. The search is clearly what drives the endeavour. The search is your task. More often than not you stumble upon the truth in the dark, colliding with it or just glimpsing an image or a shape which seems to correspond to the truth, often without realising that you have done so. But the real truth is that there never is any such thing as one truth to be found in dramatic art. There are many. These truths challenge each other, recoil from each other, reflect each other, ignore each other, tease each other, are blind to each other. Sometimes you feel you have the truth of a moment in your hand, then it slips through your fingers and is lost.

I have often been asked how my plays come about. I cannot say. Nor can I ever sum up my plays, except to say that this is what happened. That is what they said. That is what they did.

Most of the plays are engendered by a line, a word or an image. The given word is often shortly followed by the image. I shall give two examples of two lines which came right out of the blue into my head, followed by an image, followed by me.

The plays are *The Homecoming* and *Old Times*. The first line of *The Homecoming* is "What have you done with the scissors?" The first line of *Old Times* is "Dark."

In each case I had no further information.

In the first case someone was obviously looking for a pair of scissors and was demanding their whereabouts of someone else he suspected had probably stolen them. But I somehow knew that the person addressed didn't give a damn about the scissors or about the questioner either, for that matter.

"Dark" I took to be a description of someone's hair, the hair of a woman, and was the answer to a question. In each case I found myself compelled to pursue the matter. This happened visually, a very slow fade, through shadow into light.

I always start a play by calling the characters A, B and C.

In the play that became *The Homecoming* I saw a man enter a stark room and ask his question of a younger man sitting on an ugly sofa reading a racing paper. I somehow suspected that A was a father and that B was his son, but I had no proof. This was however confirmed a short time later when B (later to become Lenny) says to A (later to become Max), "Dad, do you mind if I change the subject? I want to ask you something. The dinner we had before, what was the name of it? What do you call it? Why don't you buy a dog? You're a dog cook. Honest. You think you're cooking for a lot of dogs." So since B calls A "Dad" it seemed to me reasonable to assume that they were father and son. A was also clearly the cook and his cooking did not seem to be held in high regard. Did this mean that there was no mother? I didn't know. But, as I told myself at the time, our beginnings never know our ends.

"Dark." A large window. Evening sky. A man, A (later to become Deeley), and a woman, B (later to become Kate), sitting with drinks. "Fat or thin?" the man asks. Who are they talking about? But I then see, standing at the window, a woman, C (later to become Anna), in another condition of light, her back to them, her hair dark.

It's a strange moment, the moment of creating characters who up to that moment have had no existence. What follows is fitful, uncertain, even hallucinatory, although sometimes it can be an unstoppable avalanche. The author's position is an odd one. In a sense he is not welcomed by the characters. The characters resist him, they are not easy to live with, they are impossible to define. You certainly can't dictate to them. To a certain extent you play a never-ending game with them, cat and mouse, blind man's buff, hide and seek. But finally you find that you have people of flesh and blood on your hands, people with will and an individual sensibility of their own, made out of component parts you are unable to change, manipulate or distort.

So language in art remains a highly ambiguous transaction, a quicksand, a trampoline, a frozen pool which might give way under you, the author, at any time.

But as I have said, the search for the truth can never stop. It cannot be adjourned, it cannot be postponed. It has to be faced, right there, on the spot.

Political theatre presents an entirely different set of problems. Sermonising has to be avoided at all cost. Objectivity is essential. The characters must be allowed to breathe their own air. The author cannot confine and constrict them to satisfy his own taste or disposition or prejudice. He must be prepared to approach them from a variety of angles, from a full and uninhibited range of perspectives, take them by surprise, perhaps, occasionally, but nevertheless give them the freedom to go which way they will. This does not always work. And political satire, of course, adheres to none of these precepts, in fact does precisely the opposite, which is its proper function.

In my play *The Birthday Party* I think I allow a whole range of options to operate in a dense forest of possibility before finally focussing on an act of subjugation.

Mountain Language pretends to no such range of operation. It remains brutal, short and ugly. But the soldiers in the play do get some fun out of it. One sometimes forgets that torturers become easily bored. They need a bit of a laugh to keep their spirits up. This has been confirmed of course by the events at Abu Ghraib in Baghdad. *Mountain Language* lasts only twenty minutes, but it could go on for hour after hour, on and on and on, the same pattern repeated over and over again, on and on, hour after hour.

Ashes to Ashes, on the other hand, seems to me to be taking place under water. A drowning woman, her hand reaching up through the waves, dropping down out of sight, reaching for others, but finding nobody there, either above or under the water, finding only shadows, reflections, floating; the woman a lost figure in a drowning landscape, a woman unable to escape the doom that seemed to belong only to others.

But as they died, she must die too.

Political language, as used by politicians, does not venture into any of this territory since the majority of politicians, on the evidence available to us, are interested not in truth but in power and in the maintenance of that power. To maintain that power it is essential that people remain in ignorance, that they live in ignorance of the truth, even the truth of their own lives. What surrounds us therefore is a vast tapestry of lies, upon which we feed.

The justification for the invasion of Iraq was that Saddam Hussein possessed a highly dangerous body of weapons of mass destruction, some of which could be fired in forty-five minutes, bringing about appalling devastation. We

were assured that was true. It was not true. We were told that Iraq had a re-
lationship with Al Quaeda and shared responsibility for the atrocity in New
York of September 11, 2001. We were assured that this was true. It was not
true. We were told that Iraq threatened the security of the world. We were
assured it was true. It was not true.

The truth is something entirely different. The truth is to do with how
the United States understands its role in the world and how it chooses to
embody it.

But before I come back to the present I would like to look at the recent
past, by which I mean United States foreign policy since the end of the
Second World War. I believe it is obligatory upon us to subject this period
to at least some kind of even limited scrutiny, which is all that time will
allow here.

Everyone knows what happened in the Soviet Union and throughout
Eastern Europe during the postwar period: the systematic brutality, the
widespread atrocities, the ruthless suppression of independent thought. All
this has been fully documented and verified.

But my contention here is that the U.S. crimes in the same period have
only been superficially recorded, let alone documented, let alone acknowl-
edged, let alone recognised as crimes at all. I believe this must be addressed
and that the truth has considerable bearing on where the world stands now.
Although constrained, to a certain extent, by the existence of the Soviet
Union, the United States' actions throughout the world made it clear that
it had concluded it had carte blanche to do what it liked.

Direct invasion of a sovereign state has never in fact been America's
favoured method. In the main, it has preferred what it has described as "low-
intensity conflict." Low-intensity conflict means that thousands of people
die but slower than if you dropped a bomb on them in one fell swoop. It
means that you infect the heart of the country, that you establish a malig-
nant growth and watch the gangrene bloom. When the populace has been
subdued—or beaten to death—the same thing —and your own friends, the
military and the great corporations, sit comfortably in power, you go before the camera and say that democracy has prevailed. This was a commonplace in U.S. foreign policy in the years to which I refer.

The tragedy of Nicaragua was a highly significant case. I choose to offer
it here as a potent example of America's view of its role in the world, both
then and now.

I was present at a meeting at the U.S. embassy in London in the late 1980s.

The United States Congress was about to decide whether to give more money to the Contras in their campaign against the state of Nicaragua. I was a member of a delegation speaking on behalf of Nicaragua but the most important member of this delegation was a Father John Medcalf. The leader of the U.S. body was Raymond Seitz (then number two to the ambassador, later ambassador himself). Father Medcalf said: "Sir, I am in charge of a parish in the north of Nicaragua. My parishioners built a school, a health centre, a cultural centre. We have lived in peace. A few months ago a Contra force attacked the parish. They destroyed everything: the school, the health centre, the cultural centre. They raped nurses and teachers, slaughtered doctors, in the most brutal manner. They behaved like savages. Please demand that the U.S. government withdraw its support from this shocking terrorist activity."

Raymond Seitz had a very good reputation as a rational, responsible and highly sophisticated man. He was greatly respected in diplomatic circles. He listened, paused and then spoke with some gravity. "Father," he said, "let me tell you something. In war, innocent people always suffer." There was a frozen silence. We stared at him. He did not flinch.

Innocent people, indeed, always suffer.

Finally somebody said: "But in this case 'innocent people' were the victims of a gruesome atrocity subsidised by your government, one among many. If Congress allows the Contras more money further atrocities of this kind will take place. Is this not the case? Is your government not therefore guilty of supporting acts of murder and destruction upon the citizens of a sovereign state?"

Seitz was imperturbable. "I don't agree that the facts as presented support your assertions," he said.

As we were leaving the embassy a U.S. aide told me that he enjoyed my plays. I did not reply.

I should remind you that at the time President Reagan made the following statement: "The Contras are the moral equivalent of our Founding Fathers."

The United States supported the brutal Somoza dictatorship in Nicaragua for over forty years. The Nicaraguan people, led by the Sandinistas, overthrew this regime in 1979, a breathtaking popular revolution.

The Sandinistas weren't perfect. They possessed their fair share of arrogance and their political philosophy contained a number of contradictory elements. But they were intelligent, rational and civilised. They set out to establish a stable, decent, pluralistic society. The death penalty was abolished.

Hundreds of thousands of poverty-stricken peasants were brought back from the dead. Over 100,000 families were given title to land. Two thousand schools were built. A quite remarkable literacy campaign reduced illiteracy in the country to less than one seventh. Free education was established and a free health service. Infant mortality was reduced by a third. Polio was eradicated.

The United States denounced these achievements as Marxist/Leninist subversion. In the view of the U.S. government, a dangerous example was being set. If Nicaragua was allowed to establish basic norms of social and economic justice, if it was allowed to raise the standards of health care and education and achieve social unity and national self-respect, neighbouring countries would ask the same questions and do the same things. There was of course at the time fierce resistance to the status quo in El Salvador.

I spoke earlier about "a tapestry of lies" which surrounds us. President Reagan commonly described Nicaragua as a "totalitarian dungeon." This was taken generally by the media, and certainly by the British government, as accurate and fair comment. But there was in fact no record of death squads under the Sandinista government. There was no record of torture. There was no record of systematic or official military brutality. No priests were ever murdered in Nicaragua. There were in fact three priests in the government, two Jesuits and a Maryknoll missionary. The totalitarian dungeons were actually next door, in El Salvador and Guatemala. The United States had brought down the democratically elected government of Guatemala in 1954 and it is estimated that over 200,000 people had been victims of successive military dictatorships.

Six of the most distinguished Jesuits in the world were viciously murdered at the Central American University in San Salvador in 1989 by a battalion of the Atlacatl regiment trained at Fort Benning, Georgia, USA. That extremely brave man Archbishop Romero was assassinated while saying mass. It is estimated that 75,000 people died. Why were they killed? They were killed because they believed a better life was possible and should be achieved. That belief immediately qualified them as communists. They died because they dared to question the status quo, the endless plateau of poverty, disease, degradation and oppression, which had been their birthright.

The United States finally brought down the Sandinista government. It took some years and considerable resistance but relentless economic persecution and 30,000 dead finally undermined the spirit of the Nicaraguan people. They were exhausted and poverty-stricken once again. The casinos moved back into the country. Free health and free education were over. Big business returned with a vengeance. "Democracy" had prevailed.

But this "policy" was by no means restricted to Central America. It was conducted throughout the world. It was never-ending. And it is as if it never happened.

The United States supported and in many cases engendered every right-wing military dictatorship in the world after the end of the Second World War. I refer to Indonesia, Greece, Uruguay, Brazil, Paraguay, Haiti, Turkey, the Philippines, Guatemala, El Salvador, and, of course, Chile. The horror the United States inflicted upon Chile in 1973 can never be purged and can never be forgiven.

Hundreds of thousands of deaths took place throughout these countries. Did they take place? And are they in all cases attributable to U.S. foreign policy? The answer is yes they did take place and they are attributable to American foreign policy. But you wouldn't know it.

It never happened. Nothing ever happened. Even while it was happening it wasn't happening. It didn't matter. It was of no interest. The crimes of the United States have been systematic, constant, vicious, remorseless, but very few people have actually talked about them. You have to hand it to America. It has exercised a quite clinical manipulation of power worldwide while masquerading as a force for universal good. It's a brilliant, even witty, highly successful act of hypnosis.

I put to you that the United States is without doubt the greatest show on the road. Brutal, indifferent, scornful and ruthless it may be but it is also very clever. As a salesman it is out on its own and its most saleable commodity is self-love. It's a winner. Listen to all American presidents on television say the words, "the American people," as in the sentence, "I say to the American people it is time to pray and to defend the rights of the American people and I ask the American people to trust their president in the action he is about to take on behalf of the American people."

It's a scintillating stratagem. Language is actually employed to keep thought at bay. The words "the American people" provide a truly voluptuous cushion of reassurance. You don't need to think. Just lie back on the cushion. The cushion may be suffocating your intelligence and your critical faculties but it's very comfortable. This does not apply of course to the forty million people living below the poverty line and the two million men and women imprisoned in the vast gulag of prisons, which extends across the United States.

The United States no longer bothers about low-intensity conflict. It no longer sees any point in being reticent or even devious. It puts its cards on the table without fear or favour. It quite simply doesn't give a damn about the United Nations, international law or critical dissent, which it regards as impotent and irrelevant. It also has its own bleating little lamb tagging behind it on a lead, the pathetic and supine Great Britain.

What has happened to our moral sensibility? Did we ever have any? What do these words mean? Do they refer to a term very rarely employed these days—conscience? A conscience to do not only with our own acts but to do with our shared responsibility in the acts of others? Is all this dead? Look at Guantanamo Bay. Hundreds of people detained without charge for over three years, with no legal representation or due process, technically detained forever. This totally illegitimate structure is maintained in defiance of the Geneva Convention. It is not only tolerated but hardly thought about by what's called the "international community." This criminal outrage is being committed by a country, which declares itself to be "the leader of the free world." Do we think about the inhabitants of Guantanamo Bay? What does the media say about them? They pop up occasionally—a small item on page six. They have been consigned to a no man's land from which indeed they may never return. At present many are on hunger strike, being force-fed, including British residents. No niceties in these force-feeding procedures. No sedative or anaesthetic. Just a tube stuck up your nose and into your throat. You vomit blood. This is torture. What has the British foreign secretary said about this? Nothing. What has the British prime minister said about this? Nothing. Why not? Because the United States has said: to criticise our conduct in Guantanamo Bay constitutes an unfriendly act. You're either with us or against us. So Blair shuts up.

The invasion of Iraq was a bandit act, an act of blatant state terrorism, demonstrating absolute contempt for the concept of international law. The invasion was an arbitrary military action inspired by a series of lies upon lies and gross manipulation of the media and therefore of the public; an act intended to consolidate American military and economic control of the Middle East masquerading —as a last resort—all other justifications having failed to justify themselves—as liberation. A formidable assertion of military force responsible for the death and mutilation of thousands and thousands of innocent people.

We have brought torture, cluster bombs, depleted uranium, innumerable acts of random murder, misery, degradation and death to the Iraqi people and call it "bringing freedom and democracy to the Middle East."

How many people do you have to kill before you qualify to be described as a mass murderer and a war criminal? One hundred thousand? More than enough, I would have thought. Therefore it is just that Bush and Blair be arraigned before the International Criminal Court of Justice. But Bush has been clever. He has not ratified the International Criminal Court of Justice. Therefore if any American soldier or for that matter politician finds himself in the dock Bush has warned that he will send in the marines. But Tony Blair has ratified the Court and is therefore available for prosecution. We can let the Court have his address if they're interested. It is Number 10, Downing Street, London.

Death in this context is irrelevant. Both Bush and Blair place death well away on the back burner. At least 100,000 Iraqis were killed by American bombs and missiles before the Iraq insurgency began. These people are of no moment. Their deaths don't exist. They are blank. They are not even recorded as being dead. "We don't do body counts," said the American general Tommy Franks.

Early in the invasion there was a photograph published on the front page of British newspapers of Tony Blair kissing the cheek of a little Iraqi boy. "A grateful child," said the caption. A few days later there was a story and photograph, on an inside page, of another four-year-old boy with no arms. His family had been blown up by a missile. He was the only survivor. "When do I get my arms back?" he asked. The story was dropped. Well, Tony Blair wasn't holding him in his arms, nor the body of any other mutilated child, nor the body of any bloody corpse. Blood is dirty. It dirties your shirt and tie when you're making a sincere speech on television.

The two thousand American dead are an embarrassment. They are transported to their graves in the dark. Funerals are unobtrusive, out of harm's way. The mutilated rot in their beds, some for the rest of their lives. So the dead and the mutilated both rot, in different kinds of graves.

Here is an extract from a poem by Pablo Neruda, "I'm Explaining a Few Things":

A FEW THINGS EXPLAINED

Till one morning everything blazed:
one morning bonfires
sprang out of earth
and devoured all the living;
since then, only fire,
since then, the blood and the gunpowder,
ever since then.

Bandits in airplanes, Moors
and marauders with seal rings and duchesses,
black friars and brigands signed with the cross, coming
out of the clouds to a slaughter of innocents:
the blood of the children was seen in the streets,
flowing easily out, in the habit of children.

Jackals abhorred by the jackal!
Spittle of stones that the thirst of the thistle rejected,
vipers despised by the viper!

In sight of you now, I have seen
Spain uplifting its blood
in a torrent
of knives and defiance, to carry you under!

Turncoats
and generals:
see the death of my house,
look well at the havoc of Spain:
out of dead houses it is metal that blazes
in place of the flowers,
out of the ditches of Spain
it is Spain that emerges,
out of the murder of children, a gunsight with eyes,
out of your turpitude; bullets are born
that one day will strike for the mark
of your hearts.

Would you know why his poems
never mention the soil or the leaves,
the gigantic volcanoes of the country that bore him?

Come see the blood in the streets,
come see
the blood in the streets,
come see the blood
in the streets!

Let me make it quite clear that in quoting from Neruda's poem I am in
no way comparing Republican Spain to Saddam Hussein's Iraq. I quote
Neruda because nowhere in contemporary poetry have I read such a pow-
erful visceral description of the bombing of civilians.

I have said earlier that the United States is now totally frank about putting its cards on the table. That is the case. Its official declared policy is now
defined as "full-spectrum dominance." That is not my term, it is theirs. "Full-
spectrum dominance" means control of land, sea, air and space and all attendant resources.

The United States now occupies 702 military installations throughout
the world in 132 countries, with the honourable exception of Sweden, of
course. We don't quite know how they got there but they are there all
right.

The United States possesses eight thousand active and operational nuclear
warheads. Two thousand are on hair-trigger alert, ready to be launched with
fifteen minutes' warning. It is developing new systems of nuclear force,
known as bunker busters. The British, ever cooperative, are intending to
replace their own nuclear missile, Trident. Who, I wonder, are they aim-
ing at? Osama bin Laden? You? Me? Joe Dokes? China? Paris? Who knows?
What we do know is that this infantile insanity—the possession and threatened use of nuclear weapons—is at the heart of present American political
philosophy. We must remind ourselves that the United States is on a per-
manent military footing and shows no sign of relaxing it.

Many thousands, if not millions, of people in the United States itself are
demonstrably sickened, shamed and angered by their government's actions,
but as things stand they are not a coherent political force—yet. But the
anxiety, uncertainty and fear which we can see growing daily in the United
States is unlikely to diminish.

I know that President Bush has many extremely competent speech writers but I would like to volunteer for the job myself. I propose the following short address which he can make on television to the nation. I see him grave, hair carefully combed, serious, winning, sincere, often beguiling, sometimes employing a wry smile, curiously attractive, a man's man.

"God is good. God is great. God is good. My God is good. Bin Laden's God is bad. His is a bad God. Saddam's God was bad, except he didn't have one. He was a barbarian. We are not barbarians. We don't chop people's heads off. We believe in freedom. So does God. I am not a barbarian. I am the democratically elected leader of a freedom-loving democracy. We are a compassionate society. We give compassionate electrocution and compassionate lethal injection. We are a great nation. I am not a dictator. He is. I am not a barbarian. He is. And he is. They all are. I possess moral authority. You see this fist? This is my moral authority. And don't you forget it."

A writer's life is a highly vulnerable, almost naked activity. We don't have to weep about that. The writer makes his choice and is stuck with it. But it is true to say that you are open to all the winds, some of them icy indeed. You are out on your own, out on a limb. You find no shelter, no protection—unless you lie—in which case of course you have constructed your own protection and, it could be argued, become a politician.

I have referred to death quite a few times in this speech. I shall now quote a poem of my own called "Death."

Where was the dead body found?
Who found the dead body?
Was the dead body dead when found?
How was the dead body found?

Who was the dead body?

Who was the father or daughter or brother
Or uncle or sister or mother or son
Of the dead and abandoned body?

Was the body dead when abandoned?
Was the body abandoned?
By whom had it been abandoned?

Was the dead body naked or dressed for a journey?

What made you declare the dead body dead?
Did you declare the dead body dead?
How well did you know the dead body?
How did you know the dead body was dead?

Did you wash the dead body
Did you close both its eyes
Did you bury the body
Did you leave it abandoned
Did you kiss the dead body

When we look into a mirror we think the image that confronts us is accurate. But move a millimetre and the image changes. We are actually looking at a never-ending range of reflections. But sometimes a writer has to smash the mirror—for it is on the other side of that mirror that the truth stares at us.

I believe that despite the enormous odds which exist, unflinching, unswerving, fierce intellectual determination, as citizens, to define the *real* truth of our lives and our societies is a crucial obligation which devolves upon us all. It is in fact mandatory.

If such a determination is not embodied in our political vision we have no hope of restoring what is so nearly lost to us—the dignity of man.

THE BIRTHDAY PARTY

The Birthday Party was first presented by Michael Codron and David Hall at the Arts Theatre, Cambridge, on April 28, 1958, and subsequently at the Lyric Opera House, Hammersmith, with the following cast:

PETEY, *a man in his sixties*   Willoughby Gray
MEG, *a woman in her sixties*   Beatrix Lehmann
STANLEY, *a man in his late thirties*   Richard Pearson
LULU, *a girl in her twenties*   Wendy Hutchinson
GOLDBERG, *a man in his fifties*   John Slater
MCCANN, a *man of thirty*   John Stratton

Directed by Peter Wood

The Birthday Party was revived by the Royal Shakespeare Company at the Aldwych Theatre, London, on June 18, 1964 with the following cast:

PETEY   Newton Buck
MEG   Doris Hare
STANLEY   Bryan Pringle
LULU   Janet Suzman
GOLDBERG   Brewster Mason
MCCANN   Patrick Magee

Directed by Harold Pinter

ACT I   A morning in summer
ACT II   Evening of the same day
ACT III   The next morning

ACT ONE

The living-room of a house in a seaside town. A door leading to the hall down left. Back door and small window up left. Kitchen hatch, centre back. Kitchen door up right. Table and chairs, centre.

PETEY enters from the door on the left with a paper and sits at the table. He begins to read. MEG's voice comes through the kitchen hatch.

MEG   Is that you, Petey?

Pause.

MEG (*cont.*)   Petey, is that you?

Pause.

MEG (*cont.*)   Petey?

PETEY   What?

MEG   Is that you?

PETEY   Yes, it's me.

MEG   What? (*Her face appears at the hatch.*) Are you back?

PETEY   Yes.

MEG   I've got your cornflakes ready. (*She disappears and reappears.*) Here's your cornflakes.

He rises and takes the plate from her, sits at the table, props up the paper and begins to eat. Meg enters by the kitchen door.

MEG (*cont.*)   Are they nice?

PETEY   Very nice.

MEG   I thought they'd be nice. (*She sits at the table.*) You got your paper?

PETEY   Yes.

MEG   Is it good?

PETEY   Not bad.

MEG   What does it say?

19

PETEY   Nothing much.

MEG   You read me out some nice bits yesterday.

PETEY   Yes, well, I haven't finished this one yet.

MEG   Will you tell me when you come to something good?

PETEY   Yes.

Pause.

MEG   Have you been working hard this morning?

PETEY   No. Just stacked a few of the old chairs. Cleaned up a bit.

MEG   Is it nice out?

PETEY   Very nice.

Pause.

MEG   Is Stanley up yet?

PETEY   I don't know. Is he?

MEG   I don't know. I haven't seen him down yet.

PETEY   Well then, he can't be up.

MEG   Haven't you seen him down?

PETEY   I've only just come in.

MEG   He must be still asleep.

She looks round the room, stands, goes to the sideboard and takes a pair of socks from a drawer, collects wool and a needle and goes back to the table.

MEG (*cont.*)   What time did you go out this morning, Petey?

PETEY   Same time as usual.

MEG   Was it dark?

PETEY   No, it was light.

MEG (*beginning to darn*)   But sometimes you go out in the morning and it's dark.

PETEY   That's in the winter.

MEG Oh, in winter.

PETEY Yes, it gets light later in winter.

MEG Oh.

Pause.

MEG (*cont.*) What are you reading?

PETEY Someone's just had a baby.

MEG Oh, they haven't! Who?

PETEY Some girl.

MEG Who, Petey, who?

PETEY I don't think you'd know her.

MEG What's her name?

PETEY Lady Mary Splatt.

MEG I don't know her.

PETEY No.

MEG What is it?

PETEY (*studying the paper*) Er—a girl.

MEG Not a boy?

PETEY No.

MEG Oh, what a shame. I'd be sorry. I'd much rather have a little boy.

PETEY A little girl's all right.

MEG I'd much rather have a little boy.

Pause.

PETEY I've finished my cornflakes.

MEG Were they nice?

PETEY Very nice.

MEG I've got something else for you.

PETEY Good.

She rises, takes his plate and exits into the kitchen. She then appears at the hatch with two pieces of fried bread on a plate.

MEG Here you are, Petey.

He rises, collects the plate, looks at it, sits at the table. Meg re-enters.

MEG (*cont.*) Is it nice?

PETEY I haven't tasted it yet.

MEG I bet you don't know what it is.

PETEY Yes, I do.

MEG What is it, then?

PETEY Fried bread.

MEG That's right.

He begins to eat.

She watches him eat.

PETEY Very nice.

MEG I knew it was.

PETEY (*turning to her*) Oh, Meg, two men came up to me on the beach last night.

MEG Two men?

PETEY Yes. They wanted to know if we could put them up for a couple of nights.

MEG Put them up? Here?

PETEY Yes.

MEG How many men?

PETEY Two.

MEG What did you say?

PETEY Well, I said I didn't know. So they said they'd come round to find out.

MEG   Are they coming?

PETEY   Well, they said they would.

MEG   Had they heard about us, Petey?

PETEY   They must have done.

MEG   Yes, they must have done. They must have heard this was a very good boarding house. It is. This house is on the list.

PETEY   It is.

MEG   I know it is.

PETEY   They might turn up today. Can you do it?

MEG   Oh, I've got that lovely room they can have.

PETEY   You've got a room ready?

MEG   I've got the room with the armchair all ready for visitors.

PETEY   You're sure?

MEG   Yes, that'll be all right then, if they come today.

PETEY   Good.

She takes the socks, etc. back to the sideboard drawer.

MEG   I'm going to wake that boy.

PETEY   There's a new show coming to the Palace.

MEG   On the pier?

PETEY   No. The Palace, in the town.

MEG   Stanley could have been in it, if it was on the pier.

PETEY   This is a straight show.

MEG   What do you mean?

PETEY   No dancing or singing.

MEG   What do they do then?

PETEY   They just talk.

Pause.

MEG   Oh.

PETEY   You like a song, eh, Meg?

MEG   I like listening to the piano. I used to like watching Stanley play the piano. Of course, he didn't sing. (*looking at the door*) I'm going to call that boy.

PETEY   Didn't you take him up his cup of tea?

MEG   I always take him up his cup of tea. But that was a long time ago.

PETEY   Did he drink it?

MEG   I made him. I stood there till he did. I'm going to call him. (*She goes to the door.*) Stan! Stanny! (*She listens.*) Stan! I'm coming up to fetch you if you don't come down! I'm coming up! I'm going to count three! One! Two! Three! I'm coming to get you! (*She exits and goes upstairs. In a moment, shouts from* STANLEY, *wild laughter from Meg. Petey takes his plate to the hatch. Shouts. Laughter. Petey sits a the table. Silence. She returns.*) He's coming down. (*She is panting and arranges her hair.*) I told him if he didn't hurry up he'd get no breakfast.

PETEY   That did it, eh?

MEG   I'll get his cornflakes.

Meg exits to the kitchen. Petey reads the paper. Stanley enters. He is unshaven, in his pyjama jacket and wears glasses. He sits at the table.

PETEY   Morning, Stanley.

STANLEY   Morning.

Silence. Meg enters with the bowl of cornflakes, which she sets on the table.

MEG   So he's come down at last, has he? He's come down at last for his breakfast. But he doesn't deserve any, does he, Petey? (*Stanley stares at the cornflakes.*) Did you sleep well?

STANLEY   I didn't sleep at all.

MEG   You didn't sleep at all? Did you hear that, Petey? Too tired to eat your breakfast, I suppose? Now you eat up those cornflakes like a good boy. Go on.

24

He begins to eat.

STANLEY What's it like out today?

PETEY Very nice.

STANLEY Warm?

PETEY Well, there's a good breeze blowing.

STANLEY Cold?

PETEY No, no, I wouldn't say it was cold.

MEG What are the cornflakes like, Stan?

STANLEY Horrible.

MEG Those flakes? Those lovely flakes? You're a liar, a little liar. They're refreshing. It says so. For people when they get up late.

STANLEY The milk's off.

MEG It's not. Petey ate his, didn't you, Petey?

PETEY That's right.

MEG There you are then.

STANLEY All right, I'll go on to the second course.

MEG He hasn't finished the first course and he wants to go on to the second course!

STANLEY I feel like something cooked.

MEG Well, I'm not going to give it to you.

PETEY Give it to him.

MEG (*sitting at the table, right*) I'm not going to.

Pause.

STANLEY No breakfast.

Pause.

STANLEY (*cont.*) All night long I've been dreaming about this breakfast.

MEG I thought you said you didn't sleep.

STANLEY   Day-dreaming. All night long. And now she won't give me any. Not even a crust of bread on the table.

Pause.

STANLEY (*cont.*)   Well, I can see I'll have to go down to one of those smart hotels on the front.

MEG (*rising quickly*)   You won't get a better breakfast there than here.

She exits to the kitchen. Stanley yawns broadly. Meg appears at the hatch with a plate.

MEG (*cont.*)   Here you are. You'll like this.

Petey rises, collects the plate, brings it to the table, puts it in front of Stanley, and sits.

STANLEY   What's this?

PETEY   Fried bread.

MEG (*entering*)   Well, I bet you don't know what it is.

STANLEY   Oh yes I do

MEG   What?

STANLEY   Fried bread.

MEG   He knew.

STANLEY   What a wonderful surprise.

MEG   You didn't expect that, did you?

STANLEY   I bloody well didn't.

PETEY (*rising*)   Well, I'm off.

MEG   You going back to work?

PETEY   Yes.

MEG   Your tea! You haven't had your tea!

PETEY   That's all right. No time now.

MEG   I've got it made inside.

PETEY   No, never mind. See you later. Ta-ta, Stan.

STANLEY   Ta-ta.

Petey exits, left.

STANLEY (*cont.*)   Tch, tch, tch, tch.

MEG (*defensively*)   What do you mean?

STANLEY   You're a bad wife.

MEG   I'm not. Who said I am?

STANLEY   Not to make your husband a cup of tea. Terrible.

MEG   He knows I'm not a bad wife.

STANLEY   Giving him sour milk instead.

MEG   It wasn't sour.

STANLEY   Disgraceful.

MEG   You mind your own business, anyway. (*Stanley eats.*) You won't find many better wives than me, I can tell you. I keep a very nice house and I keep it clean.

STANLEY   Whoo!

MEG   Yes! And this house is very well known, for a very good boarding house for visitors.

STANLEY   Visitors? Do you know how many visitors you've had since I've been here?

MEG   How many?

STANLEY   One.

MEG   Who?

STANLEY   Me! I'm your visitor.

MEG   You're a liar. This house is on the list.

STANLEY   I bet it is.

MEG   I know it is.

He pushes his plate away and picks up the paper.

MEG (*cont.*)   Was it nice?

STANLEY   What?

MEG   The fried bread.

STANLEY   Succulent.

MEG   You shouldn't say that word.

STANLEY   What word?

MEG   That word you said.

STANLEY   What, succulent—?

MEG   Don't say it!

STANLEY   What's the matter with it?

MEG   You shouldn't say that word to a married woman.

STANLEY   Is that a fact?

MEG   Yes.

STANLEY   Well, I never knew that.

MEG   Well, it's true.

STANLEY   Who told you that?

MEG   Never you mind.

STANLEY   Well, if I can't say it to a married woman who can I say it to?

MEG   You're bad.

STANLEY   What about some tea?

MEG   Do you want some tea? (*Stanley reads the paper.*) Say please.

STANLEY   Please.

MEG   Say sorry first.

STANLEY   Sorry first.

MEG   No. Just sorry.

STANLEY   Just sorry!

MEG   You deserve the strap.

STANLEY   Don't do that!

She takes his plate and ruffles his hair as she passes. Stanley exclaims and throws her arm away. She goes into the kitchen. He rubs his eyes under his glasses and picks up the paper. She enters.

MEG   I brought the pot in.

STANLEY (*absently*)   I don't know what I'd do without you.

MEG   You don't deserve it though.

STANLEY   Why not?

MEG (*pouring the tea, coyly*)   Go on. Calling me that.

STANLEY   How long has that tea been in the pot?

MEG   It's good tea. Good strong tea.

STANLEY   This isn't tea. It's gravy!

MEG   It's not.

STANLEY   Get out of it. You succulent old washing bag.

MEG   I am not! And it isn't your place to tell me if I am!

STANLEY   And it isn't your place to come into a man's bedroom and— wake him up.

MEG   Stanny! Don't you like your cup of tea of a morning—the one I bring you?

STANLEY   I can't drink this muck. Didn't anyone ever tell you to warm the pot, at least?

MEG   That's good strong tea, that's all.

STANLEY (*putting his head in his hands*)   Oh God, I'm tired.

Silence. Meg goes to the sideboard, collects a duster, and vaguely dusts the room, watching him. She comes to the table and dusts it.

STANLEY (*cont.*)   Not the bloody table!

Pause.

MEG   Stan?

STANLEY What?

MEG (*shyly*) Am I really succulent?

STANLEY Oh, you are. I'd rather have you than a cold in the nose any day.

MEG You're just saying that.

STANLEY (*violently*) Look, why don't you get this place cleared up! It's a pigsty. And another thing, what about my room? It needs sweeping. It needs papering. I need a new room!

MEG (*sensual, stroking his arm*) Oh, Stan, that's a lovely room. I've had some lovely afternoons in that room.

He recoils from her hand in disgust, stands and exits quickly by the door on the left. She collects his cup and the teapot and takes them to the hatch shelf. The street door slams. Stanley returns.

MEG Is the sun shining? (*Stanley crosses to the window, takes a cigarette and matches from his pyjama jacket, and lights his cigarette.*) What are you smoking?

STANLEY A cigarette.

MEG Are you going to give me one?

STANLEY No.

MEG I like cigarettes. (*Stanley stands at the window, smoking. Meg crosses behind him and tickles the back of his neck.*) Tickle, tickle.

STANLEY (*pushing her*) Get away from me.

MEG Are you going out?

STANLEY Not with you.

MEG But I'm going shopping in a minute.

STANLEY Go.

MEG You'll be lonely, all by yourself.

STANLEY Will I?

MEG Without your old Meg. I've got to get things in for the two gentlemen.

A pause. Stanley slowly raises his head. He speaks without turning.

STANLEY   What two gentlemen?

MEG   I'm expecting visitors.

He turns.

STANLEY   What?

MEG   You didn't know that, did you?

STANLEY   What are you talking about?

MEG   Two gentlemen asked Petey if they could come and stay for a couple of nights. I'm expecting them. (*She picks up the duster and begins to wipe the cloth on the table.*)

STANLEY   I don't believe it.

MEG   It's true.

STANLEY (*moving to her*)   You're saying it on purpose.

MEG   Petey told me this morning.

STANLEY (*grinding his cigarette*)   When was this? When did he see them?

MEG   Last night.

STANLEY   Who are they?

MEG   I don't know.

STANLEY   Didn't he tell you their names?

MEG   No.

STANLEY (*pacing the room*)   Here? They wanted to come here?

MEG   Yes, they did. (*She takes the curlers out of her hair.*)

STANLEY   Why?

MEG   This house is on the list.

STANLEY   But who are they?

MEG   You'll see when they come.

STANLEY (*decisively*)   They won't come.

MEG Why not?

STANLEY (*quickly*) I tell you they won't come. Why didn't they come last night, if they were coming?

MEG Perhaps they couldn't find the place in the dark. It's not easy to find in the dark.

STANLEY They won't come. Someone's taking the Michael. Forget all about it. It's a false alarm. A false alarm. (*He sits at the table.*) Where's my tea?

MEG I took it away. You didn't want it.

STANLEY What do you mean, you took it away?

MEG I took it away.

STANLEY What did you take it away for?

MEG You didn't want it!

STANLEY Who said I didn't want it?

MEG You did!

STANLEY Who gave you the right to take away my tea?

MEG You wouldn't drink it.

Stanley stares at her.

STANLEY (*quietly*) Who do you think you're talking to?

MEG (*uncertainly*) What?

STANLEY Come here.

MEG What do you mean?

STANLEY Come over here.

MEG No.

STANLEY I want to ask you something. (*Meg fidgets nervously. She does not go to him.*) Come on. (*Pause.*) All right. I can ask it from here just as well. (*deliberately*) Tell me, Mrs Boles, when you address yourself to me, do you ever ask yourself who exactly you are talking to? Eh?

Silence. He groans, his trunk falls forward, his head falls into his hands.

MEG (*in a small voice*) Didn't you enjoy your breakfast, Stan? (*She approaches the table.*) Stan? When are you going to play the piano again? (*Stanley grunts.*) Like you used to? (*Stanley grunts.*) I used to like watching you play the piano. When are you going to play it again?

STANLEY I can't, can I?

MEG Why not?

STANLEY I haven't got a piano, have I?

MEG No, I meant like when you were working. That piano.

STANLEY Go and do your shopping.

MEG But you wouldn't have to go away if you got a job, would you? You could play the piano on the pier.

He looks at her, then speaks airily.

STANLEY I've . . . er . . . I've been offered a job, as a matter of fact.

MEG What?

STANLEY Yes. I'm considering a job at the moment.

MEG You're not.

STANLEY A good one, too. A night club. In Berlin.

MEG Berlin?

STANLEY Berlin. A night club. Playing the piano. A fabulous salary. And all found.

MEG How long for?

STANLEY We don't stay in Berlin. Then we go to Athens.

MEG How long for?

STANLEY Yes. Then we pay a flying visit to . . . er . . . whatsisname. . . .

MEG Where?

STANLEY Constantinople. Zagreb. Vladivostock. It's a round the world tour.

MEG (*sitting at the table*)   Have you played the piano in those places before?

STANLEY   Played the piano? I've played the piano all over the world. All over the country. (*Pause.*) I once gave a concert.

MEG   A concert?

STANLEY (*reflectively*)   Yes. It was a good one, too. They were all there that night. Every single one of them. It was a great success. Yes. A concert. At Lower Edmonton.

MEG   What did you wear?

STANLEY (*to himself*)   I had a unique touch. Absolutely unique. They came up to me. They came up to me and said they were grateful. Champagne we had that night, the lot. (*Pause.*) My father nearly came down to hear me. Well, I dropped him a card anyway. But I don't think he could make it. No, I—I lost the address, that was it. (*Pause.*) Yes. Lower Edmonton. Then after that, you know what they did? They carved me up. Carved me up. It was all arranged, it was all worked out. My next concert. Somewhere else it was. In winter. I went down there to play. Then, when I got there, the hall was closed, the place was shuttered up, not even a caretaker. They'd locked it up. (*takes off his glasses and wipes them on his pyjama jacket*) A fast one. They pulled a fast one. I'd like to know who was responsible for that. (*bitterly*) All right, Jack, I can take a tip. They want me to crawl down on my bended knees. Well, I can take a tip . . . any day of the week. (*He replaces his glasses, then looks at Meg.*) Look at her. You're just an old piece of rock cake, aren't you? (*He rises and leans across the table to her.*) That's what you are, aren't you?

MEG   Don't you go away again, Stan. You stay here. You'll be better off. You stay with your old Meg. (*He groans and lies across the table.*) Aren't you feeling well this morning, Stan? Did you pay a visit this morning?

He stiffens, then lifts himself slowly, turns to face her and speaks lightly, casually.

STANLEY   Meg. Do you know what?

MEG   What?

STANLEY   Have you heard the latest?

34

MEG No.

STANLEY I'll bet you have.

MEG I haven't.

STANLEY Shall I tell you?

MEG What latest?

STANLEY You haven't heard it?

MEG No.

STANLEY (*advancing*) They're coming today. They're coming in a van.

MEG Who?

STANLEY And do you know what they've got in that van?

MEG What?

STANLEY They've got a wheelbarrow in that van.

MEG (*breathlessly*) They haven't.

STANLEY Oh yes they have.

MEG You're a liar.

STANLEY (*advancing upon her*) A big wheelbarrow. And when the van stops they wheel it out, and they wheel it up the garden path, and then they knock at the front door.

MEG They don't.

STANLEY They're looking for someone.

MEG They're not.

STANLEY They're looking for someone. A certain person.

MEG (*hoarsely*) No, they're not!

STANLEY Shall I tell you who they're looking for?

MEG No!

STANLEY You don't want me to tell you?

MEG You're a liar!

A sudden knock on the front door. LULU's voice: Ooh-ooh! Meg edges past Stanley and collects her shopping bag. Meg goes out. Stanley sidles to the door and listens.

VOICE (*through letter box*) Hullo, Mrs Boles . . .

MEG Oh, has it come?

VOICE Yes, it's just come.

MEG What, is that it?

VOICE Yes. I thought I'd bring it round.

MEG Is it nice?

VOICE Very nice. What shall I do with it?

MEG Well, I don't . . . (*whispers*)

VOICE No, of course not . . . (*whispers*)

MEG All right, but . . . (*whispers*)

VOICE I won't . . . (*whispers*) Ta-ta, Mrs Boles.

Stanley quickly sits at the table. Enter Lulu.

LULU Oh, hullo.

STANLEY Ay-ay.

LULU I just want to leave this in here.

STANLEY Do. (*Lulu crosses to the sideboard and puts a solid, round parcel upon it.*) That's a bulky object.

LULU You're not to touch it.

STANLEY Why would I want to touch it?

LULU Well, you're not to, anyway.

Lulu walks upstage.

LULU (*cont.*) Why don't you open the door? It's all stuffy in here. (*She opens the back door.*)

STANLEY (*rising*) Stuffy? I disinfected the place this morning.

LULU (*at the door*) Oh, that's better.

STANLEY   I think it's going to rain to-day. What do you think?

LULU   I hope so. You could do with it.

STANLEY   Me! I was in the sea at half past six.

LULU   Were you?

STANLEY   I went right out to the headland and back before breakfast. Don't you believe me!

She sits, takes out a compact and powders her nose.

LULU (*offering him the compact*)   Do you want to have a look at your face? (*Stanley withdraws from the table.*) You could do with a shave, do you know that? (*Stanley sits, right at the table.*) Don't you ever go out? (*He does not answer.*) I mean, what do you do, just sit around the house like this all day long? (*Pause.*) Hasn't Mrs Boles got enough to do without having you under her feet all day long?

STANLEY   I always stand on the table when she sweeps the floor.

LULU   Why don't you have a wash? You look terrible.

STANLEY   A wash wouldn't make any difference.

LULU (*rising*)   Come out and get a bit of air. You depress me, looking like that.

STANLEY   Air? Oh, I don't know about that.

LULU   It's lovely out. And I've got a few sandwiches.

STANLEY   What sort of sandwiches?

LULU   Cheese.

STANLEY   I'm a big eater, you know.

LULU   That's all right. I'm not hungry.

STANLEY (*abruptly*)   How would you like to go away with me?

LULU   Where.

STANLEY   Nowhere. Still, we could go.

LULU   But where could we go?

STANLEY   Nowhere. There's nowhere to go. So we could just go. It wouldn't matter.

LULU   We might as well stay here.

STANLEY   No. It's no good here.

LULU   Well, where else is there?

STANLEY   Nowhere.

LULU   Well, that's a charming proposal. (*He gets up.*) Do you have to wear those glasses?

STANLEY   Yes.

LULU   So you're not coming out for a walk?

STANLEY   I can't at the moment.

LULU   You're a bit of a washout, aren't you?

She exits, left. Stanley stands. He then goes to the mirror and looks in it. He goes into the kitchen, takes off his glasses and begins to wash his face. A pause. Enter, by the back door, GOLDBERG and McCANN. McCann carries two suitcases, Goldberg a briefcase. They halt inside the door, then walk downstage. Stanley, wiping his face, glimpses their backs through the hatch. Goldberg and McCann look round the room. Stanley slips on his glasses, sidles through the kitchen door and out of the back door.

McCANN   Is this it?

GOLDBERG   This is it.

McCANN   Are you sure?

GOLDBERG   Sure I'm sure.

Pause.

McCANN   What now?

GOLDBERG   Don't worry yourself, McCann. Take a seat.

McCANN   What about you?

GOLDBERG   What about me?

McCANN   Are you going to take a seat?

GOLDBERG   We'll both take a seat. (*McCann puts down the suitcase and sits at the table, left.*) Sit back, McCann. Relax. What's the matter with you? I bring you down for a few days to the seaside. Take a holiday. Do yourself a favour. Learn to relax, McCann, or you'll never get anywhere.

McCANN   Ah sure, I do try, Nat.

GOLDBERG   (*sitting at the table, right*)   The secret is breathing. Take my tip. It's a well-known fact. Breathe in, breathe out, take a chance, let yourself go, what can you lose? Look at me. When I was an apprentice yet, McCann, every second Friday of the month my Uncle Barney used to take me to the seaside, regular as clockwork. Brighton, Canvey Island, Rottingdean—Uncle Barney wasn't particular. After lunch on Shabbuss we'd go and sit in a couple of deck chairs—you know, the ones with canopies—we'd have a little paddle, we'd watch the tide coming in, going out, the sun coming down—golden days, believe me, McCann. (*reminiscent*) Uncle Barney. Of course, he was an impeccable dresser. One of the old school. He had a house just outside Basingstoke at the time. Respected by the whole community. Culture? Don't talk to me about culture. He was an all-round man, what do you mean? He was a cosmopolitan.

McCANN   Hey, Nat. . . .

GOLDBERG   (*reflectively*)   Yes. One of the old school.

McCANN   Nat. How do we know this is the right house?

GOLDBERG   What?

McCANN   How do we know this is the right house?

GOLDBERG   What makes you think it's the wrong house?

McCANN   I didn't see a number on the gate.

GOLDBERG   I wasn't looking for a number.

McCANN   No?

GOLDBERG   (*settling in the armchair*)   You know one thing Uncle Barney taught me? Uncle Barney taught me that the word of a gentleman is enough. That's why, when I had to go away on business I never carried any money. One of my sons used to come with me. He used to carry a few coppers. For a paper, perhaps, to see how the M.C.C. was getting on overseas. Otherwise my name was good. Besides, I was a very busy man.

MCCANN   What about this, Nat? Isn't it about time someone came in?

GOLDBERG   McCann, what are you so nervous about? Pull yourself together. Everywhere you go these days it's like a funeral.

MCCANN   That's true.

GOLDBERG   True? Of course it's true. It's more than true. It's a fact.

MCCANN   You may be right.

GOLDBERG   What is it, McCann? You don't trust me like you did in the old days?

MCCANN   Sure I trust you, Nat.

GOLDBERG   But why is it that before you do a job you're all over the place, and when you're doing the job you're as cool as a whistle?

MCCANN   I don't know, Nat. I'm just all right once I know what I'm doing. When I know what I'm doing, I'm all right.

GOLDBERG   Well, you do it very well.

MCCANN   Thank you, Nat.

GOLDBERG   You know what I said when this job came up. I mean naturally they approached me to take care of it. And you know who I asked for?

MCCANN   Who?

GOLDBERG   You.

MCCANN   That was very good of you, Nat.

GOLDBERG   No, it was nothing. You're a capable man, McCann.

MCCANN   That's a great compliment, Nat, coming from a man in your position.

GOLDBERG   Well, I've got a position, I won't deny it.

MCCANN   You certainly have.

GOLDBERG   I would never deny that I had a position.

McCANN   And what a position!

GOLDBERG   It's not a thing I would deny.

McCANN   Yes, it's true, you've done a lot for me. I appreciate it.

GOLDBERG   Say no more.

McCANN   You've always been a true Christian.

GOLDBERG   In a way.

McCANN   No, I just thought I'd tell you that I appreciate it.

GOLDBERG   It's unnecessary to recapitulate.

McCANN   You're right there.

GOLDBERG   Quite unnecessary.

Pause. McCann leans forward.

McCANN   Hey Nat, just one thing. . . .

GOLDBERG   What now?

McCANN   This job—no, listen—this job, is it going to be like anything
we've ever done before?

GOLDBERG   Tch, tch, tch.

McCANN   No, just tell me that. Just that, and I won't ask any more.

*Goldberg sighs, stands, goes behind the table, ponders, looks at McCann and
then speaks in a quiet, fluent, official tone.*

GOLDBERG   The main issue is a singular issue and quite distinct from
your previous work. Certain elements, however, might well
approximate in points of procedure to some of your other activities.
All is dependent on the attitude of our subject. At all events, McCann,
I can assure you that the assignment will be carried out and the
mission accomplished with no excessive aggravation to you or myself.
Satisfied?

McCANN   Sure. Thank you, Nat.

Meg enters, left.

GOLDBERG   Ah, Mrs Boles?

MEG   Yes?

GOLDBERG   We spoke to your husband last night. Perhaps he mentioned us? We heard that you kindly let rooms for gentlemen. So I brought my friend along with me. We were after a nice place, you understand. So we came to you. I'm Mr Goldberg and this is Mr McCann.

MEG   Very pleased to meet you.

They shake hands.

GOLDBERG   We're pleased to meet you, too.

MEG   That's very nice.

GOLDBERG   You're right. How often do you meet someone it's a pleasure to meet?

MCCANN   Never.

GOLDBERG   But today it's different. How are you keeping, Mrs Boles?

MEG   Oh, very well, thank you.

GOLDBERG   Yes? Really?

MEG   Oh yes, really.

GOLDBERG   I'm glad.

Goldberg sits at the table, right.

GOLDBERG (*cont.*)   Well, so what do you say? You can manage to put us up, eh, Mrs Boles?

MEG   Well, it would have been easier last week.

GOLDBERG   It would, eh?

MEG   Yes.

GOLDBERG   Why? How many have you got here at the moment?

MEG   Just one at the moment.

GOLDBERG   Just one?

MEG   Yes. Just one. Until you came.

GOLDBERG   And your husband, of course?

MEG   Yes, but he sleeps with me.

GOLDBERG   What does he do, your husband?

MEG   He's a deck-chair attendant.

GOLDBERG   Oh, very nice.

MEG   Yes, he's out in all weathers.

She begins to take her purchases from her bag.

GOLDBERG   Of course. And your guest? Is he a man?

MEG   A man?

GOLDBERG   Or a woman?

MEG   No. A man.

GOLDBERG   Been here long?

MEG   He's been here about a year now.

GOLDBERG   Oh yes. A resident. What's his name?

MEG   Stanley Webber.

GOLDBERG   Oh yes? Does he work here?

MEG   He used to work. He used to be a pianist. In a concert party on the pier.

GOLDBERG   Oh yes? On the pier, eh? Does he play a nice piano?

MEG   Oh, lovely. (*She sits at the table.*) He once gave a concert.

GOLDBERG   Oh? Where?

MEG (*falteringly*)   In . . . a big hall. His father gave him champagne. But then they locked the place up and he couldn't get out. The caretaker had gone home. So he had to wait until the morning before he could get out. (*With confidence.*) They were very grateful. (*Pause.*) And then they all wanted to give him a tip. And so he took the tip. And then he got a fast train and he came down here.

43

GOLDBERG Really?

MEG Oh yes. Straight down.

Pause.

MEG (*cont.*) I wish he could have played tonight.

GOLDBERG Why tonight?

MEG It's his birthday today.

GOLDBERG His birthday?

MEG Yes. Today. But I'm not going to tell him until tonight.

GOLDBERG Doesn't he know it's his birthday?

MEG He hasn't mentioned it.

GOLDBERG (*thoughtfully*) Ah! Tell me. Are you going to have a party?

MEG A party?

GOLDBERG Weren't you going to have one?

MEG (*her eyes wide*) No.

GOLDBERG Well, of course, you must have one. (*He stands.*) We'll have a party, eh? What do you say?

MEG Oh yes!

GOLDBERG Sure. We'll give him a party. Leave it to me.

MEG Oh, that's wonderful, Mr Gold—

GOLDBERG Berg.

MEG Berg.

GOLDBERG You like the idea?

MEG Oh, I'm so glad you came today.

GOLDBERG If we hadn't come today we'd have come tomorrow. Still, I'm glad we came today. Just in time for his birthday.

MEG I wanted to have a party. But you must have people for a party.

GOLDBERG And now you've got McCann and me. McCann's the life and soul of any party.

MCCANN What?

GOLDBERG What do you think of that, McCann? There's a gentleman living here. He's got a birthday today, and he's forgotten all about it. So we're going to remind him. We're going to give him a party.

MCCANN Oh, is that a fact?

MEG Tonight.

GOLDBERG Tonight.

MEG I'll put on my party dress.

GOLDBERG And I'll get some bottles.

MEG And I'll invite Lulu this afternoon. Oh, this is going to cheer Stanley up. It will. He's been down in the dumps lately.

GOLDBERG We'll bring him out of himself.

MEG I hope I look nice in my dress.

GOLDBERG Madam, you'll look like a tulip.

MEG What colour?

GOLDBERG Er—well, I'll have to see the dress first.

MCCANN Could I go up to my room?

MEG Oh, I've put you both together. Do you mind being both together?

GOLDBERG I don't mind. Do you mind, McCann?

MCCANN No.

MEG What time shall we have the party?

GOLDBERG Nine o'clock.

MCCANN (*at the door*) Is this the way?

MEG (*rising*) I'll show you. If you don't mind coming upstairs.

GOLDBERG With a tulip? It's a pleasure.

Meg and Goldberg exit laughing, followed by McCann. Stanley appears at the window. He enters by the back door. He goes to the door on the left, opens it and listens. Silence. He walks to the table. He stands. He sits, as Meg enters. She crosses and hangs her shopping bag on a hook. He lights a match and watches it burn.

STANLEY   Who is it?

MEG   The two gentlemen.

STANLEY   What two gentlemen?

MEG   The ones that were coming. I just took them to their room. They were thrilled with their room.

STANLEY   They've come?

MEG   They're very nice, Stan.

STANLEY   Why didn't they come last night?

MEG   They said the beds were wonderful.

STANLEY   Who are they?

MEG (*sitting*)   They're very nice, Stanley.

STANLEY   I said, who are they?

MEG   I've told you, the two gentlemen.

STANLEY   I didn't think they'd come.

He rises and walks to the window.

MEG   They have. They were here when I came in.

STANLEY   What do they want here?

MEG   They want to stay.

STANLEY   How long for?

MEG   They didn't say.

STANLEY (*turning*)   But why here? Why not somewhere else?

MEG   This house is on the list.

STANLEY (*coming down*)   What are they called? What are their names?

MEG   Oh, Stanley, I can't remember.

STANLEY They told you, didn't they? Or didn't they tell you?

MEG Yes, they. . . .

STANLEY Then what are they? Come on. Try to remember.

MEG Why, Stan? Do you know them?

STANLEY How do I know if I know them until I know their names?

MEG Well . . . he told me, I remember.

STANLEY Well?

She thinks.

MEG Gold—something.

STANLEY Goldsomething?

MEG Yes. Gold. . . .

STANLEY Yes?

MEG Goldberg.

STANLEY Goldberg?

MEG That's right. That was one of them.

Stanley slowly sits at the table, left.

MEG (*cont.*) Do you know them?

Stanley does not answer.

MEG (*cont.*) Stan, they won't wake you up, I promise. I'll tell them they must be quiet.

Stanley sits still.

MEG (*cont.*) They won't be here long, Stan. I'll still bring you up your early morning tea.

Stanley sits still.

MEG (*cont.*) You mustn't be sad today. It's your birthday.

A pause.

STANLEY (*dumbly*) Uh?

MEG It's your birthday, Stan. I was going to keep it a secret until tonight.

STANLEY No.

MEG It is. I've brought you a present. (*She goes to the sideboard, picks up the parcel, and places it on the table in front of him.*) Here. Go on. Open it.

STANLEY What's this?

MEG It's your present.

STANLEY This isn't my birthday, Meg.

MEG Of course it is. Open your present.

He stares at the parcel, slowly stands, and opens it. He takes our a boy's drum.

STANLEY (*flatly*) It's a drum. A boy's drum.

MEG (*tenderly*) It's because you haven't got a piano. (*He stares at her, then turns and walks towards the door, left.*) Aren't you going to give me a kiss? (*He turns sharply, and stops. He walks back towards her slowly. He stops at her chair, looking down upon her. Pause. His shoulders sag, he bends and kisses her on the cheek.*) There are some sticks in there. (*Stanley looks into the parcel. He takes out two drumsticks. He taps them together. He looks at her.*)

STANLEY Shall I put it round my neck?

She watches him, uncertainly. He hangs the drum around his neck, taps it gently with the sticks, then marches round the table, beating it regularly. Meg, pleased, watches him. Still beating it regularly, he begins to go round the table a second time. Halfway round the beat becomes erratic, uncontrolled. Meg expresses dismay. He arrives at her chair, banging the drum, his face and the drumbeat now savage and possessed.

Curtain

ACT TWO

McCann is sitting at the table tearing a sheet of newspaper into five equal strips. It is evening. After a few moments Stanley enters from the left. He stops upon seeing McCann, and watches him. He then walks towards the kitchen, stops, and speaks.

STANLEY Evening.

MCCANN Evening.

Chuckles are heard from outside the back door, which is open.

STANLEY Very warm tonight. (*He turns towards the back door, and back.*) Someone out there?

McCann tears another length of paper. Stanley goes into the kitchen and pours a glass of water. He drinks it, looking through the hatch. He puts the glass down, comes out of the kitchen and walks quickly towards the door, left. McCann rises and intercepts him.

MCCANN I don't think we've met.

STANLEY No, we haven't.

MCCANN My name's McCann.

STANLEY Staying here long?

MCCANN Not long. What's your name?

STANLEY Webber.

MCCANN I'm glad to meet you, sir. (*He offers his hand. Stanley takes it, and McCann holds the grip.*) Many happy returns of the day. (*Stanley withdraws his hand. They face each other.*) Were you going out?

STANLEY Yes.

MCCANN On your birthday?

STANLEY Yes. Why not?

MCCANN But they're holding a party here for you tonight.

STANLEY Oh really? That's unfortunate.

49

MCCANN   Ah no. It's very nice.

Voices from outside the back door.

STANLEY   I'm sorry. I'm not in the mood for a party tonight.

MCCANN   Oh, is that so? I'm sorry.

STANLEY   Yes, I'm going out to celebrate quietly, on my own.

MCCANN   That's a shame.

They stand.

STANLEY   Well, if you'd move out of my way—

MCCANN   But everything's laid on. The guests are expected.

STANLEY   Guests? What guests?

MCCANN   Myself for one. I had the honour of an invitation.

McCann begins to whistle "The Mountains of Morne."

STANLEY   (*moving away*)   I wouldn't call it an honour, would you? It'll just be another booze-up.

Stanley joins McCann in whistling "The Mountains of Morne." During the next five lines the whistling is continuous, one whistling while the other speaks, and both whistling together.

MCCANN   But it is an honour.

STANLEY   I'd say you were exaggerating.

MCCANN   Oh no. I'd say it was an honour.

STANLEY   I'd say that was plain stupid.

MCCANN   Ah no.

They stare at each other.

STANLEY   Who are the other guests?

MCCANN   A young lady.

STANLEY   Oh yes? And . . . ?

MCCANN   My friend.

STANLEY   Your friend?

MCCANN   That's right. It's all laid on.

Stanley walks round the table towards the door. McCann meets him.

STANLEY   Excuse me.

MCCANN   Where are you going?

STANLEY   I want to go out.

MCCANN   Why don't you stay here?

Stanley moves away, to the right of the table.

STANLEY   So you're down here on holiday?

MCCANN   A short one. (*Stanley picks up a strip of paper. McCann moves in.*) Mind that.

STANLEY   What is it?

MCCANN   Mind it. Leave it.

STANLEY   I've got a feeling we've met before.

MCCANN   No we haven't.

STANLEY   Ever been anywhere near Maidenhead?

MCCANN   No.

STANLEY   There's a Fuller's teashop. I used to have my tea there.

MCCANN   I don't know it.

STANLEY   And a Boots Library. I seem to connect you with the High Street.

MCCANN   Yes?

STANLEY   A charming town, don't you think?

MCCANN   I don't know it.

STANLEY   Oh no. A quiet, thriving community. I was born and brought up there. I lived well away from the main road.

MCCANN   Yes?

Pause.

STANLEY   You're here on a short stay?

MCCANN   That's right.

STANLEY   You'll find it very bracing.

MCCANN   Do you find it bracing?

STANLEY   Me? No. But you will. (*He sits at the table.*) I like it here, but I'll be moving soon. Back home. I'll stay there too, this time. No place like home. (*He laughs.*) I wouldn't have left, but business calls. Business called, and I had to leave for a bit. You know how it is.

MCCANN   (*sitting at the table, left*)   You in business?

STANLEY   No. I think I'll give it up. I've got a small private income, you see. I think I'll give it up. Don't like being away from home. I used to live very quietly—played records, that's about all. Everything delivered to the door. Then I started a little private business, in a small way, and it compelled me to come down here— kept me longer than I expected. You never get used to living in someone else's house. Don't you agree? I lived so quietly. You can only appreciate what you've had when things change. That's what they say, isn't it? Cigarette?

MCCANN   I don't smoke.

Stanley lights a cigarette. Voices from the back.

STANLEY   Who's out there?

MCCANN   My friend and the man of the house.

STANLEY   You know what? To look at me, I bet you wouldn't think I'd led such a quiet life. The lines on my face, eh? It's the drink. Been drinking a bit down here. But what I mean is . . . you know how it is . . . away from your own . . . all wrong, of course . . . I'll be all right when I get back . . . but what I mean is, the way some people look at me you'd think I was a different person. I suppose I have changed, but I'm still the same man that I always was. I mean, you wouldn't think, to look at me, really . . . I mean, not really, that I was the sort of bloke to—to cause any trouble, would you? (*McCann looks at him.*) Do you know what I mean?

MCCANN   No. (*As Stanley picks up a strip of paper.*) Mind that.

STANLEY (*quickly*)   Why are you down here?

MCCANN   A short holiday.

STANLEY   This is a ridiculous house to pick on. (*He rises.*)

MCCANN   Why?

STANLEY   Because it's not a boarding house. It never was.

MCCANN   Sure it is.

STANLEY   Why did you choose this house?

MCCANN   You know, sir, you're a bit depressed for a man on his birthday.

STANLEY (*sharply*)   Why do you call me sir?

MCCANN   You don't like it?

STANLEY (*to the table*)   Listen. Don't call me sir.

MCCANN   I won't, if you don't like it.

STANLEY (*moving away*)   No. Anyway, this isn't my birthday.

MCCANN   No?

STANLEY   No. It's not till next month.

MCCANN   Not according to the lady.

STANLEY   Her? She's crazy. Round the bend.

MCCANN   That's a terrible thing to say.

STANLEY (*to the table*)   Haven't you found that out yet? There's a lot you don't know. I think someone's leading you up the garden path.

MCCANN   Who would do that?

STANLEY (*leaning across the table*)   That woman is mad!

MCCANN   That's slander.

STANLEY   And you don't know what you're doing.

MCCANN   Your cigarette is near that paper.

Voices from the back.

STANLEY   Where the hell are they? (*stubbing his cigarette*) Why don't they come in? What are they doing out there?

MCCANN   You want to steady yourself.

Stanley crosses to him and grips his arm.

STANLEY   (*urgently*)   Look—

MCCANN   Don't touch me.

STANLEY   Look. Listen a minute.

MCCANN   Let go my arm.

STANLEY   Look. Sit down a minute.

MCCANN   (*savagely, hitting his arm*)   Don't do that!

Stanley backs across the stage, holding his arm.

STANLEY   Listen. You knew what I was talking about before, didn't you?

MCCANN   I don't know what you're at at all.

STANLEY   It's a mistake! Do you understand?

MCCANN   You're in a bad state, man.

STANLEY   (*whispering, advancing*)   Has he told you anything? Do you know what you're here for? Tell me. You needn't be frightened of me. Or hasn't he told you?

MCCANN   Told me what?

STANLEY   (*hissing*)   I've explained to you, damn you, that all those years I lived in Basingstoke I never stepped outside the door.

MCCANN   You know, I'm flabbergasted with you.

STANLEY   (*reasonably*)   Look. You look an honest man. You're being made a fool of, that's all. You understand? Where do you come from?

MCCANN   Where do you think?

STANLEY   I know Ireland very well. I've many friends there. I love that country and I admire and trust its people. I trust them. They respect the truth and they have a sense of humour. I think their policemen are wonderful. I've been there. I've never seen such sunsets. What about coming out to have a drink with me? There's a pub down the road serves draught Guinness. Very difficult to get in these parts —(*He breaks off. The voices draw nearer. Goldberg and Petey enter from the back door.*)

GOLDBERG   (*as he enters*)   A mother in a million. (*He sees Stanley.*) Ah.

PETEY   Oh hullo, Stan. You haven't met Stanley, have you, Mr Goldberg?

GOLDBERG   I haven't had the pleasure.

PETEY   Oh well, this is Mr Goldberg, this is Mr Webber.

GOLDBERG   Pleased to meet you.

PETEY   We were just getting a bit of air in the garden.

GOLDBERG   I was telling Mr Boles about my old mum. What days. (*He sits at the table, right.*) Yes. When I was a youngster, of a Friday, I used to go for a walk down the canal with a girl who lived down my road. A beautiful girl. What a voice that bird had! A nightingale, my word of honour. Good? Pure? She wasn't a Sunday school teacher for nothing. Anyway, I'd leave her with a little kiss on the cheek—I never took liberties—we weren't like the young men these days in those days. We knew the meaning of respect. So I'd give her a peck and I'd bowl back home. Humming away I'd be, past the children's playground. I'd tip my hat to the toddlers, I'd give a helping hand to a couple of stray dogs, everything came natural. I can see it like yesterday. The sun falling behind the dog stadium. Ah! (*He leans back contentedly.*)

MCCANN   Like behind the town hall.

GOLDBERG   What town hall?

MCCANN   In Carrikmacross.

GOLDBERG   There's no comparison. Up the street, into my gate, inside the door, home. "Simey!" my old mum used to shout, "quick before it gets cold." And there on the table what would I see? The nicest piece of gefilte fish you could wish to find on a plate.

MCCANN   I thought your name was Nat.

GOLDBERG   She called me Simey.

PETEY   Yes, we all remember our childhood.

GOLDBERG   Too true. Eh, Mr Webber, what do you say? Childhood. Hot water bottles. Hot milk. Pancakes. Soap suds. What a life.

Pause.

PETEY (*rising from the table*)   Well, I'll have to be off.

GOLDBERG   Off?

PETEY   It's my chess night.

GOLDBERG   You're not staying for the party?

PETEY   No, I'm sorry, Stan. I didn't know about it till just now. And we've got a game on. I'll try and get back early.

GOLDBERG   We'll save some drink for you, all right? Oh, that reminds me. You'd better go and collect the bottles.

MCCANN   Now?

GOLDBERG   Of course, now. Time's getting on. Round the corner, remember? Mention my name.

PETEY   I'm coming your way.

GOLDBERG   Beat him quick and come back, Mr Boles.

PETEY   Do my best. See you later, Stan.

Petey and McCann go out, left. Stanley moves to the centre.

GOLDBERG   A warm night.

STANLEY (*turning*)   Don't mess me about!

GOLDBERG   I beg your pardon?

STANLEY (*moving downstage*)   I'm afraid there's been a mistake. We're booked out. Your room is taken. Mrs Boles forgot to tell you. You'll have to find somewhere else.

GOLDBERG   Are you the manager here?

STANLEY   That's right.

GOLDBERG   Is it a good game?

STANLEY   I run the house. I'm afraid you and your friend will have to find other accommodation.

GOLDBERG (*rising*)   Oh, I forgot, I must congratulate you on your birthday. (*offering his hand*) Congratulations.

STANLEY (*ignoring hand*)   Perhaps you're deaf.

GOLDBERG   No, what makes you think that? As a matter of fact, every single one of my senses is at its peak. Not bad going, eh? For a man past fifty. But a birthday, I always feel, is a great occasion, taken too much for granted these days. What a thing to celebrate—birth! Like getting up in the morning. Marvellous! Some people don't like the idea of getting up in the morning. I've heard them. Getting up in the morning, they say, what is it? Your skin's crabby, you need a shave, your eyes are full of muck, your mouth is like a boghouse, the palms of your hands are full of sweat, your nose is clogged up, your feet stink, what are you but a corpse waiting to be washed? Whenever I hear that point of view I feel cheerful. Because I know what it is to wake up with the sun shining, to the sound of the lawnmower, all the little birds, the smell of the grass, church bells, tomato juice—

STANLEY   Get out.

Enter McCann, with bottles.

STANLEY (*cont.*)   Get that drink out. These are unlicensed premises.

GOLDBERG   You're in a terrible humour today, Mr Webber. And on your birthday too, with the good lady getting her strength up to give you a party.

McCann puts the bottles on the sideboard.

STANLEY   I told you to get those bottles out.

GOLDBERG   Mr Webber, sit down a minute.

STANLEY   Let me—just make this clear. You don't bother me. To me, you're nothing but a dirty joke. But I have a responsibility towards the people in this house. They've been down here too long. They've lost their sense of smell. I haven't. And nobody's going to take advantage of them while I'm here. (*a little less forceful*) Anyway, this house isn't your cup of tea. There's nothing here for you, from any angle, any angle. So why don't you just go, without any more fuss?

GOLDBERG Mr Webber, sit down.

STANLEY It's no good starting any kind of trouble.

GOLDBERG Sit down.

STANLEY Why should I?

GOLDBERG If you want to know the truth, Webber, you're beginning to get on my breasts.

STANLEY Really? Well, that's—

GOLDBERG Sit down.

STANLEY No.

Goldberg sighs, and sits at the table right.

GOLDBERG McCann.

MCCANN Nat?

GOLDBERG Ask him to sit down.

MCCANN Yes, Nat. (*McCann moves to Stanley.*) Do you mind sitting down?

STANLEY Yes, I do mind.

MCCANN Yes now, but—it'd be better if you did.

STANLEY Why don't you sit down?

MCCANN No, not me—you.

STANLEY No thanks.

Pause.

MCCANN Nat.

GOLDBERG What?

MCCANN He won't sit down.

GOLDBERG   Well, ask him.

MCCANN   I've asked him.

GOLDBERG   Ask him again.

MCCANN (*to Stanley*)   Sit down.

STANLEY   Why?

MCCANN   You'd be more comfortable.

STANLEY   So would you.

Pause.

MCCANN   All right. If you will I will.

STANLEY   You first.

McCann slowly sits at the table, left.

MCCANN   Well?

STANLEY   Right. Now you've both had a rest you can get out!

MCCANN (*rising*)   That's a dirty trick! I'll kick the shite out of him!

GOLDBERG (*rising*)   No! I have stood up.

MCCANN   Sit down again!

GOLDBERG   Once I'm up I'm up.

STANLEY   Same here.

MCCANN (*moving to Stanley*)   You've made Mr Goldberg stand up.

STANLEY (*his voice rising*)   It'll do him good!

MCCANN   Get in that seat.

GOLDBERG   McCann.

MCCANN   Get down in that seat!

GOLDBERG (*crossing to him*)   Webber. (*quietly*) SIT DOWN.

Silence. Stanley begins to whistle "The Mountains of Morne." He strolls casually to the chair at the table. They watch him. He stops whistling. Silence. He sits.

STANLEY   You'd better be careful.

GOLDBERG   Webber, what were you doing yesterday?

STANLEY   Yesterday?

GOLDBERG   And the day before. What did you do the day before that?

STANLEY   What do you mean?

GOLDBERG   Why are you wasting everybody's time, Webber? Why are you getting in everybody's way?

STANLEY   Me? What are you—

GOLDBERG   I'm telling you, Webber. You're a washout. Why are you getting on everybody's wick? Why are you driving that old lady off her conk?

MCCANN   He likes to do it!

GOLDBERG   Why do you behave so badly, Webber? Why do you force that old man out to play chess?

STANLEY   Me?

GOLDBERG   Why do you treat that young lady like a leper? She's not the leper, Webber!

STANLEY   What the—

GOLDBERG   What did you wear last week, Webber? Where do you keep your suits?

MCCANN   Why did you leave the organization?

GOLDBERG   What would your old mum say, Webber?

MCCANN   Why did you betray us?

GOLDBERG   You hurt me, Webber. You're playing a dirty game.

MCCANN   That's a Black and Tan fact.

GOLDBERG   Who does he think he is?

MCCANN   Who do you think you are?

STANLEY   You're on the wrong horse.

GOLDBERG   When did you come to this place?

STANLEY   Last year.

GOLDBERG   Where did you come from?

STANLEY   Somewhere else.

GOLDBERG   Why did you come here?

STANLEY   My feet hurt!

GOLDBERG   Why did you stay?

STANLEY   I had a headache!

GOLDBERG   Did you take anything for it?

STANLEY   Yes.

GOLDBERG   What?

STANLEY   Fruit salts!

GOLDBERG   Enos or Andrews?

STANLEY   En— An—

GOLDBERG   Did you stir properly? Did they fizz?

STANLEY   Now, now, wait, you—

GOLDBERG   Did they fizz? Did they fizz or didn't they fizz?

MCCANN   He doesn't know!

GOLDBERG   You don't know. When did you last have a bath?

STANLEY   I have one every—

GOLDBERG   Don't lie.

MCCANN   You betrayed the organization. I know him!

STANLEY   You don't!

GOLDBERG   What can you see without your glasses?

STANLEY   Anything.

GOLDBERG   Take off his glasses.

McCann snatches his glasses and as Stanley rises, reaching for them, takes his chair downstage centre, below the table, Stanley stumbling as he follows. Stanley clutches the chair and stays bent over it.

GOLDBERG (*cont.*)   Webber, you're a fake. (*They stand on each side of the chair.*) When did you last wash up a cup?

STANLEY   The Christmas before last.

GOLDBERG   Where?

STANLEY   Lyons Corner House.

GOLDBERG   Which one?

STANLEY   Marble Arch.

GOLDBERG   Where was your wife?

STANLEY   In—

GOLDBERG   Answer.

STANLEY (*turning, crouched*)   What wife?

GOLDBERG   What have you done with your wife?

MCCANN   He's killed his wife!

GOLDBERG   Why did you kill your wife?

STANLEY (*sitting, his back to the audience*)   What wife?

MCCANN   How did he kill her?

GOLDBERG   How did you kill her?

MCCANN   You throttled her.

GOLDBERG   With arsenic.

MCCANN   There's your man!

GOLDBERG   Where's your old mum?

STANLEY   In the sanatorium.

MCCANN   Yes!

GOLDBERG   Why did you never get married?

MCCANN   She was waiting at the porch.

GOLDBERG You skedaddled from the wedding.

MCCANN He left her in the lurch.

GOLDBERG You left her in the pudding club.

MCCANN She was waiting at the church.

GOLDBERG Webber! Why did you change your name?

STANLEY I forgot the other one.

GOLDBERG What's your name now?

STANLEY Joe Soap.

GOLDBERG You stink of sin.

MCCANN I can smell it.

GOLDBERG Do you recognise an external force?

STANLEY What?

GOLDBERG Do you recognise an external force?

MCCANN That's the question!

GOLDBERG Do you recognise an external force, responsible for you, suffering for you?

STANLEY It's late.

GOLDBERG Late! Late enough! When did you last pray?

MCCANN He's sweating!

GOLDBERG When did you last pray?

MCCANN He's sweating!

GOLDBERG Is the number 846 possible or necessary?

STANLEY Neither.

GOLDBERG Wrong! Is the number 846 possible or necessary?

STANLEY Both.

GOLDBERG Wrong! It's necessary but not possible.

STANLEY Both.

GOLDBERG Wrong! Why do you think the number 846 is necessarily possible?

STANLEY Must be.

GOLDBERG Wrong! It's only necessarily necessary! We admit possibility only after we grant necessity. It is possible because necessary but by no means necessary through possibility. The possibility can only be assumed after the proof of necessity.

McCANN Right!

GOLDBERG Right? Of course right! We're right and you're wrong, Webber, all along the line.

McCANN All along the line.

GOLDBERG Where is your lechery leading you?

McCANN You'll pay for this.

GOLDBERG You stuff yourself with dry toast.

McCANN You contaminate womankind.

GOLDBERG Why don't you pay the rent?

McCANN Mother defiler!

GOLDBERG Why do you pick your nose?

McCANN I demand justice!

GOLDBERG What's your trade?

McCANN What about Ireland?

GOLDBERG What's your trade?

STANLEY I play the piano.

GOLDBERG How many fingers do you use?

STANLEY No hands!

GOLDBERG No society would touch you. Not even a building society.

McCANN You're a traitor to the cloth.

GOLDBERG What do you use for pyjamas?

STANLEY   Nothing.

GOLDBERG   You verminate the sheet of your birth.

McCANN   What about the Albigensenist heresy?

GOLDBERG   Who watered the wicket in Melbourne?

McCANN   What about the blessed Oliver Plunkett?

GOLDBERG   Speak up, Webber. Why did the chicken cross the road?

STANLEY   He wanted to—he wanted to—he wanted to. . . .

McCANN   He doesn't know!

GOLDBERG   Why did the chicken cross the road?

STANLEY   He wanted to—he wanted to. . . .

GOLDBERG   Why did the chicken cross the road?

STANLEY   He wanted. . . .

McCANN   He doesn't know. He doesn't know which came first!

GOLDBERG   Which came first?

McCANN   Chicken? Egg? Which came first?

GOLDBERG AND McCANN   Which came first? Which came first? Which came first?

Stanley screams.

GOLDBERG   He doesn't know. Do you know your own face?

McCANN   Wake him up. Stick a needle in his eye.

GOLDBERG   You're a plague, Webber. You're an overthrow.

McCANN   You're what's left!

GOLDBERG   But we've got the answer to you. We can sterilise you.

McCANN   What about Drogheda?

GOLDBERG   Your bite is dead. Only your pong is left.

McCANN   You betrayed our land.

GOLDBERG   You betray our breed.

MCCANN   Who are you, Webber?

GOLDBERG   What makes you think you exist?

MCCANN   You're dead.

GOLDBERG   You're dead. You can't live, you can't think, you can't love. You're dead. You're a plague gone bad. There's no juice in you. You're nothing but an odour!

Silence. They stand over him. He is crouched in the chair. He looks up slowly and kicks Goldberg in the stomach. Goldberg falls. Stanley stands. McCann seizes a chair and lifts it above his head. Stanley seizes a chair and covers his head with it. McCann and Stanley circle.

GOLDBERG   Steady, McCann.

STANLEY (*circling*)   Uuuuuhhhhh!

MCCANN   Right, Judas.

GOLDBERG (*rising*)   Steady, McCann.

MCCANN   Come on!

STANLEY   Uuuuuuuhhhhh!

MCCANN   He's sweating.

STANLEY   Uuuuuhhhhh!

GOLDBERG   Easy, McCann.

MCCANN   The bastard sweatpig is sweating.

A loud drumbeat off left, descending the stairs. Goldberg takes the chair from Stanley. They put the chairs down. They stop still. Enter Meg, in evening dress, holding sticks and drum.

MEG   I brought the drum down. I'm dressed for the party.

GOLDBERG   Wonderful.

MEG   You like my dress?

GOLDBERG   Wonderful. Out of this world.

MEG   I know. My father gave it to me. (*placing drum on table*) Doesn't it make a beautiful noise?

GOLDBERG   It's a fine piece of work. Maybe Stan'll play us a little tune afterwards.

MEG   Oh yes. Will you, Stan?

STANLEY   Could I have my glasses?

GOLDBERG   Ah yes. (*He holds his hand out to McCann. McCann passes him his glasses.*) Here they are. (*He holds them out for Stanley, who reaches for them.*) Here they are. (*Stanley takes them.*) Now. What have we got here? Enough to scuttle a liner. We've got four bottles of Scotch and one bottle of Irish.

MEG   Oh, Mr Goldberg, what should I drink?

GOLDBERG   Glasses, glasses first. Open the Scotch, McCann.

MEG   (*at the sideboard*)   Here's my very best glasses in here.

MCCANN   I don't drink Scotch.

GOLDBERG   You've got the Irish.

MEG   (*bringing the glasses*)   Here they are.

GOLDBERG   Good. Mrs Boles, I think Stanley should pour the toast, don't you?

MEG   Oh yes. Come on, Stanley. (*Stanley walks slowly to the table.*) Do you like my dress, Mr Goldberg?

GOLDBERG   It's out on its own. Turn yourself round a minute. I used to be in the business. Go on, walk up there.

MEG   Oh no.

GOLDBERG   Don't be shy. (*He slaps her bottom.*)

MEG   Oooh!

GOLDBERG   Walk up the boulevard. Let's have a look at you. What a carriage. What's your opinion, McCann? Like a Countess, nothing less. Madam, now turn about and promenade to the kitchen. What a deportment!

MCCANN (*to Stanley*)   You can pour my Irish too.

GOLDBERG   You look like a Gladiola.

MEG   Stan, what about my dress?

GOLDBERG   One for the lady, one for the lady. Now madam—your glass.

MEG   Thank you.

GOLDBERG   Lift your glasses, ladies and gentlemen. We'll drink a toast.

MEG   Lulu isn't here.

GOLDBERG   It's past the hour. Now—who's going to propose the toast? Mrs Boles, it can only be you.

MEG   Me?

GOLDBERG   Who else?

MEG   But what do I say?

GOLDBERG   Say what you feel. What you honestly feel. (*Meg looks uncertain.*) It's Stanley's birthday. Your Stanley. Look at him. Look at him and it'll come. Wait a minute, the light's too strong. Let's have proper lighting. McCann, have you got your torch?

MCCANN (*bringing a small torch from his pocket*)   Here.

GOLDBERG   Switch out the light and put on your torch. (*McCann goes to the door, switches off the light, comes back, shines the torch on Meg. Outside the window there is still a faint light.*) Not on the lady, on the gentleman! You must shine it on the birthday boy. (*McCann shines the torch in Stanley's face.*) Now, Mrs Boles, it's all yours.

Pause.

MEG   I don't know what to say.

GOLDBERG   Look at him. Just look at him.

MEG   Isn't the light in his eyes?

GOLDBERG   No, no. Go on.

MEG   Well—it's very, very nice to be here tonight, in my house, and I want to propose a toast to Stanley, because it's his birthday, and he's lived here for a long while now, and he's my Stanley now. And I think he's a good boy, although sometimes he's bad. (*an appreciative laugh from Goldberg*) And he's the only Stanley I know, and I know him better than all the world, although he doesn't think so. (*"Hear—hear" from Goldberg*) Well, I could cry because I'm so happy, having him here and not gone away, on his birthday, and there isn't anything I wouldn't do for him, and all you good people here tonight. . . . (*She sobs.*)

GOLDBERG Beautiful! A beautiful speech. Put the light on, McCann. (*McCann goes to the door. Stanley remains still.*) That was a lovely toast. (*The light goes on. Lulu enters from the door, left. Goldberg comforts Meg.*) Buck up now. Come on, smile at the birdy. That's better. Ah, look who's here.

MEG Lulu.

GOLDBERG How do you do, Lulu? I'm Nat Goldberg.

LULU Hallo.

GOLDBERG Stanley, a drink for your guest. You just missed the toast, my dear, and what a toast.

LULU Did I?

GOLDBERG Stanley, a drink for your guest. Stanley. (*Stanley hands a glass to Lulu.*) Right. Now raise your glasses. Everyone standing up? No, not you, Stanley. You must sit down.

MCCANN Yes, that's right. He must sit down.

GOLDBERG You don't mind sitting down a minute? We're going to drink to you.

MEG Come on!

LULU Come on!

Stanley sits in a chair at the table.

GOLDBERG Right. Now Stanley's sat down. (*taking the stage*) Well, I want to say first that I've never been so touched to the heart as by the toast we've just heard. How often, in this day and age, do you come across real, true warmth? Once in a lifetime. Until a few minutes ago, ladies and gentlemen, I, like all of you, was asking the same question. What's happened to the love, the bonhomie, the unashamed expression of affection of the day before yesterday, that our mums taught us in the nursery?

MCCANN   Gone with the wind.

GOLDBERG   That's what I thought, until today. I believe in a good laugh, a day's fishing, a bit of gardening. I was very proud of my old greenhouse, made out of my own spit and faith. That's the sort of man I am. Not size but quality. A little Austin, tea in Fuller's, a library book from Boots, and I'm satisfied. But just now, I say just now, the lady of the house said her piece and I for one am knocked over by the sentiments she expressed. Lucky is the man who's at the receiving end, that's what I say. (*Pause.*) How can I put it to you? We all wander on our tod through this world. It's a lonely pillow to kip on. Right!

LULU   (*admiringly*)   Right!

GOLDBERG   Agreed. But tonight, Lulu, McCann, we've known a great fortune. We've heard a lady extend the sum total of her devotion, in all its pride, plume and peacock, to a member of her own living race. Stanley, my heartfelt congratulations. I wish you, on behalf of us all, a happy birthday. I'm sure you've never been a prouder man than you are today. Mazoltov! And may we only meet at Simchahs! (*Lulu and Meg applaud.*) Turn out the light, McCann, while we drink the toast.

LULU   That was a wonderful speech.

McCann switches out the light, comes back, and shines the torch in Stanley's face. The light outside the window is fainter.

GOLDBERG   Lift your glasses. Stanley—happy birthday.

MCCANN   Happy birthday.

LULU   Happy birthday.

MEG   Many happy returns of the day, Stan.

GOLDBERG   And well over the fast.

They all drink.

MEG   (*kissing him*)   Oh, Stanny . . .

GOLDBERG   Lights!

MCCANN Right! (*He switches on the lights.*)

MEG Clink my glass, Stan.

LULU Mr Goldberg—

GOLDBERG Call me Nat.

MEG (*to McCann*) You clink my glass.

LULU (*to Goldberg*) You're empty. Let me fill you up.

GOLDBERG It's a pleasure.

LULU You're a marvellous speaker, Nat, you know that? Where did you learn to speak like that?

GOLDBERG You liked it, eh?

LULU Oh yes!

GOLDBERG Well, my first chance to stand up and give a lecture was at the Ethical Hall, Bayswater. A wonderful opportunity. I'll never forget it. They were all there that night. Charlotte Street was empty. Of course, that's a good while ago.

LULU What did you speak about?

GOLDBERG The Necessary and the Possible. It went like a bomb. Since then I always speak at weddings.

Stanley is still. Goldberg sits left of the table. Meg joins McCann downstage, right, Lulu is downstage, left. McCann pours more Irish from the bottle, which he carries, into his glass.

MEG Let's have some of yours.

MCCANN In that?

MEG Yes.

MCCANN Are you used to mixing them?

MEG No.

MCCANN Give me your glass.

Meg sits on a shoe-box, downstage, right. Lulu, at the table, pours more drink for Goldberg and herself, and gives Goldberg his glass.

GOLDBERG   Thank you.

MEG (*to McCann*)   Do you think I should?

GOLDBERG   Lulu, you're a big bouncy girl. Come and sit on my lap.

MCCANN   Why not?

LULU   Do you think I should?

GOLDBERG   Try it.

MEG (*sipping*)   Very nice.

LULU   I'll bounce up to the ceiling.

MCCANN   I don't know how you can mix that stuff.

GOLDBERG   Take a chance.

MEG (*to McCann*)   Sit down on this stool.

Lulu sits on Goldberg's lap.

MCCANN   This?

GOLDBERG   Comfortable?

LULU   Yes thanks.

MCCANN (*sitting*)   It's comfortable.

GOLDBERG   You know, there's a lot in your eyes.

LULU   And in yours, too.

GOLDBERG   Do you think so?

LULU (*giggling*)   Go on!

MCCANN (*to Meg*)   Where'd you get it?

MEG   My father gave it to me.

LULU   I didn't know I was going to meet you here tonight.

MCCANN (*to Meg*)   Ever been to Carrikmacross?

MEG (*drinking*)   I've been to King's Cross.

LULU   You came right out of the blue, you know that?

GOLDBERG (*as she moves*)   Mind how you go. You're cracking a rib.

MEG (*standing*)   I want to dance! (*Lulu and Goldberg look into each other's eyes. McCann drinks. Meg crosses to Stanley.*) Stanley. Dance. (*Stanley sits still. Meg dances round the room alone, then comes back to McCann, who fills her glass. She sits.*)

LULU (*to Goldberg*)   Shall I tell you something?

GOLDBERG   What?

LULU   I trust you.

GOLDBERG (*lifting his glass*)   Gesundheit.

LULU   Have you got a wife?

GOLDBERG   I had a wife. What a wife. Listen to this. Friday, of an afternoon, I'd take myself for a little constitutional, down over the park. Eh, do me a favour, just sit on the table a minute, will you? (*Lulu sits on the table. He stretches and continues.*) A little constitutional. I'd say hullo to the little boys, the little girls—I never made distinctions—and then back I'd go, back to my bungalow with the flat roof. "Simey," my wife used to shout, "quick, before it gets cold!" And there on the table what would I see? The nicest piece of rollmop and pickled cucumber you could wish to find on a plate.

LULU   I thought your name was Nat.

GOLDBERG   She called me Simey.

LULU   I bet you were a good husband.

GOLDBERG   You should have seen her funeral.

LULU   Why?

GOLDBERG (*draws in his breath and wags head*)   What a funeral.

MEG (*to McCann*)   My father was going to take me to Ireland once. But then he went away by himself.

LULU (*to Goldberg*)   Do you think you knew me when I was a little girl?

GOLDBERG   Were you a nice little girl?

LULU   I was.

MEG   I don't know if he went to Ireland.

GOLDBERG   Maybe I played piggy-back with you.

LULU   Maybe you did.

MEG   He didn't take me.

GOLDBERG   Or pop goes the weasel.

LULU   Is that a game?

GOLDBERG   Sure it's a game!

McCANN   Why didn't he take you to Ireland?

LULU   You're tickling me!

GOLDBERG   You should worry.

LULU   I've always liked older men. They can soothe you.

They embrace.

McCANN   I know a place. Roscrea. Mother Nolan's.

MEG   There was a night-light in my room, when I was a little girl.

McCANN   One time I stayed there all night with the boys. Singing and drinking all night.

MEG   And my Nanny used to sit up with me, and sing songs to me.

McCANN   And a plate of fry in the morning. Now where am I?

MEG   My little room was pink. I had a pink carpet and pink curtains, and I had musical boxes all over the room. And they played me to sleep. And my father was a very big doctor. That's why I never had any complaints. I was cared for, and I had little sisters and brothers in other rooms, all different colours.

McCANN   Tullamore, where are you?

MEG   (*to McCann*)   Give us a drop more.

McCANN   (*filling her glass and singing*)   Glorio, Glorio, to the bold Fenian men!

MEG   Oh, what a lovely voice.

GOLDBERG Give us a song, McCann.

LULU A love song!

McCANN (*reciting*) The night that poor Paddy was stretched, the boys
they all paid him a visit.

GOLDBERG A love song!

McCANN (*in a full voice, sings*)
    Oh, the Garden of Eden has vanished, they say,
    But I know the lie of it still.
    Just turn to the left at the foot of Ben Clay
    And stop when halfway to Coote Hill.
    It's there you will find it, I know sure enough,
    And it's whispering over to me:
    Come back, Paddy Reilly, to Bally-James-Duff,
    Come home, Paddy Reilly, to me!

LULU (*to Goldberg*) You're the dead image of the first man I ever loved.

GOLDBERG It goes without saying.

MEG (*rising*) I want to play a game!

GOLDBERG A game?

LULU What game?

MEG Any game.

LULU (*jumping up*) Yes, let's play a game.

GOLDBERG What game?

McCANN Hide and seek.

LULU Blind man's buff.

MEG Yes!

GOLDBERG You want to play blind man's buff?

LULU AND MEG Yes!

GOLDBERG All right. Blind man's buff. Come on! Everyone up! (*rising*)
McCann. Stanley—Stanley!

MEG Stanley. Up.

GOLDBERG What's the matter with him?

MEG (*bending over him*) Stanley, we're going to play a game. Oh, come on, don't be sulky, Stan.

LULU Come on.

Stanley rises. McCann rises.

GOLDBERG Right! Now—who's going to be blind first?

LULU Mrs Boles.

MEG Not me.

GOLDBERG Of course you.

MEG Who, me?

LULU (*taking her scarf from her neck*) Here you are.

McCANN How do you play this game?

LULU (*tying her scarf round Meg's eyes*) Haven't you ever played blind man's buff? Keep still, Mrs Boles. You mustn't be touched. But you can't move after she's blind. You must stay where you are after she's blind. And if she touches you then you become blind. Turn round. How many fingers am I holding up?

MEG I can't see.

LULU Right.

GOLDBERG Right! Everyone move about. McCann. Stanley. Now stop. Now still. Off you go!

Stanley is downstage, right, Meg moves about the room. Goldberg fondles Lulu at arm's length. Meg touches McCann.

MEG Caught you!

LULU Take off your scarf.

MEG What lovely hair!

LULU (*untying the scarf*) There.

MEG It's you!

GOLDBERG Put it on, McCann.

LULU (*tying it on McCann*) There. Turn round. How many fingers am I holding up?

MCCANN I don't know.

GOLDBERG Right! Everyone move about. Right. Stop! Still!

McCann begins to move.

MEG Oh, this is lovely!

GOLDBERG Quiet! Tch, tch, tch. Now—all move again. Stop! Still!

McCann moves about. Goldberg fondles Lulu at arm's length. McCann draws near Stanley. He stretches his arm and touches Stanley's glasses.

MEG It's Stanley!

GOLDBERG (*to Lulu*) Enjoying the game?

MEG It's your turn, Stan.

McCann takes off the scarf.

MCCANN (*to Stanley*) I'll take your glasses.

McCann takes Stanley's glasses.

MEG Give me the scarf.

GOLDBERG (*holding Lulu*) Tie his scarf, Mrs Boles.

MEG That's what I'm doing. (*to Stanley*) Can you see my nose?

GOLDBERG He can't. Ready? Right! Everyone move. Stop! And still!

Stanley stands blindfolded. McCann backs slowly across the stage to the left. He breaks Stanley's glasses, snapping the frames. Meg is downstage, left, Lulu and Goldberg upstage centre, close together. Stanley begins to move, very slowly, across the stage to the left. McCann picks up the drum and places it sideways in Stanley's path. Stanley walks into the drum and falls over with his foot caught in it.

MEG Ooh!

GOLDBERG Sssh!

Stanley rises. He begins to move towards Meg, dragging the drum on his foot. He reaches her and stops. His hands move towards her and they reach her throat. He begins to strangle her. McCann and Goldberg rush forward and throw him off.

Blackout

There is now no light at all through the window. The stage is in darkness.

LULU The lights!

GOLDBERG What's happened?

LULU The lights!

MCCANN Wait a minute.

GOLDBERG Where is he?

MCCANN Let go of me!

GOLDBERG Who's this?

LULU Someone's touching me!

MCCANN Where is he?

MEG Why has the light gone out?

GOLDBERG Where's your torch? (*McCann shines the torch in Goldberg's face.*) Not on me! (*McCann shifts the torch. It is knocked from his hand and falls. It goes out.*)

MCCANN My torch!

LULU Oh God!

GOLDBERG Where's your torch? Pick up your torch!

MCCANN I can't find it.

LULU Hold me. Hold me.

GOLDBERG Get down on your knees. Help him find the torch.

LULU I can't.

MCCANN It's gone.

MEG   Why has the light gone out?

GOLDBERG   Everyone quiet! Help him find the torch.

Silence. Grunts from McCann and Goldberg on their knees. Suddenly there is a sharp, sustained rat-a-tat with a stick on the side of the drum from the back of the room. Silence. Whimpers from Lulu.

GOLDBERG   Over here. McCann!

MCCANN   Here.

GOLDBERG   Come to me, come to me. Easy. Over there.

Goldberg and McCann move up left of the table. Stanley moves down right of the table. Lulu suddenly perceives him moving towards her, screams and faints. Goldberg and McCann turn and stumble against each other.

GOLDBERG   What is it?

MCCANN   Who's that?

GOLDBERG   What is it?

In the darkness Stanley picks up Lulu and places her on the table.

MEG   It's Lulu!

Goldberg and McCann move downstage, right.

GOLDBERG   Where is she?

MCCANN   She fell.

GOLDBERG   Where?

MCCANN   About here.

GOLDBERG   Help me pick her up.

MCCANN (*moving downstage, left*)   I can't find her.

GOLDBERG   She must be somewhere.

MCCANN   She's not here.

GOLDBERG (*moving downstage, left*)   She must be.

MCCANN   She's gone.

McCann finds the torch on the floor, shines it on the table and Stanley. Lulu is lying spread-eagled on the table, Stanley bent over her. Stanley, as soon as the torchlight hits him, begins to giggle. Goldberg and McCann move towards him. He backs, giggling, the torch on his face. They follow him upstage, left. He backs against the hatch, giggling. The torch draws closer. His giggle rises and grows as he flattens himself against the wall. Their figures converge upon him.

Curtain

ACT THREE

The next morning. Petey enters, left, with a newspaper and sits at the table. He begins to read. Meg's voice comes through the kitchen hatch.

MEG   Is that you, Stan? (*Pause.*) Stanny?

PETEY   Yes?

MEG   Is that you?

PETEY   It's me.

MEG (*appearing at the hatch*)   Oh, it's you. I've run out of cornflakes.

PETEY   Well, what else have you got?

MEG   Nothing.

PETEY   Nothing?

MEG   Just a minute. (*She leaves the hatch and enters by the kitchen door.*) You got your paper?

PETEY   Yes.

MEG   Is it good?

PETEY   Not bad.

MEG   The two gentlemen had the last of the fry this morning.

PETEY   Oh, did they?

MEG   There's some tea in the pot though. (*She pours tea for him.*) I'm going out shopping in a minute. Get you something nice. I've got a splitting headache.

PETEY (*reading*)   You slept like a log last night.

MEG   Did I?

PETEY   Dead out.

MEG   I must have been tired. (*She looks about the room and sees the broken drum in the fireplace.*) Oh, look. (*She rises and picks it up.*) The drum's broken. (*Petey looks up.*) Why is it broken?

81

PETEY   I don't know.

She hits it with her hand.

MEG   It still makes a noise.

PETEY   You can always get another one.

MEG (*sadly*)   It was probably broken in the party. I don't remember it being broken though, in the party. (*She puts it down.*) What a shame.

PETEY   You can always get another one, Meg.

MEG   Well, at least he did have it on his birthday, didn't he? Like I wanted him to.

PETEY (*reading*)   Yes.

MEG   Have you seen him down yet? (*Petey does not answer.*) Petey.

PETEY   What?

MEG   Have you seen him down?

PETEY   Who?

MEG   Stanley.

PETEY   No.

MEG   Nor have I. That boy should be up. He's late for his breakfast.

PETEY   There isn't any breakfast.

MEG   Yes, but he doesn't know that. I'm going to call him.

PETEY (*quickly*)   No, don't do that, Meg. Let him sleep.

MEG   But you say he stays in bed too much.

PETEY   Let him sleep . . . this morning. Leave him.

MEG   I've been up once, with his cup of tea. But Mr McCann opened the door. He said they were talking. He said he'd made him one. He must have been up early. I don't know what they were talking about. I was surprised. Because Stanley's usually fast asleep when I wake him. But he wasn't this morning. I heard him talking. (*Pause.*) Do you think they know each other? I think they're old friends. Stanley had a lot of friends. I know he did. (*Pause.*) I didn't give him his tea. He'd already had one. I came down again and went on with my work. Then, after a bit, they came down to breakfast. Stanley must have gone to sleep again.

Pause.

PETEY   When are you going to do your shopping, Meg?

MEG   Yes, I must. (*collecting the bag*) I've got a rotten headache. (*She goes to the back door, stops suddenly and turns.*) Did you see what's outside this morning?

PETEY   What?

MEG   That big car.

PETEY   Yes.

MEG   It wasn't there yesterday. Did you . . . did you have a look inside it?

PETEY   I had a peep.

MEG (*coming down tensely, and whispering*)   Is there anything in it?

PETEY   In it?

MEG   Yes.

PETEY   What do you mean, in it?

MEG   Inside it.

PETEY   What sort of thing?

MEG   Well . . . I mean . . . is there . . . is there a wheelbarrow in it?

PETEY   A wheelbarrow?

MEG   Yes.

PETEY   I didn't see one.

MEG   You didn't? Are you sure?

PETEY   What would Mr Goldberg want with a wheelbarrow?

MEG   Mr Goldberg?

PETEY   It's his car.

MEG (*relieved*) His car? Oh, I didn't know it was his car.

PETEY Of course it's his car.

MEG Oh, I feel better.

PETEY What are you on about?

MEG Oh, I do feel better.

PETEY You go and get a bit of air.

MEG Yes, I will. I will. I'll go and get the shopping. (*She goes towards the back door. A door slams upstairs. She turns.*) It's Stanley! He's coming down—what am I going to do about his breakfast? (*She rushes into the kitchen.*) Petey, what shall I give him? (*She looks through the hatch.*) There's no cornflakes. (*They both gaze at the door. Enter Goldberg. He halts at the door, as he meets their gaze, then smiles.*)

GOLDBERG A reception committee!

MEG Oh, I thought it was Stanley.

GOLDBERG You find a resemblance?

MEG Oh no. You look quite different.

GOLDBERG (*coming into the room*) Different build, of course.

MEG (*entering from the kitchen*) I thought he was coming down for his breakfast. He hasn't had his breakfast yet

GOLDBERG Your wife makes a very nice cup of tea, Mr Boles, you know that?

PETEY Yes, she does sometimes. Sometimes she forgets.

MEG Is he coming down?

GOLDBERG Down? Of course he's coming down. On a lovely sunny day like this he shouldn't come down? He'll be up and about in next to no time. (*He sits at the table.*) And what a breakfast he's going to get.

MEG Mr Goldberg.

GOLDBERG Yes?

MEG I didn't know that was your car outside.

GOLDBERG   You like it?

MEG   Are you going to go for a ride?

GOLDBERG (*to Petey*)   A smart car, eh?

PETEY   Nice shine on it all right.

GOLDBERG   What is old is good, take my tip. There's room there. Room in the front, and room in the back. (*He strokes the teapot.*) The pot's hot. More tea, Mr Boles?

PETEY   No thanks,

GOLDBERG (*pouring tea*)   That car? That car's never let me down.

MEG   Are you going to go for a ride?

Goldberg does not answer, drinks his tea.

MEG (*cont.*)   Well, I'd better be off now. (*She moves to the back door, and turns.*) Petey, when Stanley comes down. . . .

PETEY   Yes?

MEG   Tell him I won't be long.

PETEY   I'll tell him.

MEG (*vaguely*)   I won't be long. (*She exits.*)

GOLDBERG (*sipping his tea*)   A good woman. A charming woman. My mother was the same. My wife was identical.

PETEY   How is he this morning?

GOLDBERG   Who?

PETEY   Stanley. Is he any better?

GOLDBERG (*a little uncertainly*)   Oh . . . a little better, I think, a little better. Of course, I'm not really qualified to say, Mr Boles. I mean, I haven't got the . . . the qualifications. The best thing would be if someone with the proper . . . mnn . . . qualifications . . . was to have a look at him. Someone with a few letters after his name. It makes all the difference.

PETEY   Yes.

GOLDBERG Anyway, Dermot's with him at the moment. He's . . . keeping him company.

PETEY Dermot?

GOLDBERG Yes.

PETEY It's a terrible thing.

GOLDBERG (*sighs*) Yes. The birthday celebration was too much for him.

PETEY What came over him?

GOLDBERG (*sharply*) What came over him? Breakdown, Mr Boles. Pure and simple. Nervous breakdown.

PETEY But what brought it on so suddenly?

GOLDBERG (*rising, and moving upstage*) Well, Mr Boles, it can happen in all sorts of ways. A friend of mine was telling me about it only the other day. We'd both been concerned with another case—not entirely similar, of course, but . . . quite alike, quite alike. (*He pauses.*) Anyway, he was telling me, you see, this friend of mine, that sometimes it happens gradual—day by day it grows and grows and grows . . . day by day. And then other times it happens all at once. Poof! Like that! The nerves break. There's no guarantee how it's going to happen, but with certain people . . . it's a foregone conclusion.

PETEY Really?

GOLDBERG Yes. This friend of mine—he was telling me about it—only the other day. (*He stands uneasily for a moment, then brings out a cigarette case and takes a cigarette.*) Have an Abdullah.

PETEY No, no, I don't take them.

GOLDBERG Once in a while I treat myself to a cigarette. An Abdullah, perhaps, or a . . . (*He snaps his fingers.*)

PETEY What a night. (*Goldberg lights his cigarette with a lighter.*) Came in the front door and all the lights were out. Put a shilling in the slot, came in here and the party was over.

GOLDBERG (*coming downstage*) You put a shilling in the slot?

PETEY Yes.

GOLDBERG   And the lights came on.

PETEY   Yes, then I came in here.

GOLDBERG (*with a short laugh*)   I could have sworn it was a fuse.

PETEY (*continuing*)   There was dead silence. Couldn't hear a thing. So I went upstairs and your friend—Dermot—met me on the landing. And he told me.

GOLDBERG (*sharply*)   Who?

PETEY   Your friend—Dermot.

GOLDBERG (*heavily*)   Dermot. Yes. (*He sits.*)

PETEY   They get over it sometimes though, don't they? I mean, they can recover from it, can't they?

GOLDBERG   Recover? Yes, sometimes they recover, in one way or another.

PETEY   I mean, he might have recovered by now, mightn't he?

GOLDBERG   It's conceivable. Conceivable.

Petey rises and picks up the teapot and cup.

PETEY   Well, if he's no better by lunchtime I'll go and get hold of a doctor.

GOLDBERG (*briskly*)   It's all taken care of, Mr Boles. Don't worry yourself.

PETEY (*dubiously*)   What do you mean? (*enter McCann with two suitcases*) All packed up?

Petey takes the teapot and cups into the kitchen. McCann crosses left and puts down the suitcases. He goes up to the window and looks out.

GOLDBERG   Well? (*McCann does not answer.*) McCann. I asked you well.

MCCANN (*without turning*)   Well what?

GOLDBERG   What's what? (*McCann does not answer.*)

MCCANN (*turning to look at Goldberg, grimly*)   I'm not going up there again.

GOLDBERG Why not?

MCCANN I'm not going up there again.

GOLDBERG What's going on now?

MCCANN (*moving down*) He's quiet now. He stopped all that . . . talking a while ago.

Petey appears at the kitchen hatch, unnoticed.

GOLDBERG When will he be ready?

MCCANN (*sullenly*) You can go up yourself next time.

GOLDBERG What's the matter with you?

MCCANN (*quietly*) I gave him. . . .

GOLDBERG What?

MCCANN I gave him his glasses.

GOLDBERG Wasn't he glad to get them back?

MCCANN The frames are bust.

GOLDBERG How did that happen?

MCCANN He tried to fit the eyeholes into his eyes. I left him doing it.

PETEY (*at the kitchen door*) There's some Sellotape somewhere. We can stick them together.

Goldberg and McCann turn to see him. Pause.

GOLDBERG Sellotape? No, no, that's all right, Mr Boles. It'll keep him quiet for the time being, keep his mind off other things.

PETEY (*moving downstage*) What about a doctor?

GOLDBERG It's all taken care of.

McCann moves over right to the shoe-box, and takes out brush and brushes his shoes.

PETEY (*moves to the table*) I think he needs one.

GOLDBERG I agree with you. It's all taken care of. We'll give him a bit of time to settle down, and then I'll take him to Monty.

PETEY   You're going to take him to a doctor?

GOLDBERG (*staring at him*)   Sure. Monty.

Pause. McCann brushes his shoes.

GOLDBERG (*cont.*)   So Mrs Boles has gone out to get us something nice for lunch?

PETEY   That's right.

GOLDBERG   Unfortunately we may be gone by then.

PETEY   Will you?

GOLDBERG   By then we may be gone.

Pause.

PETEY   Well, I think I'll see how my peas are getting on, in the meantime.

GOLDBERG   The meantime?

PETEY   While we're waiting.

GOLDBERG   Waiting for what? (*Petey walks towards the back door.*) Aren't you going back to the beach?

PETEY   No, not yet. Give me a call when he comes down, will you, Mr Goldberg?

GOLDBERG (*earnestly*)   You'll have a crowded beach today . . . on a day like this. They'll be lying on their backs, swimming out to sea. My life. What about the deck-chairs? Are the deck-chairs ready?

PETEY   I put them all out this morning.

GOLDBERG   But what about the tickets? Who's going to take the tickets?

PETEY   That's all right. That'll be all right. Mr Goldberg. Don't you worry about that. I'll be back.

He exits. Goldberg rises, goes to the window and looks after him. McCann crosses to the table, left, sits, picks up the paper and begins to tear it into strips.

GOLDBERG   Is everything ready?

MCCANN   Sure.

Goldberg walks heavily, brooding, to the table. He sits right of it noticing what McCann is doing.

GOLDBERG   Stop doing that!

MCCANN   What?

GOLDBERG   Why do you do that all the time? It's childish, it's pointless. It's without a solitary point.

MCCANN   What's the matter with you today?

GOLDBERG   Questions, questions. Stop asking me so many questions. What do you think I am?

McCann studies him. He then folds the paper, leaving the strips inside.

MCCANN   Well?

Pause. Goldberg leans back in the chair, his eyes closed.

MCCANN (*cont.*)   Well?

GOLDBERG (*with fatigue*)   Well what?

MCCANN   Do we wait or do we go and get him?

GOLDBERG (*slowly*)   You want to go and get him?

MCCANN   I want to get it over.

GOLDBERG   That's understandable.

MCCANN   So do we wait or do we go and get him?

GOLDBERG (*interrupting*)   I don't know why, but I feel knocked out. I feel a bit . . . It's uncommon for me.

MCCANN   Is that so?

GOLDBERG   It's unusual.

MCCANN (*rising swiftly and going behind Goldberg's chair. Hissing*)   Let's finish and go. Let's get it over and go. Get the thing done. Let's finish the bloody thing. Let's get the thing done and go!

Pause.

MCCANN (*cont.*)   Will I go up?

Pause.

MCCANN (*cont.*)   Nat!

Goldberg sits humped. McCann slips to his side.

MCCANN (*cont.*)   Simey!

GOLDBERG (*opening his eyes, regarding McCann*)   What—did—you—call—me?

MCCANN   Who?

GOLDBERG (*murderously*)   Don't call me that! (*He seizes McCann by the throat.*) NEVER CALL ME THAT!

MCCANN (*writhing*)   Nat, Nat, Nat, NAT! I called you Nat. I was asking you, Nat. Honest to God. Just a question, that's all, just a question, do you see, do you follow me?

GOLDBERG (*jerking him away*)   What question?

MCCANN   Will I go up?

GOLDBERG (*violently*)   Up? I thought you weren't going to go up there again.

MCCANN   What do you mean? Why not?

GOLDBERG   You said so!

MCCANN   I never said that!

GOLDBERG   No?

MCCANN (*from the floor, to the room at large*)   Who said that? I never said that! I'll go up now!

He jumps up and rushes to the door, left.

GOLDBERG   Wait!

He stretches his arms to the arms of the chair.

GOLDBERG (*cont.*)   Come here.

McCann approaches him very slowly.

GOLDBERG (*cont.*)   I want your opinion. Have a look in my mouth.

He opens his mouth wide.

GOLDBERG (*cont.*)   Take a good look.

McCann looks.

GOLDBERG (*cont.*)   You know what I mean?

McCann peers.

GOLDBERG (*cont.*)   You know what? I've never lost a tooth. Not since the day I was born. Nothing's changed. (*He gets up.*) That's why I've reached my position, McCann. Because I've always been as fit as a fiddle. All my life I've said the same. Play up, play up, and play the game. Honour thy father and thy mother. All along the line. Follow the line, the line, McCann, and you can't go wrong. What do you think, I'm a self-made man? No! I sat where I was told to sit. I kept my eye on the ball. School? Don't talk to me about school. Top in all subjects. And for why? Because I'm telling you, I'm telling you, follow my line? Follow my mental? Learn by heart. Never write down a thing. And don't go too near the water. And you'll find—that what I say is true. Because I believe that the world . . . (*vacant*) . . . Because I believe that the world. . . (*desperate*) . . . BECAUSE I BELIEVE THAT THE WORLD . . . (*lost*) . . .

He sits in chair.

GOLDBERG (*cont.*)   Sit down, McCann, sit here where I can look at you.

McCann kneels in front of the table.

GOLDBERG (*cont.*) (*intensely, with growing certainty*)   My father said to me, Benny, Benny, he said, come here. He was dying. I knelt down. By him day and night. Who else was there? Forgive, Benny, he said, and let live. Yes, Dad. Go home to your wife. I will, Dad. Keep an eye open for low-lives, for schnorrers and for layabouts. He didn't mention names. I lost my life in the service of others, he said, I'm not ashamed. Do your duty and keep your observations. Always bid good morning to the neighbours. Never, never forget your family, for they are the rock, the constitution and the core! If you're ever in any difficulties Uncle Barney will see you in the clear. I knelt down. (*He kneels, facing McCann.*) I swore on the good book. And I knew the word I had to remember—Respect! Because McCann— (*gently*) Seamus—who came before your father? His father. And who came before him? Before him? . . . (*vacant—triumphant*) Who came before your father's father but your father's father's mother! Your great-gran-granny.

Silence. He slowly rises.

GOLDBERG (*cont.*) And that's why I've reached my position, McCann. Because I've always been as fit as a fiddle. My motto. Work hard and play hard. Not a day's illness.

Goldberg sits.

GOLDBERG (*cont.*) All the same, give me a blow. (*Pause.*) Blow in my mouth.

McCann stands, puts his hands on his knees, bends, and blows in Goldberg's mouth.

GOLDBERG (*cont.*) One for the road.

McCann blows again in his mouth. Goldberg breathes deeply, smiles.

GOLDBERG (*cont.*) Right!

Enter Lulu. McCann looks at them, and goes to the door.

MCCANN (*at the door*) I'll give you five minutes. (*He exits.*)

GOLDBERG Come over here.

LULU What's going to happen?

GOLDBERG Come over here.

LULU No, thank you.

GOLDBERG What's the matter? You got the needle to Uncle Natey?

LULU I'm going.

GOLDBERG Have a game of pontoon first, for old time's sake.

LULU I've had enough games.

GOLDBERG   A girl like you, at your age, at your time of health, and you don't take to games?

LULU   You're very smart.

GOLDBERG   Anyway, who says you don't take to them?

LULU   Do you think I'm like all the other girls?

GOLDBERG   Are all the other girls like that, too?

LULU   I don't know about any other girls.

GOLDBERG   Nor me. I've never touched another woman.

LULU (*distressed*)   What would my father say, if he knew? And what would Eddie say?

GOLDBERG   Eddie?

LULU   He was my first love, Eddie was. And whatever happened, it was pure. With him! He didn't come into my room at night with a briefcase!

GOLDBERG   Who opened the briefcase, me or you? Lulu, schmulu, let bygones be bygones, do me a turn. Kiss and make up.

LULU   I wouldn't touch you.

GOLDBERG   And today I'm leaving.

LULU   You're leaving?

GOLDBERG   Today.

LULU (*with growing anger*)   You used me for a night. A passing fancy.

GOLDBERG   Who used who?

LULU   You made use of me by cunning when my defences were down.

GOLDBERG   Who took them down?

LULU That's what you did. You quenched your ugly thirst. You taught me things a girl shouldn't know before she's been married at least three times!

GOLDBERG   Now you're a jump ahead! What are you complaining about?

Enter McCann quickly.

LULU   You didn't appreciate me for myself. You took all those liberties only to satisfy your appetite. Oh Nat, why did you do it?

GOLDBERG   You wanted me to do it, Lulula, so I did it.

McCANN   That's fair enough. (*advancing*) You had a long sleep, miss.

LULU   (*backing upstage left*)   Me?

McCANN   Your sort, you spend too much time in bed.

LULU   What do you mean?

McCANN   Have you got anything to confess?

LULU   What?

McCANN   (*savagely*)   Confess!

LULU   Confess what?

McCANN   Down on your knees and confess!

LULU   What does he mean?

GOLDBERG   Confess. What can you lose?

LULU   What, to him?

GOLDBERG   He's only been unfrocked six months.

McCANN   Kneel down, woman, and tell me the latest!

LULU   (*retreating to the back door*)   I've seen everything that's happened. I know what's going on. I've got a pretty shrewd idea.

McCANN   (*advancing*)   I've seen you hanging about the Rock of Cashel, profaning the soil with your goings-on. Out of my sight!

LULU   I'm going.

She exits. McCann goes to the door, left, and goes out. He ushers in Stanley, who is dressed in a dark well-cut suit and white collar. He holds his broken glasses in his hand. He is clean-shaven. McCann follows and closes the door. Goldberg meets Stanley, seats him in a chair.

GOLDBERG   How are you, Stan?

Pause.

GOLDBERG (*cont.*)   Are you feeling any better?

Pause.

GOLDBERG (*cont.*)   What's the matter with your glasses?

Goldberg bends to look.

GOLDBERG (*cont.*)   They're broken. A pity.

Stanley stares blankly at the floor.

McCANN (*at the table*)   He looks better, doesn't he?

GOLDBERG   Much better.

McCANN   A new man.

GOLDBERG   You know what we'll do?

McCANN   What?

GOLDBERG   We'll buy him another pair.

They begin to woo him, gently and with relish. During the following sequence Stanley shows no reaction. He remains, with no movement, where he sits.

McCANN   Out of our own pockets.

GOLDBERG   It goes without saying. Between you and me, Stan, it's about time you had a new pair of glasses.

McCANN   You can't see straight.

GOLDBERG   It's true. You've been cockeyed for years.

McCANN   Now you're even more cockeyed.

GOLDBERG   He's right. You've gone from bad to worse.

McCANN   Worse than worse.

GOLDBERG   You need a long convalescence.

McCANN   A change of air.

GOLDBERG   Somewhere over the rainbow.

McCANN   Where angels fear to tread.

GOLDBERG   Exactly.

McCANN   You're in a rut.

GOLDBERG   You look anaemic.

McCANN   Rheumatic.

GOLDBERG   Myopic.

McCANN   Epileptic.

GOLDBERG   You're on the verge.

McCANN   You're a dead duck.

GOLDBERG   But we can save you.

McCANN   From a worse fate.

GOLDBERG   True.

McCANN   Undeniable.

GOLDBERG   From now on, we'll be the hub of your wheel.

McCANN   We'll renew your season ticket.

GOLDBERG   We'll take tuppence off your morning tea.

McCANN   We'll give you a discount on all inflammable goods.

GOLDBERG   We'll watch over you.

McCANN   Advise you.

GOLDBERG   Give you proper care and treatment.

McCANN   Let you use the club bar.

GOLDBERG   Keep a table reserved.

McCANN   Help you acknowledge the fast days.

GOLDBERG   Bake you cakes.

McCANN   Help you kneel on kneeling days.

GOLDBERG   Give you a free pass.

MCCANN   Take you for constitutionals.

GOLDBERG   Give you hot tips.

MCCANN   We'll provide the skipping rope.

GOLDBERG   The vest and pants.

MCCANN   The ointment.

GOLDBERG   The hot poultice.

MCCANN   The fingerstall.

GOLDBERG   The abdomen belt.

MCCANN   The ear plugs.

GOLDBERG   The baby powder.

MCCANN   The back scratcher.

GOLDBERG   The spare tyre.

MCCANN   The stomach pump.

GOLDBERG   The oxygen tent.

MCCANN   The prayer wheel.

GOLDBERG   The plaster of Paris.

MCCANN   The crash helmet.

GOLDBERG   The crutches.

MCCANN   A day and night service.

GOLDBERG   All on the house.

MCCANN   That's it.

GOLDBERG   We'll make a man of you.

MCCANN   And a woman.

GOLDBERG   You'll be re-orientated.

MCCANN   You'll be rich.

GOLDBERG   You'll be adjusted.

MCCANN   You'll be our pride and joy.

GOLDBERG   You'll be a mensch.

MCCANN   You'll be a success.

GOLDBERG   You'll be integrated.

MCCANN   You'll give orders.

GOLDBERG   You'll make decisions.

MCCANN   You'll be a magnate.

GOLDBERG   A statesman.

MCCANN   You'll own yachts.

GOLDBERG   Animals.

MCCANN   Animals.

Goldberg looks at McCann.

GOLDBERG   I said animals. (*He turns back to Stanley.*) You'll be able to make or break, Stan. By my life. (*Silence. Stanley is still.*) Well? What do you say?

Stanley's head lifts very slowly and turns in Goldberg's direction.

GOLDBERG (*cont.*)   What do you think? Eh, boy?

Stanley begins to clench and unclench his eyes.

MCCANN   What's your opinion, sir? Of this prospect, sir?

GOLDBERG   Prospect. Sure. Sure it's a prospect.

Stanley's hands, clutching his glasses, begin to tremble.

GOLDBERG (*cont.*)   What's your opinion of such a prospect? Eh, Stanley?

Stanley concentrates, his mouth opens, he attempts to speak, fails and emits sounds from his throat.

STANLEY   Uh-gug . . . uh-gug . . . eeehhh-gag . . . (*on the breath*) Caahh . . . caahh.

They watch him. He draws a long breath which shudders down his body. He concentrates.

GOLDBERG   Well, Stanny boy, what do you say, eh?

They watch. He concentrates. His head lowers, his chin draws into his chest, he crouches.

STANLEY Ug-gughh . . . uh-gughhh . . .

MCCANN What's your opinion, sir?

STANLEY Caaahhh . . . caaahhh . . .

MCCANN Mr Webber! What's your opinion?

GOLDBERG What do you say, Stan? What do you think of the prospect?

MCCANN What's your opinion of the prospect?

Stanley's body shudders, relaxes, his head drops, he becomes still again, stooped. Petey enters from door, downstage, left.

GOLDBERG Still the same old Stan. Come with us. Come on, boy.

MCCANN Come along with us.

PETEY Where are you taking him?

They turn. Silence.

GOLDBERG We're taking him to Monty.

PETEY He can stay here.

GOLDBERG Don't be silly.

PETEY We can look after him here.

GOLDBERG Why do you want to look after him?

PETEY He's my guest.

GOLDBERG He needs special treatment.

PETEY We'll find someone.

GOLDBERG No. Monty's the best there is. Bring him, McCann.

They help Stanley out of the chair. They all three move towards the door, left.

PETEY Leave him alone!

They stop. Goldberg studies him.

GOLDBERG (*insidiously*) Why don't you come with us, Mr Boles?

MCCANN Yes, why don't you come with us?

GOLDBERG Come with us to Monty. There's plenty of room in the car.

Petey makes no move. They pass him and reach the door. McCann opens the door and picks up the suitcases.

PETEY (*broken*) Stan, don't let them tell you what to do!

They exit.

Silence. Petey stands. The front door slams. Sound of a car starting. Sound of a car going away. Silence. Petey slowly goes to the table. He sits on a chair, left. He picks up the paper and opens it. The strips fall to the floor. He looks down at them. Meg comes past the window and enters by the back door. Petey studies the front page of the paper.

MEG (*coming downstage*) The car's gone.

PETEY Yes.

MEG Have they gone?

PETEY Yes.

MEG Won't they be in for lunch?

PETEY No.

MEG Oh, what a shame. (*She puts her bag on the table.*) It's hot out. (*She hangs her coat on a hook.*) What are you doing?

PETEY Reading.

MEG Is it good?

PETEY All right.

She sits by the table.

MEG Where's Stan?

Pause.

MEG (*cont.*) Is Stan down yet, Petey?

PETEY No . . . he's . . .

MEG Is he still in bed?

PETEY Yes, he's . . . still asleep.

MEG Still? He'll be late for his breakfast.

PETEY Let him . . . sleep.

Pause.

MEG Wasn't it a lovely party last night?

PETEY I wasn't there.

MEG Weren't you?

PETEY I came in afterwards.

MEG Oh.

Pause.

MEG (*cont.*) It was a lovely party. I haven't laughed so much for years. We had dancing and singing. And games. You should have been there.

PETEY It was good, eh?

Pause.

MEG I was the belle of the ball.

PETEY Were you?

MEG Oh yes. They all said I was.

PETEY I bet you were, too.

MEG Oh, it's true. I was.

Pause.

MEG (*cont.*) I know I was.

Curtain

THE CARETAKER

This play was first presented by the Arts Theatre Club in association with Michael Codron and David Hall at the Arts Theatre, London, WC2, on April 27, 1960.

On May 30, 1960, the play was presented by Michael Codron and David Hall at the Duchess Theatre, London, with the following cast:

MICK, *a man in his late twenties*   Alan Bates
ASTON, *a man in his early thirties*   Peter Woodthorpe
DAVIES, *an old man*   Donald Pleasence

Directed by Donald McWhinnie

On March 2, 1972, a revival of the play was presented at the Mermaid Theatre, London, with the following cast:

MICK   John Hurt
ASTON   Jeremy Kemp
DAVIES   Leonard Rossiter

Directed by Christopher Morahan

The action of the play takes place in a house in west London

ACT I   A night in winter
ACT II   A few seconds later
ACT III   A fortnight later

A room. A window in the back wall, the bottom half covered by a sack. An iron bed along the left wall. Above it a small cupboard, paint buckets, boxes containing nuts, screws, etc. More boxes, vases, by the side of the bed. A door, up right. To the right of the window, a mound: a kitchen sink, a step-ladder, a coal bucket, a lawnmower, a shopping trolley, boxes, sideboard drawers. Under this mound an iron bed. In front of it a gas stove. On the gas stove a statue of Buddha. Down right, a fireplace. Around it a couple of suitcases, a rolled carpet, a blow-lamp, a wooden chair on its side, boxes, a number of ornaments, a clothes horse, a few short planks of wood, a small electric fire and a very old electric toaster. Below this a pile of old newspapers. Under Aston's bed by the left wall is an Electrolux, which is not seen till used. A bucket hangs from the ceiling.

ACT ONE

MICK *is alone in the room, sitting on the bed. He wears a leather jacket.*

Silence.

He slowly looks about the room looking at each object in turn. He looks up at the ceiling, and stares at the bucket. Ceasing, he sits quite still, expressionless, looking out front.

Silence for thirty seconds.

A door bangs. Muffled voices are heard.

Mick turns his head. He stands, moves silently to the door, goes out, and closes the door quietly.

Silence.

Voices are heard again. They draw nearer, and stop. The door opens. ASTON *and* DAVIES *enter, Aston first, Davies following, shambling, breathing heavily.*

Aston wears an old tweed overcoat, and under it a thin shabby dark-blue pinstripe suit, single-breasted, with a pullover and faded shirt and tie. Davies wears a worn brown overcoat, shapeless trousers, a waistcoat, vest, no shirt, and sandals. Aston puts the key in his pocket and closes the door. Davies looks about the room.

ASTON   Sit down.

DAVIES   Thanks. (*looking about*) Uuh . . .

ASTON   Just a minute.

Aston looks around for a chair, sees one lying on its sides by the rolled carpet at the fireplace, and starts to get it out.

DAVIES   Sit down? Huh . . . I haven't had a good sit down . . . I haven't had a proper sit down . . . well, I couldn't tell you. . . .

ASTON (*placing the chair*)   Here you are.

DAVIES   Ten minutes off for a tea-break in the middle of the night in that place and I couldn't find a seat, not one. All them Greeks had it, Poles, Greeks, Blacks, the lot of them, all them aliens had it. And they had me working there . . . they had me working. . . .

Aston sits on the bed, takes out a tobacco tin and papers, and begins to roll himself a cigarette. Davies watches him.

DAVIES (*cont.*) All them Blacks had it, Blacks, Greeks, Poles, the lot of them, that's what, doing me out of a seat, treating me like dirt. When he come at me tonight I told him.

Pause.

ASTON Take a seat.

DAVIES Yes, but what I got to do first, you see, what I got to do, I got to loosen myself up, you see what I mean? I could have got done in down there.

Davies exclaims loudly, punches downward with closed fist, turns his back to Aston and stares at the wall.

Pause. Aston lights a cigarette.

ASTON You want to roll yourself one of these?

DAVIES (*turning*) What? No, no, I never smoke a cigarette. (*Pause. He comes forward.*) I'll tell you what, though. I'll have a bit of that tobacco there for my pipe, if you like.

ASTON (*handing him the tin*) Yes. Go on. Take some out of that.

DAVIES That's kind of you, mister. Just enough to fill my pipe, that's all. (*He takes a pipe from his pocket and fills it.*) I had a tin, only . . . only a while ago. But it was knocked off. It was knocked off on the Great West Road. (*He holds out the tin.*) Where shall I put it?

ASTON I'll take it.

DAVIES (*handing the tin*) When he come at me tonight I told him. Didn't I? You heard me tell him, didn't you?

ASTON I saw him have a go at you.

DAVIES Go at me? You wouldn't grumble. The filthy skate, an old man like me, I've had dinner with the best.

Pause.

ASTON Yes, I saw him have a go at you.

DAVIES All them toe-rags, mate, got the manners of pigs. I might have been on the road a few years but you can take it from me I'm clean. I keep myself up. That's why I left my wife. Fortnight after I married her, no, not so much as that, no more than a week, I took the lid off a saucepan, you know what was in it? A pile of her underclothing, unwashed. The pan for vegetables, it was. The vegetable pan. That's when I left her and I haven't seen her since.

Davies turns, shambles across the room, comes face to face with a statue of Buddha standing on the gas stove, looks at it and turns.

DAVIES (*cont.*) I've eaten my dinner off the best of plates. But I'm not young any more. I remember the days I was as handy as any of them. They didn't take any liberties with me. But I haven't been so well lately. I've had a few attacks.

Pause.

DAVIES (*cont.*) (*coming closer*) Did you see what happened with that one?

ASTON I only got the end of it.

DAVIES Comes up to me, parks a bucket of rubbish at me tells me to take it out the back. It's not my job to take out the bucket! They got a boy there for taking out the bucket. I wasn't engaged to take out buckets. My job's cleaning the floor, clearing up the tables, doing a bit of washing-up, nothing to do with taking out buckets!

ASTON Uh.

He crosses down right, to get the electric toaster.

DAVIES (*following*) Yes, well say I had! Even if I had! Even if I was supposed to take out the bucket, who was this git to come up and give me orders? We got the same standing. He's not my boss. He's nothing superior to me.

ASTON What was he, a Greek?

DAVIES Not him, he was a Scotch. He was a Scotchman. You got an eye of him, did you?

Aston goes back to his bed with the toaster and starts to unscrew the plug. Davies follows him.

ASTON Yes.

DAVIES I told him what to do with his bucket. Didn't I? You heard. Look here, I said, I'm an old man, I said, where I was brought up we had some idea how to talk to old people with the proper respect, we was brought up with the right ideas, if I had a few years off me I'd . . . I'd break you in half. That was after the guvnor give me the bullet. Making too much commotion, he says. Commotion, me! Look here, I said to him, I got my rights. I told him that. I might have been on the road but nobody's got more rights than I have. Let's have a bit of fair play, I said. Anyway, he give me the bullet. (*He sits in the chair.*) That's the sort of place.

Pause.

DAVIES (*cont.*) If you hadn't come out and stopped that Scotch git I'd be inside the hospital now. I'd have cracked my head on that pavement if he'd have landed. I'll get him. One night I'll get him. When I find myself around that direction.

Aston crosses to the plug box to get another plug.

DAVIES (*cont.*) I wouldn't mind so much but I left all my belongings in that place, in the back room there. All of them, the lot there was, you see, in this bag. Every lousy blasted bit of all my bleeding belongings I left down there now. In the rush of it. I bet he's having a poke around in it now this very moment.

ASTON I'll pop down sometime and pick them up for you.

Aston goes back to his bed and starts to fix the plug on the toaster.

DAVIES Anyway, I'm obliged to you, letting me . . . letting me have a bit of a rest, like . . . for a few minutes. (*He looks about.*) This your room?

ASTON Yes.

DAVIES You got a good bit of stuff here.

ASTON Yes.

DAVIES Must be worth a few bob, this . . . put it all together.

Pause.

DAVIES (*cont.*)   There's enough of it.

ASTON   There's a good bit of it, all right.

DAVIES   You sleep here, do you?

ASTON   Yes.

DAVIES   What, in that?

ASTON   Yes.

DAVIES   Yes, well, you'd be well out of the draught there.

ASTON   You don't get much wind.

DAVIES   You'd be well out of it. It's different when you're kipping out.

ASTON   Would be.

DAVIES   Nothing but wind then.

Pause.

ASTON   Yes, when the wind gets up it. . . .

Pause.

DAVIES   Yes. . . .

ASTON   Mmnn. . . .

Pause.

DAVIES   Gets very draughty.

ASTON   Ah.

DAVIES   I'm very sensitive to it.

ASTON   Are you?

DAVIES   Always have been.

Pause.

DAVIES (*cont.*)   You got any more rooms then, have you?

ASTON   Where?

DAVIES   I mean, along the landing here . . . up the landing there.

ASTON They're out of commission.

DAVIES Get away.

ASTON They need a lot of doing to.

Slight pause.

DAVIES What about downstairs?

ASTON That's closed up. Needs seeing to . . . The floors . . .

Pause.

DAVIES I was lucky you come into that caff. I might have been done by that Scotch git. I been left for dead more than once.

Pause.

DAVIES (*cont.*) I noticed that there was someone was living in the house next door.

ASTON What?

DAVIES (*gesturing*) I noticed. . . .

ASTON Yes. There's people living all along the road.

DAVIES Yes, I noticed the curtains pulled down there next door as we came along.

ASTON They're neighbours.

Pause.

DAVIES This your house then, is it?

Pause.

ASTON I'm in charge.

DAVIES You the landlord, are you?

He puts a pipe in his mouth and puffs without lighting it.

DAVIES (*cont.*) Yes, I noticed them heavy curtains pulled across next door as we came along. I noticed them heavy big curtains right across the window down there. I thought there must be someone living there.

ASTON Family of Indians live there.

DAVIES   Blacks?

ASTON   I don't see much of them.

DAVIES   Blacks, eh? (*Davies stands and moves about.*) Well you've got some knick-knacks here all right, I'll say that. I don't like a bare room. (*Aston joins Davies upstage centre.*) I'll tell you what, mate, you haven't got a spare pair of shoes?

ASTON   Shoes?

Aston moves downstage right.

DAVIES   Them bastards at the monastery let me down again.

ASTON (*going to his bed*)   Where?

DAVIES   Down in Luton. Monastery down at Luton . . . I got a mate at Shepherd's Bush, you see. . . .

ASTON (*looking under his bed*)   I might have a pair.

DAVIES   I got this mate at Shepherd's Bush. In the convenience. Well, he was in the convenience. Run about the best convenience they had. (*He watches Aston.*) Run about the best one. Always slipped me a bit of soap, any time I went in there. Very good soap. They have to have the best soap. I was never without a piece of soap, whenever I happened to be knocking about the Shepherd's Bush area.

ASTON (*emerging from under the bed with shoes*)   Pair of brown.

DAVIES   He's gone now. Went. He was the one who put me on to this monastery. Just the other side of Luton. He'd heard they give away shoes.

ASTON   You've got to have a good pair of shoes.

DAVIES   Shoes? It's life and death to me. I had to go all the way to Luton in these.

ASTON   What happened when you got there, then?

Pause.

DAVIES   I used to know a bootmaker in Acton. He was a good mate to me.

Pause.

DAVIES (*cont.*)   You know what that bastard monk said to me?

Pause.

DAVIES (*cont.*)   How many more Blacks you got around here then?

ASTON   What?

DAVIES   You got any more Blacks around here?

ASTON (*holding out the shoes*)   See if these are any good.

DAVIES   You know what that bastard monk said to me? (*He looks over to the shoes.*) I think those'd be a bit small.

ASTON   Would they?

DAVIES   No, don't look the right size.

ASTON   Not bad trim.

DAVIES   Can't wear shoes that don't fit. Nothing worse. I said to this monk, here, I said, look here, mister, he opened the door, big door, he opened it, look here, mister, I said, I come all the way down here, look, I said, I showed him these, I said, you haven't got a pair of shoes, have you, a pair of shoes, I said, enough to keep me on my way. Look at these, they're nearly out, I said, they're no good to me. I heard you got a stock of shoes here. Piss off, he said to me. Now look here, I said, I'm an old man, you can't talk to me like that, I don't care who you are. If you don't piss off, he says, I'll kick you all the way to the gate. Now look here, I said, now wait a minute, all I'm asking for is a pair of shoes, you don't want to start taking liberties with me, it's taken me three days to get here, I said to him, three days without a bite, I'm worth a bite to eat, en' I? Get out round the corner to the kitchen, he says, get out round the corner, and when you've had your meal, piss off out of it. I went round to this kitchen, see? Meal they give me! A bird, I tell you, a little bird, a little tiny bird, be could have ate it in under two minutes. Right, they said to me, you've had your meal, get off out of it. Meal? I said, what do you think I am, a dog? Nothing better than a dog. What do you think I am, a wild animal? What about them shoes I come all the way here to get I heard you was giving away? I've a good mind to report you to your mother superior. One of them, an Irish hooligan, come at me. I cleared out. I took a short cut to Watford and picked up a pair there. Got onto the North Circular, just past Hendon, the sole come off, right where I was walking. Lucky I had my old ones wrapped up, still carrying them, otherwise I'd have been finished, man. So I've had to stay with these, you see, they're gone, they're no good, all the good's gone out of them.

ASTON Try these.

Davies takes the shoes, takes off his sandals and tries them on.

DAVIES Not a bad pair of shoes. (*He trudges round the room.*) They're strong, all right. Yes. Not a bad shape of shoe. This leather's hardy, en't? Very hardy. Some bloke tried to flog me some suede the other day. I wouldn't wear them. Can't beat leather, for wear. Suede goes off, it creases, it stains for life in five minutes. You can't beat leather. Yes. Good shoe this.

ASTON Good.

Davies waggles his feet.

DAVIES Don't fit though.

ASTON Oh?

DAVIES No. I got a very broad foot.

ASTON Mmnn.

DAVIES These are too pointed, you see.

ASTON Ah.

DAVIES They'd cripple me in a week. I mean these ones I got on, they're no good but at least they're comfortable. Not much cop, but I mean they don't hurt. (*He takes them off and gives them back.*) Thanks anyway, mister.

ASTON I'll see what I can look out for you.

DAVIES Good luck. I can't go on like this. Can't get from one place to another. And I'll have to be moving about, you see, try to get fixed up.

ASTON Where you going to go?

DAVIES   Oh, I got one or two things in mind. I'm waiting for the weather to break.

Pause.

ASTON (*attending to the toaster*)   Would . . . would you like to sleep here?

DAVIES   Here?

ASTON   You can sleep here if you like.

DAVIES   Here? Oh, I don't know about that.

Pause.

DAVIES (*cont.*)   How long for?

ASTON   Till you . . . get yourself fixed up.

DAVIES (*sitting*)   Ay well, that . . .

ASTON   Get yourself sorted out . . .

DAVIES   Oh, I'll be fixed up . . . pretty soon now . . .

Pause.

DAVIES (*cont.*)   Where would I sleep?

ASTON   Here. The other rooms would . . . would be no good to you.

DAVIES (*rising, looking about*)   Here? Where?

ASTON (*rising, pointing upstage right*)   There's a bed behind all that.

DAVIES   Oh, I see. Well, that's handy. Well, that's . . . I tell you what, I might do that . . . just till I get myself sorted out. You got enough furniture here.

ASTON   I picked it up. Just keeping it here for the time being. Thought it might come in handy.

DAVIES   This gas stove work, do it?

ASTON   No.

DAVIES   What do you do for a cup of tea?

ASTON   Nothing.

DAVIES That's a bit rough. (*Davies observes the planks.*) You building something?

ASTON I might build a shed out the back.

DAVIES Carpenter, eh? (*He turns to the lawnmower.*) Got a lawn.

ASTON Have a look.

Aston lifts the sack at the window. They look out.

DAVIES Looks a bit thick.

ASTON Overgrown.

DAVIES What's that, a pond?

ASTON Yes.

DAVIES What you got, fish?

ASTON No. There isn't anything in there.

Pause.

DAVIES Where you going to put your shed?

ASTON (*turning*) I'll have to clear the garden first.

DAVIES You'd need a tractor, man.

ASTON I'll get it done.

DAVIES Carpentry, eh?

ASTON (*standing still*) I like . . . working with my hands.

Davies picks up the statue of Buddha.

DAVIES What's this?

ASTON (*taking and studying it*) That's a Buddha.

DAVIES Get on.

ASTON Yes. I quite like it. Picked it up in a . . . in a shop. Looked quite nice to me. Don't know why. What do you think of these Buddhas?

DAVIES Oh, they're . . . they're all right, en't they?

ASTON   Yes, I was pleased when I got hold of this one. It's very well made.

Davies turns and peers under the sink.

DAVIES   This the bed here, is it?

ASTON (*moving to the bed*)   We'll get rid of all that. The ladder'll fit under the bed. (*They put the ladder under the bed.*)

DAVIES (*indicating the sink*)   What about this?

ASTON   I think that'll fit in under here as well.

DAVIES   I'll give you a hand. (*They lift it.*) It's a ton weight, en't?

ASTON   Under here.

DAVIES   This in use at all, then?

ASTON   No. I'll be getting rid of it. Here.

They place the sink under the bed.

ASTON (*cont.*)   There's a lavatory down the landing. It's got a sink in there. We can put this stuff over there.

They begin to move the coal bucket, shopping trolley, lawnmower and sideboard drawers to the right wall.

DAVIES (*stopping*)   You don't share it, do you?

ASTON   What?

DAVIES   I mean you don't share the toilet with them Blacks, do you?

ASTON   They live next door.

DAVIES   They don't come in?

Aston puts a drawer against the wall.

DAVIES (*cont.*)   Because, you know . . . I mean . . . fair's fair. . . .

Aston goes to the bed, blows dust and shakes a blanket.

ASTON   You see a blue case?

DAVIES   Blue case? Down here. Look. By the carpet.

Aston goes to the case, opens it, takes out a sheet and pillow and puts them on the bed.

DAVIES (*cont.*)   That's a nice sheet.

ASTON   The blanket'll be a bit dusty.

DAVIES   Don't you worry about that.

Aston stands upright, takes out his tobacco and begins to roll a cigarette. He goes to his bed and sits.

ASTON   How are you off for money?

DAVIES   Oh well . . . now, mister, if you want the truth . . . I'm a bit short.

Aston takes some coins from his pocket, sorts them, and holds out five shillings.

ASTON   Here's a few bob.

DAVIES (*taking the coins*)   Thank you, thank you, good luck. I just happen to find myself a bit short. You see, I got nothing for all that week's work I did last week. That's the position, that's what it is.

Pause.

ASTON   I went into a pub the other day. Ordered a Guinness. They gave it to me in a thick mug. I sat down but I couldn't drink it. I can't drink Guinness from a thick mug. I only like it out of a thin glass. I had a few sips but I couldn't finish it.

Aston picks up a screwdriver and plug from the bed and begins to poke the plug.

DAVIES (*with great feeling*)   If only the weather would break! Then I'd be able to get down to Sidcup!

ASTON   Sidcup?

DAVIES   The weather's so blasted bloody awful, how can I get down to Sidcup in these shoes?

ASTON   Why do you want to get down to Sidcup?

DAVIES   I got my papers there!

Pause.

ASTON   Your what?

DAVIES   I got my papers there!

Pause.

ASTON   What are they doing at Sidcup?

DAVIES   A man I know has got them. I left them with him. You see?
They prove who I am! I can't move without them papers. They tell
you who I am. You see! I'm stuck without them.

ASTON   Why's that?

DAVIES   You see, what it is, you see, I changed my name! Years ago. I
been going around under an assumed name! That's not my real name.

ASTON   What name you been going under?

DAVIES   Jenkins. Bernard Jenkins. That's my name. That's the name I'm
known, anyway. But it's no good me going on with that name. I got
no rights. I got an insurance card here. (*He takes a card from his pocket.*)
Under the name of Jenkins. See? Bernard Jenkins. Look. It's got four
stamps on it. Four of them. But I can't go along with these. That's not
my real name, they'd find out, they'd have me in the nick. Four
stamps. I haven't paid out pennies. I've paid out pounds. I've paid out
pounds, not pennies. There's been other stamps, plenty, but they
haven't put them on, the nigs, I never had enough time to go into it.

ASTON   They should have stamped your card.

DAVIES   It would have done no good! I'd have got nothing anyway.
That's not my real name. If I take that card along I go in the nick.

ASTON   What's your real name, then?

DAVIES   Davies. Mac Davies. That was before I changed my name.

Pause.

ASTON   It looks as though you want to sort all that out.

DAVIES   If only I could get down to Sidcup! I've been waiting for the
weather to break. He's got my papers, this man I left them with, it's
got it all down there, I could prove everything.

ASTON   How long's he had them?

DAVIES What?

ASTON How long's he had them?

DAVIES Oh, must be . . . it was in the war . . . must be . . . about near on fifteen year ago.

He suddenly becomes aware of the bucket and looks up.

ASTON Any time you want to . . . get into bed, just get in. Don't worry about me.

DAVIES (*taking off his overcoat*) Eh, well, I think I will. I'm a bit . . . a bit done in. (*He steps out of his trousers, and holds them out.*) Shall I put these on here?

ASTON Yes.

Davies puts the coat and trousers on the clothes horse.

DAVIES I see you got a bucket up here.

ASTON Leak.

Davies looks up.

DAVIES Well, I'll try your bed then. You getting in?

ASTON I'm mending this plug.

Davies looks at him and then at the gas stove.

DAVIES You . . . you can't move this, eh?

ASTON Bit heavy.

DAVIES Yes.

Davies gets into bed. He tests his weight and length.

DAVIES (*cont.*) Not bad. Not bad. A fair bed. I think I'll sleep in this.

ASTON I'll have to fix a proper shade on that bulb. The light's a bit glaring.

DAVIES Don't you worry about that, mister, don't you worry about that. (*He turns and puts the cover up.*)

Aston sits, poking his plug.

The lights fade out. Darkness.

Lights up. Morning.

Aston is fastening his trousers, standing by the bed. He straightens his bed. He turns, goes to the centre of the room and looks at Davies. He turns, puts his jacket on, turns, goes towards Davies and looks down on him.

He coughs. Davies sits up abruptly.

DAVIES   What? What's this? What's this?

ASTON   It's all right.

DAVIES (*staring*)   What's this?

ASTON   It's all right.

Davies looks about.

DAVIES   Oh, yes.

Aston goes to his bed, picks up the plug and shakes it.

ASTON   Sleep well?

DAVIES   Yes. Dead out. Must have been dead out.

Aston goes downstage right, collects the toaster and examines it.

ASTON   You . . . er . . .

DAVIES   Eh?

ASTON   Were you dreaming or something?

DAVIES   Dreaming?

ASTON   Yes.

DAVIES   I don't dream. I've never dreamed.

ASTON   No, nor have I.

DAVIES   Nor me.

Pause.

DAVIES (*cont.*)   Why you ask me that, then?

ASTON   You were making noises.

DAVIES Who was?

ASTON You were.

Davies gets out of bed. He wears long underpants.

DAVIES Now, wait a minute. Wait a minute, what do you mean? What kind of noises?

ASTON You were making groans. You were jabbering.

DAVIES Jabbering? Me?

ASTON Yes.

DAVIES I don't jabber, man. Nobody ever told me that before.

Pause.

DAVIES (*cont.*) What would I be jabbering about?

ASTON I don't know.

DAVIES I mean, where's the sense in it?

Pause.

DAVIES (*cont.*) Nobody ever told me that before.

Pause.

DAVIES (*cont.*) You got hold of the wrong bloke, mate.

ASTON (*crossing to the bed with the toaster*) No. You woke me up. I thought you might have been dreaming.

DAVIES I wasn't dreaming. I never had a dream in my life.

Pause.

ASTON Maybe it was the bed.

DAVIES Nothing wrong with this bed.

ASTON Might be a bit unfamiliar.

DAVIES There's nothing unfamiliar about me with beds. I slept in beds. I don't make noises just because I sleep in a bed. I slept in plenty of beds.

Pause.

DAVIES (*cont.*)   I tell you what, maybe it were them Blacks.

ASTON   What?

DAVIES   Them noises.

ASTON   What Blacks?

DAVIES   Them you got. Next door. Maybe it were them Blacks making noises, coming up through the walls.

ASTON   Hmmnn.

DAVIES   That's my opinion.

Aston puts down the plug and moves to the door.

DAVIES (*cont.*)   Where you going, you going out?

ASTON   Yes.

DAVIES (*seizing the sandals*)   Wait a minute then, just a minute.

ASTON   What you doing?

DAVIES (*putting on the sandals*)   I better come with you.

ASTON   Why?

DAVIES   I mean, I better come out with you, anyway.

ASTON   Why?

DAVIES   Well . . . don't you want me to go out?

ASTON   What for?

DAVIES   I mean . . . when you're out. Don't you want me to get out . . . when you're out?

ASTON   You don't have to go out.

DAVIES   You mean . . . I can stay here?

ASTON   Do what you like. You don't have to come out just because I go out.

DAVIES   You don't mind me staying here?

ASTON   I've got a couple of keys. (*He goes to a box by his bed and finds them.*) This door and the front door. (*He hands them to Davies.*)

DAVIES Thanks very much, the best of luck.

Pause. Aston stands.

ASTON I think I'll take a stroll down the road. A little . . . kind of a shop. Man there'd got a jig saw the other day. I quite liked the look of it.

DAVIES A jig saw, mate?

ASTON Yes. Could be very useful.

DAVIES Yes.

Slight pause.

DAVIES (*cont.*) What's that then, exactly, then?

Aston walks up to the window and looks out.

ASTON A jig saw? Well, it comes from the same family as the fret saw. But it's an appliance, you see. You have to fix it on to a portable drill.

DAVIES Ah, that's right. They're very handy.

ASTON They are, yes.

Pause.

ASTON (*cont.*) You know, I was sitting in a café the other day. I happened to be sitting at the same table as this woman. Well, we started to . . . we started to pick up a bit of a conversation. I don't know . . . about her holiday, it was, where she'd been. She'd been down to the south coast. I can't remember where though. Anyway, we were just sitting there, having this bit of a conversation . . . then suddenly she put her hand over to mine . . . and she said, how would you like me to have a look at your body?

DAVIES Get out of it.

Pause.

ASTON Yes. To come out with it just like that, in the middle of this conversation. Struck me as a bit odd.

DAVIES They've said the same thing to me.

ASTON Have they?

DAVIES   Women? There's many a time they've come up to me and asked me more or less the same question.

Pause.

ASTON   What did you say your name was?

DAVIES   Bernard Jenkins is my assumed one.

ASTON   No, your other one?

DAVIES   Davies. Mac Davies.

ASTON   Welsh, are you?

DAVIES   Eh?

ASTON   You Welsh?

Pause.

DAVIES   Well, I been around, you know . . . what I mean . . . I been about. . . .

ASTON   Where were you born then?

DAVIES   (*darkly*)   What do you mean?

ASTON   Where were you born?

DAVIES   I was . . . uh . . . oh, it's a bit hard, like, to set your mind back . . . see what I mean . . . going back . . . a good way. . . lose a bit of track, like . . . you know. . . .

ASTON   (*going to below the fireplace*)   See this plug? Switch it on here, if you like. This little fire.

DAVIES   Right, mister.

ASTON   Just plug in here.

DAVIES   Right, mister.

Aston goes towards the door.

DAVIES   (*cont.*) (*anxiously*)   What do I do?

ASTON   Just switch it on, that's all. The fire'll come on.

DAVIES   I tell you what. I won't bother about it.

ASTON No trouble.

DAVIES No, I don't go in for them things much.

ASTON Should work. (*turning*) Right.

DAVIES Eh, I was going to ask you, mister, what about this stove? I mean, do you think it's going to be letting out any . . . what do you think?

ASTON It's not connected.

DAVIES You see, the trouble is, it's right on top of my bed, you see? What I got to watch is nudging . . . one of them gas taps with my elbow when I get up, you get my meaning?

He goes round to the other side of stove and examines it.

ASTON There's nothing to worry about.

DAVIES Now look here, don't you worry about it. All I'll do, I'll keep an eye on these taps every now and again, like, you see. See they're switched off. You leave it to me.

ASTON I don't think . . .

DAVIES (*coming round*) Eh, mister, just one thing . . . eh . . . you couldn't slip me a couple of bob, for a cup of tea, just, you know?

ASTON I gave you a few bob last night.

DAVIES Eh, so you did. So you did. I forgot. Went clean out of my mind. That's right. Thank you, mister. Listen. You're sure now, you're sure you don't mind me staying here? I mean, I'm not the sort of man who wants to take any liberties.

ASTON No, that's all right.

DAVIES I might get down to Wembley later on in the day.

ASTON Uh-uh.

DAVIES There's a caff down there, you see, might be able to get fixed up there. I was there, see? I know they were a bit short-handed. They might be in the need of a bit of staff.

ASTON When was that?

DAVIES Eh? Oh, well, that was . . . near on . . . that'll be . . . that'll be
a little while ago now. But of course what it is, they can't find the
right kind of people in these places. What they want to do, they're
trying to do away with these foreigners, you see, in catering. They
want an Englishman to pour their tea, that's what they want, that's
what they're crying out for. It's only common sense, en't? Oh, I got
all that under way . . . that's . . . uh . . . that's . . . what I'll be doing.

Pause.

DAVIES (*cont.*)   If only I could get down there.

ASTON   Mmnn. (*Aston moves to the door.*) Well, I'll be seeing you then.

DAVIES   Yes. Right.

Aston goes out and closes the door.

*Davies stands still. He waits a few seconds, then goes to the door, opens it, looks
out, closes it, stands with his back to it, turns swiftly, opens it, looks out, comes
back, closes the door, finds the keys in his pocket, tries one, tries the other, locks
the door. He looks about the room. He then goes quickly to Aston's bed, bends,
brings out the pair of shoes and examines them.*

DAVIES (*cont.*)   Not a bad pair of shoes. Bit pointed.

*He puts them back under the bed. He examines the area by Aston's bed, picks
up a vase and looks into it, then picks up a box and shakes it.*

DAVIES (*cont.*)   Screws!

He sees paint buckets at the top of the bed, goes to them, and examines them.

DAVIES (*cont.*)   Paint. What's he going to paint?

*He puts the bucket down, comes to the centre of the room, looks up at bucket, and
grimaces.*

DAVIES (*cont.*)   I'll have to find out about that. (*He crosses right, and picks
up a blow-lamp.*) He's got some stuff in here. (*He picks up the Buddha and
looks at it.*) Full of stuff. Look at all this. (*His eye falls on the piles of papers.*)
What's he got all those papers for? Damn pile of papers.

He goes to a pile and touches it. The pile wobbles. He steadies it.

DAVIES (*cont.*)   Hold it, hold it!

He holds the pile and pushes the papers back into place.

The door opens.

Mick comes in, puts the key in his pocket, and closes the door silently. He stands at the door and watches Davies.

DAVIES (*cont.*)   What's he got all these papers for? (*Davies climbs over the rolled carpet to the blue case.*) Had a sheet and pillow ready in here. (*He opens the case.*) Nothing. (*He shuts the case.*) Still, I had a sleep though. I don't make no noises. (*He looks at the window.*) What's this?

He picks up another case and tries to open it. Mick moves upstage, silently.

DAVIES (*cont.*)   Locked. (*He puts it down and moves downstage.*) Must be something in it. (*He picks up a sideboard drawer, rummages in the contents, then puts it down.*)

Mick slides across the room.

Davies half turns, Mick seizes his arm and forces it up his back. Davies screams.

DAVIES (*cont.*)   Uuuuuuuhlth! Uuuuuuuhhh! What! What! What! Uuuuuuuhhh!

Mick swiftly forces him to the floor, with Davies struggling, grimacing, whimpering and staring.

Mick holds his arm, puts his other hand to his lips, then puts his hand to Davies' lips. Davies quietens. Mick lets him go. Davies writhes. Mick holds out a warning finger. He then squats down to regard Davies. He regards him, then stands looking down on him. Davies massages his arm, watching Mick. Mick turns slowly to look at the room. He goes to Davies' bed and uncovers it. He turns, goes to the clothes horse and picks up Davies' trousers. Davies starts to rise. Mick presses him down with his foot and stands over him. Finally he removes his foot. He examines the trousers and throws them back. Davies remains on the floor, crouched. Mick slowly goes to the chair, sits, and watches Davies, expressionless.

Silence.

MICK   What's the game?

Curtain.

ACT TWO

A few seconds later.

Mick is seated, Davies on the floor, half seated, crouched.

Silence.

MICK Well?

DAVIES Nothing, nothing. Nothing.

A drip sounds in the bucket overhead. They look up. Mick looks back to Davies.

MICK What's your name?

DAVIES I don't know you. I don't know who you are.

Pause.

MICK Eh?

DAVIES Jenkins.

MICK Jenkins?

DAVIES Yes.

MICK Jen . . . kins.

Pause.

MICK (*cont.*) You sleep here last night?

DAVIES Yes.

MICK Sleep well?

DAVIES Yes.

MICK I'm awfully glad. It's awfully nice to meet you.

Pause.

MICK (*cont.*) What did you say your name was?

DAVIES Jenkins.

MICK I beg your pardon?

DAVIES Jenkins!

Pause.

MICK Jen . . . kins.

A drip sounds in the bucket. Davies looks up.

MICK (*cont.*)   You remind me of my uncle's brother. He was always on the move, that man. Never without his passport. Had an eye for the girls. Very much your build. Bit of an athlete. Long-jump specialist. He had a habit of demonstrating different run-ups in the drawing-room round about Christmas time. Had a penchant for nuts. That's what it was. Nothing else but a penchant. Couldn't eat enough of them. Peanuts, walnuts, Brazil nuts, monkey nuts, wouldn't touch a piece of fruitcake. Had a marvellous stop-watch. Picked it up in Hong Kong. The day after they chucked him out of the Salvation Army. Used to go in number four for Beckenham Reserves. That was before he got his Gold Medal. Had a funny habit of carrying his fiddle on his back. Like a papoose. I think there was a bit of the Red Indian in him. To be honest, I've never made out how he came to be my uncle's brother. I've often thought that maybe it was the other way round. I mean that my uncle was his brother and he was my uncle. But I never called him uncle. As a matter of fact I called him Sid. My mother called him Sid too. It was a funny business. Your spitting image he was. Married a Chinaman and went to Jamaica.

Pause.

MICK (*cont.*)   I hope you slept well last night.

DAVIES Listen! I don't know who you are!

MICK What bed you sleep in?

DAVIES Now look here—

MICK Eh?

DAVIES That one.

MICK Not the other one?

DAVIES No.

MICK Choosy.

Pause.

MICK (*cont.*)   How do you like my room?

DAVIES   Your room?

MICK   Yes.

DAVIES   This ain't your room. I don't know who you are. I ain't never seen you before.

MICK   You know, believe it or not, you've got a funny kind of resemblance to a bloke I once knew in Shoreditch. Actually he lived in Aldgate. I was staying with a cousin in Camden Town. This chap, he used to have a pitch in Finsbury Park, just by the bus depot. When I got to know him I found out he was brought up in Putney. That didn't make any difference to me. I know quite a few people who were born in Putney. Even if they weren't born in Putney they were born in Fulham. The only trouble was, he wasn't born in Putney, he was only brought up in Putney. It turned out he was born in the Caledonian Road, just before you get to the Nag's Head. His old mum was still living at the Angel. All the buses passed right by the door. She could get a 38, 581, 30 or 38A, take her down the Essex Road to Dalston Junction in next to no time. Well, of course, if she got the 30 he'd take her up Upper Street way, round by Highbury Corner and down to St. Paul's Church, but she'd get to Dalston Junction just the same in the end. I used to leave my bike in her garden on my way to work. Yes, it was a curious affair. Dead spit of you he was. Bit bigger round the nose but there was nothing in it.

Pause.

MICK (*cont.*)   Did you sleep here last night?

DAVIES   Yes.

MICK   Sleep well?

DAVIES   Yes!

MICK   Did you have to get up in the night?

DAVIES   No!

Pause.

MICK What's your name?

DAVIES (*shifting, about to rise*) Now look here!

MICK What?

DAVIES Jenkins!

MICK Jen . . . kins.

Davies makes a sudden move to rise. A violent bellow from Mick sends him back.

MICK (*cont.*) (*a shout*) Sleep here last night?

DAVIES Yes. . . .

MICK (*continuing at great pace*) How'd you sleep?

DAVIES I slept—

MICK Sleep well?

DAVIES Now look—

MICK What bed?

DAVIES That—

MICK Not the other?

DAVIES No!

MICK Choosy.

Pause.

MICK (*cont.*) (*quietly*) Choosy.

Pause.

MICK (*cont.*) (*again amiable*) What sort of sleep did you have in that bed?

DAVIES (*banging on floor*) All right!

MICK You weren't uncomfortable?

DAVIES (*groaning*) All right!

Mick stands, and moves to him.

MICK You a foreigner?

DAVIES No.

MICK Born and bred in the British Isles?

DAVIES I was!

MICK What did they teach you?

Pause.

MICK (*cont.*) How did you like my bed?

Pause.

MICK (*cont.*) That's my bed. You want to mind you don't catch a draught.

DAVIES From the bed?

MICK No, now, up your arse.

Davies stares warily at Mick, who turns. Davies scrambles to the clothes horse and seizes his trousers. Mick turns swiftly and grabs them. Davies lunges for them. Mick holds out a hand warningly.

MICK (*cont.*) You intending to settle down here?

DAVIES Give me my trousers then.

MICK You settling down for a long stay?

DAVIES Give me my bloody trousers!

MICK Why, where you going?

DAVIES Give me and I'm going, I'm going to Sidcup!

Mick flicks the trousers in Davies' face several times.

Davies retreats.

Pause.

MICK You know, you remind me of a bloke I bumped into once, just the other side of the Guildford by-pass—

DAVIES I was brought here!

Pause.

MICK Pardon?

DAVIES I was brought here! I was brought here!

MICK Brought here? Who brought you here?

DAVIES Man who lives here . . . he . . .

Pause.

MICK Fibber.

DAVIES I was brought here, last night . . . met him in a caff . . . I was working . . . I got the bullet . . . I was working there . . . bloke saved me from a punch up, brought me here, brought me right here.

Pause.

MICK I'm afraid you're a born fibber, en't you? You're speaking to the owner. This is my room. You're standing in my house.

DAVIES It's his . . . he seen me all right . . . he . . .

MICK (*pointing to Davies' bed*) That's my bed.

DAVIES What about that, then?

MICK That's my mother's bed.

DAVIES Well she wasn't in it last night!

MICK (*moving to him*) Now don't get perky, son, don't get perky. Keep your hands off my old mum.

DAVIES I ain't . . . I haven't. . . .

MICK Don't get out of your depth, friend, don't start taking liberties with my old mother, let's have a bit of respect.

DAVIES I got respect, you won't find anyone with more respect.

MICK Well, stop telling me all these fibs.

DAVIES Now listen to me, I never seen you before, have I?

MICK Never seen my mother before either, I suppose?

Pause.

MICK (*cont.*) I think I'm coming to the conclusion that you're an old rogue. You're nothing but an old scoundrel.

DAVIES Now wait—

MICK Listen, son. Listen, sonny. You stink.

DAVIES You ain't got no right to—

MICK You're stinking the place out. You're an old robber, there's no getting away from it. You're an old skate. You don't belong in a nice place like this. You're an old barbarian. Honest. You got no business wandering about in an unfurnished flat. I could charge seven quid a week for this if I wanted to. Get a taker tomorrow. Three hundred and fifty a year exclusive. No argument. I mean, if that sort of money's in your range don't be afraid to say so. Here you are. Furniture and fittings, I'll take four hundred or the nearest offer. Rateable value ninety quid for the annum. You can reckon water, heating and lighting at close on fifty. That'll cost you eight hundred and ninety if you're all that keen. Say the word and I'll have my solicitors draft you out a contract. Otherwise I've got the van outside, I can run you to the police station in five minutes, have you in for trespassing, loitering with intent, daylight robbery, filching, thieving and stinking the place out. What do you say? Unless you're really keen on a straightforward purchase. Of course, I'll get my brother to decorate it up for you first. I've got a brother who's a number one decorator. He'll decorate it up for you. If you want more space, there's four more rooms along the landing ready to go. Bathroom, living-room, bedroom and nursery. You can have this as your study. This brother I mentioned, he's just about to start on the other rooms. Yes, just about to start. So what do you say? Eight hundred odd for this room or three thousand down for the whole upper storey. On the other hand, if you prefer to approach it in the long-term way I know an insurance firm in West Ham'll be pleased to handle the deal for you. No strings attached, open and above board, untarnished record; twenty per cent interest, fifty per cent deposit; down payments, back payments, family allowances, bonus schemes, remission of term for good behaviour, six months lease, yearly examination of the relevant archives, tea laid on, disposal of shares, benefit extension, compensation on cessation, comprehensive indemnity against Riot, Civil Commotion, Labour Disturbances, Storm, Tempest, Thunderbolt, Larceny or

Cattle all subject to a daily check and double check. Of course we'd need a signed declaration from your personal medical attendant as assurance that you possess the requisite fitness to carry the can, won't we? Who do you bank with?

Pause.

MICK (*cont.*)   Who do you bank with?

The door opens. Aston comes in. Mick turns and drops the trousers. Davies picks them up and puts them on. Aston, after a glance at the other two, goes to his bed, places a bag which he is carrying on it, sits down and resumes fixing the toaster. Davies retreats to his corner. Mick sits in the chair.

Silence.

A drip sounds in the bucket. They all look up.

Silence.

MICK (*cont.*)   You still got that leak.

ASTON   Yes.

Pause.

ASTON (*cont.*)   It's coming from the roof.

MICK   From the roof, eh?

ASTON   Yes.

Pause.

ASTON (*cont.*)   I'll have to tar it over.

MICK   You're going to tar it over?

ASTON   Yes.

MICK   What?

ASTON   The cracks.

Pause.

MICK   You'll be tarring over the cracks on the roof.

ASTON   Yes.

Pause.

MICK Think that'll do it?

ASTON It'll do it, for the time being.

MICK Uh.

Pause.

DAVIES (*abruptly*) What do you do—?

They both look as him.

DAVIES (*cont.*) What do you do . . . when that bucket's full?

Pause.

ASTON Empty it.

Pause.

MICK I was telling my friend you were about to start decorating the other rooms.

ASTON Yes.

Pause.

ASTON (*cont.*) (*to Davies*) I got your bag.

DAVIES Oh. (*crossing to him and taking it*) Oh thanks, mister, thanks. Give it to you, did they?

Davies crosses back with the bag. Mick rises and snatches it.

MICK What's this?

DAVIES Give us it, that's my bag!

MICK (*warding him off*) I've seen this bag before.

DAVIES That's my bag!

MICK (*eluding him*) This bag's very familiar.

DAVIES What do you mean?

MICK Where'd you get it?

ASTON (*rising, to them*) Scrub it.

DAVIES That's mine.

MICK Whose?

DAVIES It's mine! Tell him it's mine!

MICK This your bag?

DAVIES Give me it!

ASTON Give it to him.

MICK What? Give him what?

DAVIES That bloody bag!

MICK (*slipping it behind the gas stove*) What bag? (*to Davies*) What bag?

DAVIES (*moving*) Look here!

MICK (*facing him*) Where you going?

DAVIES I'm going to get ... my old ...

MICK Watch your step, sonny! You're knocking at the door when no one's at home. Don't push it too hard. You come busting into a private house, laying your hands on anything you can lay your hands on. Don't overstep the mark, son.

Aston picks up the bag.

DAVIES You thieving bastard ... you thieving skate ... let me get my—

ASTON Here you are. (*Aston offers the bag to Davies.*)

Mick grabs it. Aston takes it.

Mick grabs it. Davies reaches for it.

Aston takes it. Mick reaches for it.

Aston gives it to Davies. Mick grabs it.

Pause.

Aston takes it. Davies takes it. Mick takes it. Davies reaches for it. Aston takes it.

Pause.

Aston gives it to Mick. Mick gives it to Davies.

Davies grasps it to him.

Pause.

Mick looks at Aston. Davies moves away with the bag. He drops it.

Pause.

They watch him. He picks it up. Goes to his bed, and sits. Aston goes to his bed, sits, and begins to roll a cigarette. Mick stands still.

Pause.

A drip sounds in the bucket. They all look up.

Pause.

ASTON (*cont.*)   How did you get on at Wembley?

DAVIES   Well, I didn't get down there.

Pause.

DAVIES (*cont.*)   No. I couldn't make it.

Mick goes to the door and exits.

ASTON   I had a bit of bad luck with that jig saw. When I got there it had gone.

Pause.

DAVIES   Who was that feller?

ASTON   He's my brother.

DAVIES   Is he? He's a bit of a joker, en'he?

ASTON   Uh.   -

DAVIES   Yes . . . he's a real joker.

ASTON   He's got a sense of humour.

DAVIES   Yes, I noticed.

Pause.

DAVIES (*cont.*)   He's a real joker, that lad, you can see that.

Pause.

ASTON Yes, he tends . . . he tends to see the funny side of things.

DAVIES Well, he's got a sense of humour, en' he?

ASTON Yes.

DAVIES Yes, you could tell that.

Pause.

DAVIES (*cont.*) I could tell the first time I saw him he had his own way of looking at things.

Aston stands, goes to the sideboard drawer, right, picks up the statue of Buddha, and puts it on the gas stove.

ASTON I'm supposed to be doing up the upper part of the house for him.

DAVIES What . . . you mean . . . you mean it's his house?

ASTON Yes. I'm supposed to be decorating this landing for him. Make a flat out of it.

DAVIES What does he do, then?

ASTON He's in the building trade. He's got his own van.

DAVIES He don't live here, do he?

ASTON Once I get that shed up outside . . . I'll be able to give a bit more thought to the flat, you see. Perhaps I can knock up one or two things for it. (*He walks to the window.*) I can work with my hands, you see. That's one thing I can do. I never knew I could. But I can do all sorts of things now, with my bands. You know, manual things. When I get that shed up out there . . . I'll have a workshop, you see. I . . . could do a bit of woodwork. Simple woodwork, to start. Working with . . . good wood.

Pause.

ASTON (*cont.*) Of course, there's a lot to be done to this place. What I think, though, I think I'll put in a partition . . . in one of the rooms along the landing. I think it'll take it. You know . . . they've got these screens . . . you know . . . Oriental. They break up a room with them. Make it into two parts. I could either do that or I could have a partition. I could knock them up, you see, if I had a workshop.

Pause.

ASTON (*cont.*)   Anyway, I think I've decided on the partition.

Pause.

DAVIES   Eh, look here, I been thinking. This ain't my bag.

ASTON   Oh. No.

DAVIES   No, this ain't my bag. My bag, it was another kind of bag altogether, you see. I know what they've done. What they done, they kept my bag, and they given you another one altogether.

ASTON   No . . . what happened was, someone had gone off with your bag.

DAVIES (*rising*)   That's what I said!

ASTON   Anyway, I picked that bag up somewhere else. It's got a few . . . pieces of clothes in it too. He let me have the whole lot cheap.

DAVIES (*opening the bag*)   Any shoes?

Davies takes two check shirts, bright red and bright green, from the bag. He holds them up.

DAVIES (*cont.*)   Check.

ASTON   Yes.

DAVIES   Yes . . . well, I know about these sort of shirts, you see. Shirts like these, they don't go far in the wintertime. I mean, that's one thing I know for a fact. No, what I need, is a kind of a shirt with stripes, a good solid shirt, with stripes going down. That's what I want. (*He takes from the bag a deep-red velvet smoking-jacket.*) What's this?

ASTON   It's a smoking-jacket.

DAVIES   A smoking-jacket? (*He feels it.*) This ain't a bad piece of cloth. I'll see how it fits.

He tries it on.

DAVIES (*cont.*)   You ain't got a mirror here, have you?

ASTON   I don't think I have.

DAVIES   Well, it don't fit too bad. How do you think it looks?

ASTON   Looks all right.

DAVIES   Well, I won't say no to this, then.

Aston picks up the plug and examines it.

DAVIES (*cont.*)   No, I wouldn't say no to this.

Pause.

ASTON   You could be . . . caretaker here, if you liked.

DAVIES   What?

ASTON   You could . . . look after the place, if you liked . . . you know, the stairs and the landing, the front steps, keep an eye on it. Polish the bells.

DAVIES   Bells?

ASTON   I'll be fixing a few, down by the front door. Brass.

DAVIES   Caretaking, eh?

ASTON   Yes.

DAVIES   Well, I . . . I never done caretaking before, you know . . . I mean to say . . . I never . . . what I mean to say is . . . I never been a caretaker before.

Pause.

ASTON   How do you feel about being one, then?

DAVIES   Well, I reckon . . . Well, I'd have to know . . . you know. . . .

ASTON   What sort of . . .

DAVIES   Yes, what sort of . . . you know . . .

Pause.

ASTON   Well, I mean. . . .

DAVIES   I mean, I'd have to . . . I'd have to. . . .

ASTON   Well, I could tell you. . . .

DAVIES   That's . . . that's it . . . you see . . . you get my meaning?

ASTON   When the time comes . . .

DAVIES   I mean, that's what I'm getting at, you see. . . .

ASTON   More or less exactly what you . . .

DAVIES   You see, what I mean to say . . . what I'm getting at is . . . I mean, what sort of jobs . . .

Pause.

ASTON   Well, there's things like the stairs . . . and the . . . the bells. . . .

DAVIES   But it'd be a matter . . . wouldn't it . . . it'd be a matter of a broom . . . isn't it?

ASTON   Yes, and of course, you'd need a few brushes.

DAVIES   You'd need implements . . . you see . . . you'd need a good few implements. . . .

Aston takes a white overall from a nail over his bed, and shows it to Davies.

ASTON   You could wear this, if you liked.

DAVIES   Well . . . that's nice, en't?

ASTON   It'd keep the dust off.

DAVIES   (*putting it on*)   Yes, this'd keep the dust off, all right. Well off. Thanks very much, mister.

ASTON   You see, what we could do, we could . . . I could fit a bell at the bottom, outside the front door, with "Caretaker" on it. And you could answer any queries.

DAVIES   Oh, I don't know about that.

ASTON   Why not?

DAVIES   Well, I mean, you don't know who might come up them front steps, do you? I got to be a bit careful.

ASTON   Why, someone after you?

DAVIES   After me? Well, I could have that Scotch git coming looking after me, couldn't I? All I'd do, I'd hear the bell, I'd go down there, open the door, who might be there, any Harry might be there. I could be buggered as easy as that, man. They might be there after my card, I mean look at it, here I am, I only got four stamps, on this card, here it is, look, four stamps, that's all I got, I ain't got any more, that's all I got, they ring the bell called Caretaker, they'd have me in, that's what they'd do, I wouldn't stand a chance. Of course I got plenty of other cards lying about, but they don't know that, and I can't tell them, can I, because then they'd find out I was going about under an assumed name. You see, the name I call myself now, that's not my real name. My real name's not the one I'm using, you see. It's different. You see, the name I go under now ain't my real one. It's assumed.

Silence.

The lights fade to blackout.

Then up to dim light through the window.

A door bangs.

Sound of a key in the door of the room.

Davies enters, closes the door, and tries the light switch, on, off, on, off.

DAVIES (*muttering*)   What's this? (*He switches on and off.*) What's the matter with this damn light? (*He switches on and off.*) Aaah. Don't tell me the damn light's gone now.

Pause.

DAVIES (*cont.*)   What'll I do? Damn light's gone now. Can't see a thing.
Pause.

DAVIES (*cont.*)   What'll I do now? (*He moves, stumbles.*) Ah God, what's that? Give me a light. Wait a minute.

He feels for matches in his pocket, takes out a box and lights one. The match goes out. The box falls.

DAVIES (*cont.*)   Aah! Where is it? (*stooping*) Where's the bloody box?

The box is kicked.

DAVIES (*cont.*) What's that? What? Who's that? What's that?

Pause. He moves.

DAVIES (*cont.*) Where's my box? It was down here. Who's this? Who's moving it?

Silence.

DAVIES (*cont.*) Come on. Who's this? Who's this got my box?

Pause.

DAVIES (*cont.*) Who's in here!

Pause.

DAVIES (*cont.*) I got a knife here. I'm ready. Come on then, who are you?

He moves, stumbles, falls and cries out.

Silence.

A faint whimper from Davies. He gets up.

DAVIES (*cont.*) All right!

He stands. Heavy breathing.

Suddenly the Electrolux starts to hum. A figure moves with it, guiding it. The nozzle moves along the floor after Davies, who skips, dives away from it and falls, breathlessly.

DAVIES (*cont.*) Ah, ah, ah, ah, ah, ah! Get away-y-y-y-y!

The Electrolux stops. The figure jumps on Aston's bed.

DAVIES (*cont.*) I'm ready for you! I'm . . . I'm . . . I'm here!

The figure takes out the Electrolux plug from the light socket and fits the bulb. The light goes on. Davies flattens himself against right wall, knife in hand. Mick stands on the bed, holding the plug.

MICK I was just doing some spring cleaning. (*He gets down.*) There used to be a wall plug for this Electrolux. But it doesn't work. I had to fit it in the light socket. (*He puts the Electrolux under Aston's bed.*) How do you think the place is looking? I gave it a good going over.

Pause.

MICK (*cont.*)   We take it in turns, once a fortnight, my brother and me, to give the place a thorough going over. I was working late tonight, I only just got here. But I thought I better get on with it, as it's my turn.

Pause.

MICK (*cont.*)   It's not that I actually live here. I don't. As a matter of fact I live somewhere else. But after all, I'm responsible for the upkeep of the premises, en' I? Can't help being house-proud.

He moves towards Davies and indicates the knife.

MICK (*cont.*)   What are you waving that about for?

DAVIES   You come near me . . .

MICK   I'm sorry if I gave you a start. But I had you in mind too, you know. I mean, my brother's guest. We got to think of your comfort, en't we? Don't want the dust to get up your nose. How long you thinking of staying here, by the way? As a matter of fact, I was going to suggest that we'd lower your rent, make it just a nominal sum, I mean until you get fixed up. Just nominal, that's all.

Pause.

MICK (*cont.*)   Still, if you're going to be spiky, I'll have to reconsider the whole proposition.

Pause.

MICK (*cont.*)   Eh, you're not thinking of doing any violence on me, are you? You're not the violent sort, are you?

DAVIES (*vehemently*)   I keep myself to myself, mate. But if anyone starts with me though, they know what they got coming.

MICK   I can believe that.

DAVIES   You do. I been all over, see? You understand my meaning? I don't mind a bit of a joke now and then, but anyone'll tell you . . . that no one starts anything with me.

MICK   I get what you mean, yes.

DAVIES   I can be pushed so far . . . but . . .

MICK   No further.

DAVIES   That's it.

Mick sits on junk down right.

DAVIES (*cont.*)   What you doing?

MICK   No, I just want to say that . . . I'm very impressed by that.

DAVIES   Eh?

MICK   I'm very impressed by what you've just said.

Pause.

MICK (*cont.*)   Yes, that's impressive, that is.

Pause.

MICK (*cont.*)   I'm impressed, anyway.

DAVIES   You know what I'm talking about then?

MICK   Yes, I know. I think we understand one another.

DAVIES   Uh? Well . . . I'll tell you . . . I'd . . . I'd like to think that. You been playing me about, you know. I don't know why. I never done you no harm.

MICK   No, you know what it was? We just got off on the wrong foot. That's all it was.

DAVIES   Ay, we did.

Davies joins Mick in junk.

MICK   Like a sandwich?

DAVIES   What?

MICK (*taking a sandwich from his pocket*)   Have one of these.

DAVIES   Don't you pull anything.

MICK   No, you're still not understanding me. I can't help being interested in any friend of my brother's. I mean, you're my brother's friend, aren't you?

DAVIES   Well, I . . . I wouldn't put it as far as that.

MICK   Don't you find him friendly, then?

DAVIES   Well, I wouldn't say we was all that friends. I mean, he done me no harm, but I wouldn't say he was any particular friend of mine. What's in that sandwich, then?

MICK   Cheese.

DAVIES   That'll do me.

MICK   Take one.

DAVIES   Thank you, mister.

MICK   I'm sorry to hear my brother's not very friendly.

DAVIES   He's friendly, he's friendly, I didn't say he wasn't. . . .

MICK   (*taking a salt-cellar from his pocket*)   Salt?

DAVIES   No thanks. (*He munches the sandwich.*) I just can't exactly . . . make him out.

MICK   (*feeling in his pocket*)   I forgot the pepper.

DAVIES   Just can't get the hang of him, that's all.

MICK   I had a bit of beetroot somewhere. Must have mislaid it.

Pause.

Davies chews the sandwich. Mick watches him eat. He then rises and strolls downstage.

MICK   (*cont.*)   Uuh . . . listen . . . can I ask your advice? I mean, you're a man of the world. Can I ask your advice about something?

DAVIES   You go right ahead.

MICK   Well, what it is, you see, I'm . . . I'm a bit worried about my brother.

DAVIES   Your brother?

MICK   Yes . . . you see, his trouble is . . .

DAVIES   What?

MICK   Well, it's not a very nice thing to say.

DAVIES (*rising, coming downstage*)   Go on now, you say it.

Mick looks at him.

MICK   He doesn't like work.

Pause.

DAVIES   Go on!

MICK   No, he just doesn't like work, that's his trouble.

DAVIES   Is that a fact?

MICK   It's a terrible thing to have to say about your own brother.

DAVIES   Ay.

MICK   He's just shy of it. Very shy of it.

DAVIES   I know that sort.

MICK   You know the type?

DAVIES   I've met them.

MICK   I mean, I want to get him going in the world.

DAVIES   Stands to reason, man.

MICK   If you got an older brother you want to push him on, you want to see him make his way. Can't have him idle, he's only doing himself harm. That's what I say.

DAVIES   Yes.

MICK   But he won't buckle down to the job.

DAVIES   He don't like work.

MICK   Work shy.

DAVIES   Sounds like it to me.

MICK   You've met the type, have you?

DAVIES   Me? I know that sort.

MICK   Yes.

DAVIES I know that sort. I've met them.

MICK Causing me great anxiety. You see, I'm a working man: I'm a tradesman. I've got my own van.

DAVIES Is that a fact?

MICK He's supposed to be doing a little job for me . . . I keep him here to do a little job . . . but I don't know . . . I'm coming to the conclusion he's a slow worker.

Pause.

MICK (*cont.*) What would your advice be?

DAVIES Well . . . he's a funny bloke, your brother.

MICK What?

DAVIES I was saying, he's . . . he's a bit of a funny bloke, your brother.

Mick stares at him.

MICK Funny? Why?

DAVIES Well . . . he's funny. . . .

MICK What's funny about him?

Pause.

DAVIES Not liking work.

MICK What's funny about that?

DAVIES Nothing.

Pause.

MICK I don't call it funny.

DAVIES Nor me.

MICK You don't want to start getting hypercritical.

DAVIES No, no, I wasn't that, I wasn't . . . I was only saying . . .

MICK Don't get too glib.

DAVIES Look, all I meant was—

MICK Cut it! (*briskly*) Look! I got a proposition to make to you. I'm thinking of taking over the running of this place, you see? I think it could be run a bit more efficiently. I got a lot of ideas, a lot of plans. (*He eyes Davies.*) How would you like to stay on here, as caretaker?

DAVIES What?

MICK I'll be quite open with you. I could rely on a man like you around the place, keeping an eye on things.

DAVIES Well now . . . wait a minute . . . I . . . I ain't never done no caretaking before, you know. . . .

MICK Doesn't matter about that. It's just that you look a capable sort of man to me.

DAVIES I am a capable sort of man. I mean to say, I've had plenty offers in my time, you know, there's no getting away from that.

MICK Well, I could see before, when you took out that knife, that you wouldn't let anyone mess you about.

DAVIES No one messes me about, man.

MICK I mean, you've been in the services, haven't you?

DAVIES The what?

MICK You been in the services. You can tell by your stance.

DAVIES Oh . . . yes. Spent half my life there, man. Overseas . . . like . . . serving . . . I was.

MICK In the colonies, weren't you?

DAVIES I was over there. I was one of the first over there.

MICK That's it. You're just the man I been looking for.

DAVIES What for?

MICK Caretaker.

DAVIES Yes, well . . . look . . . listen . . . who's the landlord here, him or you?

MICK Me. I am. I got deeds to prove it.

DAVIES Ah . . . (*decisively*) Well listen, I don't mind doing a bit of caretaking, I wouldn't mind looking after the place for you.

MICK Of course, we'd come to a small financial agreement, mutually beneficial.

DAVIES I leave you to reckon that out, like.

MICK Thanks. There's only one thing.

DAVIES What's that?

MICK Can you give me any references?

DAVIES Eh?

MICK Just to satisfy my solicitor.

DAVIES I got plenty of references. All I got to do is to go down to Sidcup tomorrow. I got all the references I want down there.

MICK Where's that?

DAVIES Sidcup. He ain't only got my references down there, he got all my papers down there. I know that place like the back of my hand. I'm going down there anyway, see what I mean, I got to get down there, or I'm done.

MICK So we can always get hold of these references if we want them.

DAVIES I'll be down there any day, I tell you. I was going down today, but I'm . . . I'm waiting for the weather to break.

MICK Ah.

DAVIES Listen. You can't pick me up a pair of good shoes, can you? I got a bad need for a good pair of shoes. I can't get anywhere without a pair of good shoes, see? Do you think there's any chance of you being able to pick me up a pair?

The lights fade to blackout.

Lights up. Morning.

Aston is pulling on his trousers over long underwear. A slight grimace. He looks around at the head of his bed, takes a towel from the rail and waves it about. He pulls it down, goes to Davies and wakes him. Davies sits up abruptly.

ASTON   You said you wanted me to get you up.

DAVIES   What for?

ASTON   You said you were thinking of going to Sidcup.

DAVIES   Ay, that'd be a good thing, if I got there.

ASTON   Doesn't look much of a day.

DAVIES   Ay, well, that's shot it, en't it?

ASTON   I . . . I didn't have a very good night again.

DAVIES   I slept terrible.

Pause.

ASTON   You were making . . .

DAVIES   Terrible. Had a bit of rain in the night, didn't it?

ASTON   Just a bit.

He goes to his bed, picks up a small plank and begins to sandpaper it.

DAVIES   Thought so. Come in on my head.

Pause.

DAVIES (*cont.*)   Draught's blowing right in on my head, anyway.

Pause.

DAVIES (*cont.*)   Can't you close that window behind that sack?

ASTON   You could.

DAVIES   Well then, what about it, then? The rain's coming right in on my bead.

ASTON   Got to have a bit of air.

Davies gets out of bed. He is wearing his trousers, waistcoat and vest.

DAVIES (*putting on his sandals*)   Listen. I've lived all my life in the air, boy. You don't have to tell me about air. What I'm saying is, there's too much air coming in that window when I'm asleep.

ASTON   Gets very stuffy in here without that window open.

Aston crosses to the chair, puts the plank on it, and continues sandpapering.

DAVIES Yes, but listen, you don't know what I'm telling you. That bloody rain, man, come right in on my head. Spoils my sleep. I could catch my death of cold with it, with that draught. That's all I'm saying. Just shut that window and no one's going to catch any colds, that's all I'm saying.

Pause.

ASTON I couldn't sleep in here without that window open.

DAVIES Yes, but what about me? What . . . what you got to say about my position?

ASTON Why don't you sleep the other way round?

DAVIES What do you mean?

ASTON Sleep with your feet to the window.

DAVIES What good would that do?

ASTON The rain wouldn't come in on your head.

DAVIES No, I couldn't do that. I couldn't do that.

Pause.

DAVIES (*cont.*) I mean, I got used to sleeping this way. It isn't me has to change, it's that window. You see, it's raining now. Look at it. It's coming down now.

Pause.

ASTON I think I'll have a walk down to Goldhawk Road. I got talking to a man there. He had a saw bench. It looked in pretty good condition to me. Don't think it's much good to him.

Pause.

ASTON (*cont.*) Have a walk down there, I think.

DAVIES Listen to that. That's done my trip to Sidcup. Eh, what about closing that window now? It'll be coming in here.

ASTON Close it for the time being.

Davies closes the window and looks out.

DAVIES What's all that under that tarpaulin out there?

ASTON Wood.

DAVIES What for?

ASTON To build my shed.

Davies sits on his bed.

DAVIES You haven't come across that pair of shoes you was going to look out for me, have you?

ASTON Oh. No. I'll see if I can pick some up today.

DAVIES I can't go out in this with these, can I? I can't even go out and get a cup of tea.

ASTON There's a café just along the road.

DAVIES There may be, mate.

During Aston's speech the room grows darker.

By the close of the speech only Aston can be seen clearly. Davies and all the other objects are in the shadow. The fade-down of the light must be as gradual, as protracted and as unobtrusive as possible.

ASTON I used to go there quite a bit. Oh, years ago now. But I stopped. I used to like that place. Spent quite a bit of time in there. That was before I went away. Just before. I think that . . . place had a lot to do with it. They were all . . . a good bit older than me. But they always used to listen. I thought . . . they understood what I said. I mean I used to talk to them. I talked too much. That was my mistake. The same in the factory. Standing there, or in the breaks, I used to . . . talk about things. And these men, they used to listen, whenever I . . . had anything to say. It was all right. The trouble was, I used to have kind of hallucinations. They weren't hallucinations, they . . . I used to get the feeling I could see things . . . very clearly . . . everything . . . was so clear . . . everything used . . . everything used to get very quiet . . . everything got very quiet . . . all this . . . quiet . . . and . . . this clear sight . . . it was . . . but maybe I was wrong. Anyway, someone must have said something. I didn't know

anything about it. And . . . some kind of lie must have got around.
And this lie went round. I thought people started being funny. In that
café. The factory. I couldn't understand it. Then one day they took
me to a hospital, right outside London. They . . . got me there. I
didn't want to go. Anyway . . . I tried to get out, quite a few times.
But . . . it wasn't very easy. They asked me questions, in there. Got
me in and asked me all sorts of questions. Well, I told them . . . when
they wanted to know. . . what my thoughts were. Hmmnn. Then one
day . . . this man . . . doctor, I suppose . . . the head one . . . he was
quite a man of . . . distinction . . . although I wasn't so sure about
that. He called me in. He said . . . he told me I had something. He
said they'd concluded their examination. That's what he said. And he
showed me a pile of papers and he said that I'd got something, some
complaint. He said . . . he just said that, you see. You've got . . . this
thing. That's your complaint. And we've decided, he said, that in
your interests there's only one course we can take. He said . . . but I
can't . . . exactly remember . . . how he put it . . . he said, we're
going to do something to your brain. He said . . . if we don't, you'll
be in here for the rest of your life, but if we do, you stand a chance.
You can go out, he said, and live like the others. What do you want
to do to my brain, I said to him. But he just repeated what he'd said.
Well, I wasn't a fool. I knew I was a minor. I knew he couldn't do
anything to me without getting permission. I knew he had to get
permission from my mother. So I wrote to her and told her what they
were trying to do. But she signed their form, you see, giving them
permission. I know that because he showed me her signature when I
brought it up. Well, that night I tried to escape, that night. I spent
five hours sawing at one of the bars on the window in this ward.
Right throughout the dark. They used to shine a torch over the beds
every half hour. So I timed it just right. And then it was nearly done,
and a man had a . . . he had a fit, right next to me, And they caught
me, anyway. About a week later they started to come round and do
this thing to the brain. We were all supposed to have it done, in this
ward. And they came round and did it one at a time. One a night. I
was one of the last. And I could see quite clearly what they did to the
others. They used to come round with these . . . I don't know what
they were . . . they looked like big pincers, with wires on, the wires
were attached to a little machine. It was electric. They used to hold
the man down, and this chief . . . the chief doctor, used to fit the

pincers, something like earphones, he used to fit them on either side of the man's skull. There was a man holding the machine, you see, and he'd . . . turn it on, and the chief would just press these pincers on either side of the skull and keep them there. Then he'd take them off. They'd cover the man up . . . and they wouldn't touch him again until later on. Some used to put up a fight, but most of them didn't. They just lay there. Well, they were coming round to me, and the night they came I got up and stood against the wall. They told me to get on the bed, and I knew they had to get me on the bed because if they did it while I was standing up they might break my spine. So I stood up and then one or two of them came for me, well, I was younger then, I was much stronger than I am now, I was quite strong then, I laid one of them out and I had another one round the throat, and then suddenly this chief had these pincers on my skull and I knew he wasn't supposed to do it while I was standing up, that's why I. . . . anyway, he did it. So I did get out. I got out of the place . . . but I couldn't walk very well. I don't think my spine was damaged. That was perfectly all right. The trouble was . . . my thoughts . . . had become very slow . . . I couldn't think at all . . . I couldn't . . . get . . . my thoughts . . . together . . . uuuhh . . . I could . . . never quite get it . . . together. The trouble was, I couldn't hear what people were saying. I couldn't look to the right or the left, I had to look straight in front of me, because if I turned my head round . . . I couldn't keep . . . upright. And I had these headaches. I used to sit in my room. That was when I lived with my mother. And my brother. He was younger than me. And I laid everything out, in order, in my room, all the things I knew were mine, but I didn't die. The thing is, I should have been dead. I should have died. Anyway, I feel much better now. But I don't talk to people now. I steer clear of places like that café. I never go into them now. I don't talk to anyone . . . like that. I've often thought of going back and trying to find the man who did that to me. But I want to do something first. I want to build that shed out in the garden.

Curtain

ACT THREE

Two weeks later.

Mick is lying on the floor, down left, his head resting on the rolled carpet, looking up at the ceiling.

Davies is sitting in the chair, holding his pipe. He is wearing the smoking-jacket. It is afternoon.

Silence.

DAVIES   I got a feeling he's done something to them cracks.

Pause.

DAVIES (*cont.*)   See, there's been plenty of rain in the last week, but it ain't been dripping into the bucket.

Pause.

DAVIES (*cont.*)   He must have tarred it over up there.

Pause.

DAVIES (*cont.*)   There was someone walking about on the roof the other night. It must have been him.

Pause.

DAVIES (*cont.*)   But I got a feeling he's tarred it over on the roof up there. Ain't said a word to me about it. Don't say a word to me.

Pause.

DAVIES (*cont.*)   He don't answer me when I talk to him.

He lights a match, holds it to his pipe, and blows it.

DAVIES (*cont.*)   He don't give me no knife!

Pause.

DAVIES (*cont.*)   He don't give me no knife to cut my bread.

Pause.

DAVIES (*cont.*)   How can I cut a loaf of bread without no knife?

Pause.

DAVIES (*cont.*)   It's an impossibility.

Pause.

MICK   You've got a knife.

DAVIES   What?

MICK   You've got a knife.

DAVIES   I got a knife, sure I got a knife, but how do you expect me to cut a good loaf of bread with that? That's not a bread-knife. It's nothing to do with cutting bread. I picked it up somewhere. I don't know where it's been, do I? No, what I want—

MICK   I know what you want.

Pause. Davies rises and goes to the gas stove.

DAVIES   What about this gas stove? He tells me it's not connected. How do I know it's not connected? Here I am, I'm sleeping right with it, I wake up in the middle of the night, I'm looking right into the oven, man! It's right next to my face, how do I know, I could be lying there in bed, it might blow up, it might do me harm!

Pause.

DAVIES (*cont.*)   But he don't seem to take any notice of what I say to him. I told him the other day, see, I told him about them Blacks, about them Blacks coming up from next door, and using the lavatory. I told him, it was all dirty in there, all the banisters were dirty, they were black, all the lavatory was black. But what did he do? He's supposed to be in charge of it here, he had nothing to say, he hadn't got a word to say.

Pause.

DAVIES (*cont.*)   Couple of weeks ago . . . he sat there, he give me a long chat . . . about a couple of weeks ago. A long chat he give me. Since then he ain't said hardly a word. He went on talking there . . . I don't know what he was . . . he wasn't looking at me, he wasn't talking to me, he don't care about me. He was talking to himself! That's all he worries about. I mean, you come up to me, you ask my advice, he

wouldn't never do a thing like that. I mean, we don't have any
conversation, you see? You can't live in the same room with someone
who . . . who don't have any conversation with you.

Pause.

DAVIES (*cont.*)   I just can't get the hang of him.

Pause.

DAVIES (*cont.*)   You and me, we could get this place going.

MICK (*ruminatively*)   Yes, you're quite right. Look what I could do with
this place.

Pause.

MICK (*cont.*)   I could turn this place into a penthouse. For instance . . .
this room. This room you could have as the kitchen. Right size, nice
window, sun comes in. I'd have . . . I'd have teal-blue, copper and
parchment linoleum squares. I'd have those colours re-echoed in the
walls. I'd offset the kitchen units with charcoal-grey worktops. Plenty
of room for cupboards for the crockery. We'd have a small wall
cupboard, a large wall cupboard, a corner wall cupboard with
revolving shelves. You wouldn't be short of cupboards. You could
put the dining-room across the landing, see? Yes. Venetian blinds on
the window, cork floor, cork tiles. You could have an off-white pile
linen rug, a table in . . . in afromosia teak veneer, sideboard with
matt-black drawers, curved chairs with cushioned seats, armchairs in
oatmeal tweed, a beech frame settee with a woven sea-grass seat,
white-topped heat-resistant coffee table, white tile surround. Yes.
Then the bedroom. What's a bedroom? It's a retreat. It's a place to go
for rest and peace. So you want quiet decoration. The lighting
functional. Furniture . . . mahogany and rosewood. Deep azure-blue
carpet, unglazed blue and white curtains, a bedspread with a pattern of
small blue roses on a white ground, dressing-table with a lift-up top
containing a plastic tray, table lamp of white raffia . . . (*Mick sits up.*) it
wouldn't be a flat it'd be a palace.

DAVIES   I'd say it would, man.

MICK   A palace.

DAVIES   Who would live there?

MICK   I would. My brother and me.

Pause.

DAVIES   What about me?

MICK (*quietly*)   All this junk here, it's no good to anyone. It's just a lot
   of old iron, that's all. Clobber. You couldn't make a home out of this.
   There's no way you could arrange it. It's junk. He could never sell it,
   either, he wouldn't get tuppence for it.

Pause.

MICK (*cont.*)   Junk.

Pause.

MICK (*cont.*)   But he doesn't seem to be interested in what I got in
   mind, that's the trouble. Why don't you have a chat with him, see if
   he's interested?

DAVIES   Me?

MICK   Yes. You're a friend of his.

DAVIES   He's no friend of mine.

MICK   You're living in the same room with him, en't you?

DAVIES   He's no friend of mine. You don't know where you are with
   him. I mean, with a bloke like you, you know where you are.

Mick looks a him.

DAVIES (*cont.*)   I mean, you got your own ways, I'm not saying you ain't
   got your own ways, anyone can see that. You may have some funny
   ways, but that's the same with all of us, but with him it's different, see? I
   mean at least with you, the thing with you is you're . . .

MICK   Straightforward.

DAVIES   That's it, you're straightforward.

MICK   Yes.

DAVIES   But with him, you don't know what he's up to half the time!

MICK   Uh.

DAVIES   He's got no feelings!

Pause.

DAVIES (*cont.*)   See, what I need is a clock! I need a clock to tell the time! How can I tell the time without a clock? I can't do it! I said to him, I said, look here, what about getting in a clock, so's I can tell what time it is? I mean, if you can't tell what time you're at you don't know where you are, you understand my meaning? See, what I got to do now, if I'm walking about outside, I got to get my eye on a clock, and keep the time in my head for when I come in. But that's no good, I mean I'm not in here five minutes and I forgotten it. I forgotten what time it was!

Davies walks up and down the room.

DAVIES (*cont.*)   Look at it this way. If I don't feel well I have a bit of a lay down, then, when I wake up, I don't know what time it is to go and have a cup of tea! You see, it's not so bad when I'm coming in. I can see the clock on the corner, the moment I'm stepping into the house I know what the time is, but when I'm *in*! It's when I'm *in* . . . that I haven't the foggiest idea what time it is!

Pause.

DAVIES (*cont.*)   No, what I need is a clock in here, in this room, and then I stand a bit of a chance. But he don't give me one.

Davies sits in the chair.

DAVIES (*cont.*)   He wakes me up! He wakes me up in the middle of the night! Tells me I'm making noises! I tell you I've half a mind to give him a mouthful one of these days.

MICK   He don't let you sleep?

DAVIES   He don't let me sleep! He wakes me up!

MICK   That's terrible.

DAVIES   I been plenty of other places. They always let me sleep. It's the same the whole world over. Except here.

MICK   Sleep's essential. I've always said that.

DAVIES   You're right, it's essential. I get up in the morning, I'm worn
out! I got business to see to. I got to move myself, I got to sort myself
out, I got to get fixed up. But when I wake up in the morning, I ain't
got no energy in me. And on top of that I ain't got no clock.

MICK   Yes.

DAVIES (*standing, moving*)   He goes out, I don't know where he goes to,
where's he go, he never tells me. We used to have a bit of a chat, not
any more. I never see him, he goes out, he comes in late, next thing I
know he's shoving me about in the middle of the night.

Pause.

DAVIES (*cont.*)   Listen! I wake up in the morning . . . I wake up in the
morning and he's smiling at me! He's standing there, looking at me,
smiling! I can see him, you see, I can see him through the blanket. He
puts on his coat, he turns himself round, he looks down at my bed,
there's a smile on his face! What the hell's he smiling at? What he
don't know is that I'm watching him through that blanket. He don't
know that! He don't know I can see him, he thinks I'm asleep, but I
got my eye on him all the time through the blanket, see? But he don't
know that! He just looks at me and he smiles, but he don't know that
I can see him doing it!

Pause.

DAVIES (*cont.*) (*bending, close to Mick*)   No, what you want to do, you
want to speak to him, see? I got . . . I got that worked out. You want
to tell him . . . that we got ideas for this place, we could build it up,
we could get it started. You see, I could decorate it out for you, I
could give you a hand in doing it . . . between us.

Pause.

DAVIES (*cont.*)   Where do you live now, then?

MICK   Me? Oh, I've got a little place. Not bad. Everything laid on. You
must come up and have a drink some time. Listen to some
Tchaikovsky.

DAVIES   No, you see, you're the bloke who wants to talk to him. I
mean, you're his brother.

Pause.

MICK   Yes . . . maybe I will.

A door bangs.

Mick rises, goes to the door and exits.

DAVIES   Where you going? This is him!

Silence.

Davies stands, then goes to the window and looks out.

Aston enters. He is carrying a paper bag. He takes off his overcoat, opens the bag and takes out a pair of shoes.

ASTON   Pair of shoes.

DAVIES (*turning*)   What?

ASTON   I picked them up. Try them.

DAVIES   Shoes? What sort?

ASTON   They might do you.

Davies comes downstage, takes off his sandals and tries the shoes on. He walks about, waggling his feet, bends, and presses the leather.

DAVIES   No, they're not right.

ASTON   Aren't they?

DAVIES   No, they don't fit.

ASTON   Mmnn.

Pause.

DAVIES   Well, I'll tell you what, they might do . . . until I get another pair.

Pause.

DAVIES (*cont.*)   Where's the laces?

ASTON   No laces.

DAVIES   I can't wear them without laces.

ASTON   I just got the shoes.

DAVIES   Well now, look that puts the lid on it, don't it? I mean, you couldn't keep these shoes on right without a pair of laces. The only way to keep a pair of shoes on, if you haven't got no laces, is to tighten the foot, see? Walk about with a tight foot, see? Well, that's no good for the foot. Puts a bad strain on the foot. If you can do the shoes up proper there's less chance of you getting a strain.

Aston goes round to the top of his bed.

ASTON   I might have some somewhere.

DAVIES   You see what I'm getting at?

Pause.

ASTON   Here's some. (*He hands them to Davies.*)

DAVIES   These are brown.

ASTON   That's all I got.

DAVIES   These shoes are black.

Aston does not answer.

DAVIES (*cont.*)   Well, they can do, anyway, until I get another pair.

Davies sits in the chair and begins to lace his shoes.

DAVIES (*cont.*)   Maybe they'll get me down to Sidcup tomorrow. If I get down there I'll be able to sort myself out.

Pause.

DAVIES (*cont.*)   I've been offered a good job. Man has offered it to me, he's . . . he's got plenty of ideas. He's got a bit of a future. But they want my papers, you see, they want my references. I'd have to get down to Sidcup before I could get hold of them. That's where they are, see. Trouble is, getting there. That's my problem. The weather's dead against it.

Aston quietly exits, unnoticed.

DAVIES (*cont.*)   Don't know as these shoes'll be much good. It's a hard road, I been down there before. Coming the other way, like. Last time I left there, it was . . . last time . . . getting on a while back . . . the road was bad, the rain was coming down, lucky I didn't die there on the road, but I got here, I kept going, all along . . . yes . . . I kept going all along. But all the same, I can't go on like this, what I got to do, I got to get back there, find this man—

He turns and looks about the room.

DAVIES (*cont.*)   Christ! That bastard, he ain't even listening to me!

Blackout.

Dim light through the window.

It is night. Aston and Davies are in bed, Davies groaning. Aston sits up, gets out of bed, switches on the light, goes over to Davies and shakes him.

ASTON   Hey, stop it, will you? I can't sleep.

DAVIES   What? What? What's going on?

ASTON   You're making noises.

DAVIES   I'm an old man, what do you expect me to do, stop breathing?

ASTON   You're making noises.

DAVIES   What do you expect me to do, stop breathing?

Aston goes to his bed, and puts on his trousers.

ASTON   I'll get a bit of air.

DAVIES   What do you expect me to do? I tell you, mate, I'm not surprised they took you in. Waking an old man up in the middle of the night, you must be off your nut! Giving me bad dreams, who's responsible, then, for me having bad dreams? If you wouldn't keep mucking me about I wouldn't make no noises! How do you expect me to sleep peaceful when you keep poking me all the time? What do you want me to do, stop breathing?

He throws the cover off and gets out of bed, wearing his vest, waistcoat and trousers.

DAVIES (*cont.*)   It's getting so freezing in here I have to keep my trousers on to go to bed. I never done that before in my life. But that's what I got to do here. Just because you won't put in any bleeding heating! I've had just about enough with you mucking me about. I've seen better days than you have, man. Nobody ever got me inside one of them places, anyway. I'm a sane man! So don't you start mucking me about. I'll be all right as long as you keep your place. Just you keep your place, that's all. Because I can tell you, your brother's got his eye on you. He knows all about you. I got a friend there, don't you worry about that. I got a true pal there. Treating me like dirt! Why'd you invite me in here in the first place if you was going to treat me like this? You think you're better than me you got another think coming. I know enough. They had you inside one of them places before, they can have you: inside again. Your brother's got his eye on you! They can put the pincers on your head again, man! They can have them on again! Any time. All they got to do is get the word. They'd carry you in there, boy. They'd come here and pick you up and carry you in! They'd keep you fixed! They'd put them pincers on your head, they'd have you fixed! They'd take one look at all this junk I got to sleep with they'd know you were a creamer. That was the greatest mistake they made, you take my tip, letting you get out of that place. Nobody knows what you're at, you go out you come in, nobody knows what you're at! Well, nobody messes me about for long. You think I'm going to do your dirty work? Haaaaahhhhh! You better think again! You want me to do all the dirty work all up and down them stairs just so I can sleep in this lousy filthy hole every night? Not me, boy. Not for you boy. You don't know what you're doing half the time. You're up the creek! You're half off! You can tell it by looking at you. Who ever saw you slip me a few bob? Treating me like a bloody animal! I never been inside a nuthouse!

Aston makes a slight move towards him. Davies takes his knife from his back pocket.

DAVIES (*cont.*)   Don't come nothing with me, mate. I got this here. I used it. I used it. Don't come it with me.

A pause. They stare at each other.

DAVIES (*cont.*)   Mind what you do now.

Pause.

DAVIES (*cont.*)   Don't you try anything with me.

Pause.

ASTON   I . . . I think it's about time you found somewhere else. I don't think we're hitting it off.

DAVIES   Find somewhere else?

ASTON   Yes.

DAVIES   Me? You talking to me? Not me, man! You!

ASTON   What?

DAVIES   You! You better find somewhere else!

ASTON   I live here. You don't.

DAVIES   Don't I? Well, I live here. I been offered a job here.

ASTON   Yes . . . well, I don't think you're really suitable.

DAVIES   Not suitable? Well, I can tell you, there's someone here thinks I am suitable. And I'll tell you. I'm staying on here as caretaker! Get it! Your brother, he's told me, see, he's told me the job is mine. Mine! So that's where I am. I'm going to be his caretaker.

ASTON   My brother?

DAVIES   He's staying, he's going to run this. place, and I'm staying with him.

ASTON   Look. If I give you . . . a few bob you can get down to Sidcup.

DAVIES   You build your shed first! A few bob! When I can earn a steady wage here! You build your stinking shed first! That's what!

Aston stares at him.

ASTON   That's not a stinking shed.

Silence.

Aston moves to him.

ASTON (*cont.*)   It's clean. It's all good wood. I'll get it up. No trouble.

DAVIES   Don't come too near!

ASTON (*cont.*)   You've no reason to call that shed stinking.

Davies points the knife.

ASTON (*cont.*)   You stink.

DAVIES   What!

ASTON   You've been stinking the place out.

DAVIES   Christ, you say that to me!

ASTON   For days. That's one reason I can't sleep.

DAVIES   You call me that! You call me stinking!

ASTON   You better go.

DAVIES   I'LL STINK YOU!

He thrusts his arm out, the arm trembling, the knife pointing at Aston's stomach. Aston does not move. Silence. Davies' arm moves no farther. They stand.

DAVIES (*cont.*)   I'll stink you. . . .

Pause.

ASTON   Get your stuff.

Davies draws the knife in to his chest, breathing heavily. Aston goes to Davies' bed, collects his bag and puts a few of Davies' things into it.

DAVIES   You ain't . . . you ain't got the right . . . Leave that alone, that's mine!

Davies takes the bag and presses the contents down.

DAVIES (*cont.*)   All right . . . I been offered a job here . . . you wait . . . (*He puts on his smoking-jacket.*) . . . you wait . . . your brother . . . he'll sort you out . . . you call me that . . . you call me that . . . no one's ever called me that. . . . (*He puts on his overcoat.*) You'll be sorry you called me that . . . you ain't heard the last of this . . . (*He picks up his bag and goes to the door.*) You'll be sorry you called me that. . . .

He opens the door, Aston watching him.

DAVIES (*cont.*)   Now I know who I can trust.

Davies goes out. Aston stands.

Blackout.

Lights up. Early evening.

Voices on the stairs.

Mick and Davies enter.

DAVIES Stink! You hear that! Me! I told you what he said, didn't I? Stink! You hear that? That's what he said to me!

MICK Tch, tch, tch.

DAVIES That's what he said to me.

MICK You don't stink.

DAVIES No, sir!

MICK If you stank I'd be the first one to tell you.

DAVIES I told him, I told him he . . . I said to him, you ain't heard the last of this man! I said, don't you forget your brother. I told him you'd be coming along to sort him out. He don't know what he's started, doing that. Doing that to me. I said to him, I said to him, he'll be along, your brother'll be along, he's got sense, not like you—

MICK What do you mean?

DAVIES Eh?

MICK You saying my brother hasn't got any sense?

DAVIES What? What I'm saying is, you got ideas for this place, all this . . . all this decorating, see? I mean, he's got no right to order me about. I take orders from you, I do my caretaking for you, I mean, you look upon me . . . you don't treat me like a lump of dirt . . . we can both . . . we can both see him for what he is.

Pause.

MICK What did he say then, when you told him I'd offered you the job as caretaker?

DAVIES He . . . he said . . . he said . . . something about . . . he lived here.

MICK Yes, he's got a point, en' he?

DAVIES A point! This is your house, en't? You let him live here!

MICK I could tell him to go, I suppose.

DAVIES That's what I'm saying.

MICK Yes. I could tell him to go. I mean, I'm the landlord. On the other hand, he's the sitting tenant. Giving him notice, you see, what it is, it's a technical matter, that's what it is. It depends how you regard this room. I mean it depends whether you regard this room as furnished or unfurnished. See what I mean?

DAVIES No, I don't.

MICK All this furniture, you see, in here, it's all his, except the beds, of course. So what it is, it's a fine legal point, that's what it is.

Pause.

DAVIES I tell you he should go back where he come from!

MICK (*turning to look at kin*) Come from?

DAVIES Yes.

MICK Where did he come from?

DAVIES Well ... he ... he ...

MICK You get a bit out of your depth sometimes, don't you?

Pause.

MICK (*cont.*) (*rising, briskly*) Well, anyway, as things stand, I don't mind having a go at doing up the place. ...

DAVIES That's what I wanted to hear!

MICK No, I don't mind.

He turns to face Davies.

MICK (*cont.*) But you better be as good as you say you are.

DAVIES What do you mean?

MICK Well, you say you're an interior decorator, you'd better be a good one.

DAVIES A what?

MICK   What do you mean, a what? A decorator. An interior decorator.

DAVIES   Me? What do you mean? I never touched that. I never been that.

MICK   You've never what?

DAVIES   No, no, not me, man. I'm not an interior decorator. I been too busy. Too many other things to do, you see. But I . . . but I could always turn my hand to most things . . . give me. . . give me a bit of time to pick it up.

MICK   I don't want you to pick it up. I want a first-class experienced interior decorator. I thought you were one.

DAVIES   Me? Now wait a minute—wait a minute—you got the wrong man.

MICK   How could I have the wrong man? You're the only man I've spoken to. You're the only man I've told, about my dreams, about my deepest wishes, you're the only one I've told, and I only told you because I understood you were an experienced first-class professional interior and exterior decorator.

DAVIES   Now look here—

MICK   You mean you wouldn't know how to fit teal-blue, copper and parchment linoleum squares and have those colours re-echoed in the walls?

DAVIES   Now, look here, where'd you get—?

MICK   You wouldn't be able to decorate out a table in afromosia teak veneer, an armchair in oatmeal tweed and a beech frame settee with a woven sea-grass seat?

DAVIES   I never said that!

MICK   Christ! I must have been under a false impression!

DAVIES   I never said it!

MICK   You're a bloody impostor, mate!

DAVIES   Now you don't want to say that sort of thing to me. You took me on here as caretaker. I was going to give you a helping hand, that's

all, for a small . . . for a small wage, I never said nothing about that
. . . you start calling me names—

MICK   What is your name?

DAVIES   Don't start that—

MICK   No, what's your real name?

DAVIES   My real name's Davies.

MICK   What's the name you go under?

DAVIES   Jenkins!

MICK   You got two names. What about the rest? Eh? Now come on,
why did you tell me all this dirt about you being an interior
decorator?

DAVIES   I didn't tell you nothing! Won't you listen to what I'm saying?

Pause.

DAVIES (*cont.*)   It was him who told you. It was your brother who must
have told you. He's nutty! I He'd tell you anything, out of spite, he's
nutty, he's halfway gone, it was him who told you.

Mick walks slowly to him.

MICK   What did you call my brother?

DAVIES   When?

MICK   He's what?

DAVIES   I . . . now get this straight. . . .

MICK   Nutty? Who's nutty?

Pause.

MICK (*cont.*)   Did you call my brother nutty? My brother. That's a bit of
. . . that's a bit of an impertinent thing to say, isn't it?

DAVIES   But he says so himself!

*Mick walks slowly round Davies' figure, regarding him, once. He circles him,
once.*

174

MICK   What a strange man you are. Aren't you? You're really strange. Ever since you come into this house there's been nothing but trouble. Honest. I can take nothing you say at face value. Every word you speak is open to any number of different interpretations. Most of what you say is lies. You're violent, you're erratic, you're just completely unpredictable. You're nothing else but a wild animal, when you come down to it. You're a barbarian. And to put the old tin lid on it, you stink from arsehole to breakfast time. Look at it. You come here recommending yourself as an interior decorator, whereupon I take you on, and what happens? You make a long speech about all the references you've got down at Sidcup, and what happens? I haven't noticed you go down to Sidcup to obtain them. It's all most regrettable but it looks as though I'm compelled to pay you off for your caretaking work. Here's half a dollar.

He feels in his pocket, takes out a half-crown and tosses it at Davies' feet. Davies stands still. Mick walks to the gas stove and picks up the Buddha.

DAVIES (*slowly*)   All right then . . . you do that . . . you do it . . . if that's what you want. . . .

MICK   THAT'S WHAT I WANT!

He hurls the Buddha against the gas stove. It breaks.

MICK (*cont.*) (*passionately*)   Anyone would think this house was all I got to worry about. I got plenty of other things I can worry about. I've got other things. I've got plenty of other interests. I've got my own business to build up, haven't I? I got to think about expanding . . . in all directions. I don't stand still. I'm moving about, all the time. I'm moving . . . all the time. I've got to think about the future. I'm not worried about this house. I'm not interested. My brother can worry about it. He can do it up, he can decorate it, he can do what he likes with it. I'm not bothered. I thought I was doing him a favour, letting him live here. He's got his own ideas. Let him have them. I'm going to chuck it in.

Pause.

DAVIES   What about me?

Silence. Mick does not look at him.

A door bangs.

Silence. They do not move.

Aston comes in. He closes the door, moves into the room and faces Mick. They look at each other. Both are smiling, faintly.

MICK (*beginning to speak to Aston*)   Look . . . uh . . .

He stops, goes to the door and exits. Aston leaves the door open, crosses behind Davies, sees the broken Buddha, and looks at the pieces for a moment. He then goes to his bed, takes off his overcoat, sits, takes the screwdriver and plug and pokes the plug.

DAVIES   I just come back for my pipe.

ASTON   Oh yes.

DAVIES   I got out and . . . halfway down I . . . I suddenly . . . found out . . . you see . . . that I hadn't got my pipe. So I come back to get it. . . .

Pause. He moves to Aston.

DAVIES (*cont.*)   That ain't the same plug, is it, you been . . . ?

Pause.

DAVIES (*cont.*)   Still can't get anywhere with it, eh?

Pause.

DAVIES (*cont.*)   Well, if you . . . persevere, in my opinion, you'll probably . . .

Pause.

DAVIES (*cont.*)   Listen. . . .

Pause.

DAVIES (*cont.*)   You didn't mean that, did you, about me stinking, did you?

Pause.

DAVIES (*cont.*)   Did you? You been a good friend to me. You took me in. You took me in, you didn't ask me no questions, you give me a bed, you been a mate to me. Listen. I been thinking, why I made all

176

them noises, it was because of the draught, see, that draught was on me as I was sleeping, made me make noises without me knowing it, so I been thinking, what I mean to say, if you was to give me your bed, and you have my bed, there's not all that difference between them, they're the same sort of bed, if I was to have yourn, you sleep, wherever bed you're in, so you have mine, I have yourn, and that'll be all right, I'll be out of the draught, see, I mean, you don't mind a bit of wind, you need a bit of air, I can understand that, you being in that place that time, with all them doctors and all they done, closed up, I know them places, too hot, you see, they're always too hot, I had a peep in one once, nearly suffocated me, so I reckon that'd be the best way out of it, we swap beds, and then we could get down to what we was saying, I'd look after the place for you, I'd keep an eye on it for you, for you, like, not for the other . . . not for . . . for your brother, you see, not for him, for you, I'll be your man, you say the word, just say the word. . . .

Pause.

DAVIES (*cont.*)   What do you think of this I'm saying?

Pause.

ASTON   No, I like sleeping in this bed.

DAVIES   But you don't understand my meaning!

ASTON   Anyway, that one's my brother's bed.

DAVIES   Your brother?

ASTON   Any time he stays here. This is my bed. It's the only bed I can sleep in.

DAVIES   But your brother's gone! He's gone!

Pause.

ASTON   No. I couldn't change beds.

DAVIES   But you don't understand my meaning!

ASTON   Anyway, I'm going to be busy. I've got that shed to get up. If I don't get it up now it'll never go up. Until it's up I can't get started.

DAVIES   I'll give you a hand to put up your shed, that's what I'll do!

Pause.

DAVIES (*cont.*)   I'll give you a hand! We'll both put up that shed together! See? Get it done in next to no time! Do you see what I'm saying?

Pause.

ASTON   No. I can get it up myself.

DAVIES   But listen. I'm with you, I'll be here, I'll do it for you!

Pause.

DAVIES (*cont.*)   We'll do it together!

Pause.

DAVIES (*cont.*)   Christ, we'll change beds!

Aston moves to the window and stands with his back to Davies.

DAVIES (*cont.*)   You mean you're throwing me out? You can't do that. Listen man, listen man, I don't mind, you see, I don't mind, I'll stay, I don't mind, I'll tell you what, if you don't want to change beds, we'll keep it as it is, I'll stay in the same bed, maybe if I can get a stronger piece of sacking, like, to go over the window, keep out the draught, that'll do it, what do you say, we'll keep it as it is?

Pause.

ASTON   No.

DAVIES   Why . . . not?

Aston turns to look at him.

ASTON   You make too much noise.

DAVIES   But . . . but . . . look . . . listen . . . listen here . . . I mean . . .

Aston turns back to the window.

DAVIES (*cont.*)   What am I going to do?

Pause.

DAVIES (*cont.*)   What shall I do?

Pause.

DAVIES (*cont.*) Where am I going to go?

Pause.

DAVIES (*cont.*) If you want me to go . . . I'll go. You just say the word.

Pause.

DAVIES (*cont.*) I'll tell you what though . . . them shoes . . . them shoes you give me . . . they're working out all right . . . they're all right. Maybe I could . . . get down . . .

Aston remains still, his back to him, at the window.

DAVIES (*cont.*) Listen . . . if I . . . got down . . . if I was to . . . get my papers . . . would you . . . would you let . . . would you . . . if I got down . . . and got my . . .

Long silence.

Curtain.

THE HOMECOMING

The Homecoming was first presented by the Royal Shakespeare Company at the Aldwych Theatre on June 3, 1965, with the following cast:

MAX, *a man of seventy*   Paul Rogers
LENNY, *a man in his early thirties*   Ian Holm
SAM, *a man of sixty-three*   John Normington
JOEY, a *man in his middle twenties*   Terence Rigby
TEDDY, *a man in his middle thirties*   Michael Bryant
RUTH, a *woman in her early thirties*   Vivien Merchant

Directed by Peter Hall

The play was presented by the Royal Shakespeare Company and Alexander H. Cohen at the Music Box Theatre, New York, on 5 January, 1967 with one change in the cast: the part of Teddy was played by Michael Craig.

SUMMER

An old house in North London.

A large room, extending the width of the stage.

The back wall, which contained the door, has been removed. A square arch shape remains. Beyond it, the hall. In the hall a staircase, ascending up left, well in view. The front door up right. A coatstand, hooks, etc.

In the room a window, right. Odd tables, chairs. Two large armchairs. A large sofa, left. Against the right wall a large sideboard, the upper half of which contains a mirror. Up left, a radiogram.

ACT ONE

Evening.

LENNY *is sitting on the sofa with a newspaper, a pencil in his hand. He wears a dark suit. He makes occasional marks on the back page.*

MAX *comes in, from the direction of the kitchen. He goes to sideboard, opens top drawer, rummages in it, closes it.*

He wears an old cardigan and a cap, and carries a stick.

He walks downstage, stands, looks about the room.

MAX   What have you done with the scissors?

Pause.

MAX *(cont.)*   I said I'm looking for the scissors. What have you done with them?

Pause.

MAX *(cont.)*   Did you hear me? I want to cut something out of the paper.

LENNY   I'm reading the paper.

MAX   Not that paper. I haven't even read that paper. I'm talking about last Sunday's paper. I was just having a look at it in the kitchen.

Pause.

MAX *(cont.)*   Do you hear what I'm saying? I'm talking to you! Where's the scissors?

LENNY *(looking up, quietly)*   Why don't you shut up, you daft prat?

Max lifts his stick and points it at him.

MAX   Don't you talk to me like that. I'm warning you.

He sits in large armchair.

MAX *(cont.)*   There's an advertisement in the paper about flannel vests. Cut price. Navy surplus. I could do with a few of them.

Pause.

MAX (*cont.*) I think I'll have a fag. Give me a fag.

Pause.

MAX (*cont.*) I just asked you to give me a cigarette.

Pause.

MAX (*cont.*) Look what I'm lumbered with.

He takes a crumpled cigarette from his pocket.

MAX (*cont.*) I'm getting old, my word of honour.

He lights it.

MAX (*cont.*) You think I wasn't a tearaway? I could have taken care of you, twice over. I'm still strong. You ask your Uncle Sam what I was. But at the same time I always had a kind heart. Always.

Pause.

MAX (*cont.*) I used to knock about with a man called MacGregor. I called him Mac. You remember Mac? Eh?

Pause.

MAX (*cont.*) Huhh! We were two of the worst-hated men in the West End of London. I tell you, I still got the scars. We'd walk into a place, the whole room'd stand up, they'd make way to let us pass. You never heard such silence. Mind you, he was a big man, he was over six foot tall. His family were all MacGregors, they came all the way from Aberdeen, but he was the only one they called Mac.

Pause.

MAX (*cont.*) He was very fond of your mother, Mac was. Very fond. He always had a good word for her.

Pause.

MAX (*cont.*) Mind you, she wasn't such a bad woman. Even though it made me sick just to look at her rotten stinking face, she wasn't such a bad bitch. I gave her the best bleeding years of my life, anyway.

LENNY Plug it, will you, you stupid sod, I'm trying to read the paper.

MAX Listen! I'll chop your spine off, you talk to me like that! You understand? Talking to your lousy filthy father like that!

LENNY You know what, you're getting demented.

Pause.

LENNY (*cont.*) What do you think of Second Wind for the three-thirty?

MAX Where?

LENNY Sandown Park.

MAX Don't stand a chance.

LENNY Sure he does.

MAX Not a chance.

LENNY He's the winner.

Lenny ticks the paper.

MAX He talks to me about horses.

Pause.

MAX (*cont.*) I used to live on the course. One of the loves of my life. Epsom? I knew it like the back of my hand. I was one of the best-known faces down at the paddock. What a marvellous open-air life.

Pause.

MAX (*cont.*) He talks to me about horses. You only read their names in the papers. But I've stroked their manes, I've held them, I've calmed them down before a big race. I was the one they used to call for. Max, they'd say, there's a horse here, he's highly strung, you're the only man on the course who can calm him. It was true. I had a . . . I had an instinctive understanding of animals. I should have been a trainer. Many times I was offered the job—you know, a proper post, by the Duke of . . . I forget his name . . . one of the Dukes. But I had family obligations, my family needed me at home.

Pause.

MAX (*cont.*) The times I've watched those animals thundering past the post. What an experience. Mind you, I didn't lose, I made a few bob out of it, and you know why? Because I always had the smell of a horse. I could smell him. And not only the colts but the fillies. Because the fillies are more highly strung than the colts, they're more unreliable, did you know that? No, what do you know? Nothing. But I was always able to tell a good filly by one particular trick. I'd look her in the eye. You see? I'd stand in front of her and look her straight in the eye, it was a kind of hypnotism, and by the look deep down in her eye I could tell whether she was a stayer or not. It was a gift. I had a gift.

Pause.

MAX (*cont.*) And he talks to me about horses.

LENNY Dad, do you mind if I change the subject?

Pause.

LENNY (*cont.*) I want to ask you something. The dinner we had before, what was the name of it? What do you call it?

Pause.

LENNY (*cont.*) Why don't you buy a dog? You're a dog cook. Honest. You think you're cooking for a lot of dogs.

MAX If you don't like it get out

LENNY I am going out. I'm going out to buy myself a proper dinner.

MAX Well, get out! What are you waiting for?

Lenny looks at him.

LENNY What did you say?

MAX I said shove off out of it, that's what I said.

LENNY You'll go before me, Dad, if you talk to me in that tone of voice.

MAX Will I, you bitch?

Max grips his stick.

LENNY Oh, Daddy, you're not going to use your stick on me, are you? Eh? Don't use your stick on me, Daddy. No, please. It wasn't my fault, it was one of the others. I haven't done anything wrong, Dad, honest. Don't clout me with that stick, Dad.

Silence.

Max sits hunched. Lenny reads the paper.

SAM comes in the front door. He wears a chauffeur's uniform. He hangs his hat on a hook in the hall and comes into the room. He goes to a chair, sits in it and sighs.

LENNY (*cont.*)   Hullo, Uncle Sam.

SAM   Hullo.

LENNY   How are you, Uncle?

SAM   Not bad. A bit tired.

LENNY   Tired? I bet you're tired. Where you been?

SAM   I've been to London Airport.

LENNY   All the way up to London Airport? What, right up the M4?

SAM   Yes, all the way up there.

LENNY   Tch, tch, tch. Well, I think you're entitled to be tired, Uncle.

SAM   Well, it's the drivers.

LENNY   I know. That's what I'm talking about. I'm talking about the drivers.

SAM   Knocks you out.

Pause.

MAX   I'm here, too, you know.

Sam looks at him.

MAX (*cont.*)   I said I'm here, too. I'm sitting here.

SAM   I know you're here.

Pause.

SAM (*cont.*)   I took a Yankee out there today . . . to the Airport.

LENNY   Oh, a Yankee, was it?

SAM   Yes, I been with him all clay. Picked him up at the Savoy at half past twelve, took him to the Caprice for his lunch. After lunch I picked him up again, took him down to a house in Eaton Square— he had to pay a visit to a friend there—and then round about tea-time I took him right the way out to the Airport.

LENNY   Had to catch a plane there, did he?

SAM   Yes. Look what he gave me. He gave me a box of cigars.

Sam takes a box of cigars from his pocket.

MAX   Come here. Let's have a look at them.

Sam shows Max the cigars. Max takes one from the box, pinches it and sniffs it.

MAX   (*cont.*)   It's a fair cigar.

SAM   Want to try one?

Max and Sam light cigars.

SAM   (*cont.*)   You know what he said to me? He told me I was the best chauffeur he'd ever had. The best one.

MAX   From what point of view?

SAM   Eh?

MAX   From what point of view?

LENNY   From the point of view of his driving, Dad, and his general sense of courtesy, I should say.

MAX   Thought you were a good driver, did he, Sam? Well, he gave you a first-class cigar.

SAM   Yes, he thought I was the best he'd ever had. They all say that, you know. They won't have anyone else, they only ask for me. They say I'm the best chauffeur in the firm.

LENNY   I bet the other drivers tend to get jealous, don't they, Uncle?

SAM   They do get jealous. They get very jealous.

MAX   Why?

Pause.

SAM   I just told you.

MAX   No, I just can't get it clear, Sam. Why do the other drivers get jealous?

SAM   Because (a) I'm the best driver, and because . . . (b) I don't take liberties.

Pause.

SAM (*cont.*)   I don't press myself on people, you see. These big businessmen, men of affairs, they don't want the driver jawing all the time, they like to sit in the back, have a bit of peace and quiet. After all, they're sitting in a Humber Super Snipe, they can afford to relax. At the same time, though, this is what really makes me special . . . I do know how to pass the time of day when required.

Pause.

SAM (*cont.*)   For instance, I told this man today I was in the second world war. Not the first. I told him I was too young for the first. But I told him I fought in the second.

Pause.

SAM (*cont.*)   So did he, it turned out.

Lenny stands, goes to the mirror and straightens his tie.

LENNY   He was probably a colonel, or something, in the American Air Force.

SAM   Yes.

LENNY   Probably a navigator, or something like that, in a Flying Fortress. Now he's most likely a high executive in a worldwide group of aeronautical engineers.

SAM   Yes.

LENNY   Yes, I know the kind of man you're talking about.

Lenny goes out, turning to his right.

SAM   After all, I'm experienced. I was driving a dust cart at the age of nineteen. Then I was in long-distance haulage. I had ten years as a taxi-driver and I've had five as a private chauffeur.

MAX   It's funny you never got married, isn't it? A man with all your
gifts.

Pause.

MAX *(cont.)*   Isn't it? A man like you?

SAM   There's still time.

MAX   Is there?

Pause.

SAM   You'd be surprised.

MAX   What you been doing, banging away at your lady customers, have
you?

SAM   Not me.

MAX   In the back of the Snipe? Been having a few crafty reefs in a
layby, have you?

SAM   Not me.

MAX   On the back seat? What about the armrest, was it up or down?

SAM   I've never done that kind of thing in my car.

MAX   Above all that kind of thing, are you, Sam?

SAM   Too true.

MAX   Above having a good bang on the back seat, are you?

SAM   Yes, I leave that to others.

MAX   You leave it to others? What others? You paralysed prat!

SAM   I don't mess up my car! Or my . . . my boss's car! Like other
people.

MAX   Other people? What other people?

Pause.

MAX *(cont.)*   What other people?

Pause.

SAM Other people.

Pause.

MAX When you find the right girl, Sam, let your family know, don't forget, we'll give you a number one send-off, I promise you. You can bring her to live here, she can keep us all happy. We'd take it in turns to give her a walk round the park.

SAM I wouldn't bring her here.

MAX Sam, it's your decision. You're welcome to bring your bride here, to the place where you live, or on the other hand you can take a suite at the Dorchester. It's entirely up to you.

SAM I haven't got a bride.

Sam stands, goes to the sideboard, takes an apple from the bowl, bites into it.

SAM (*cont.*) Getting a bit peckish.

He looks out of the window.

SAM (*cont.*) Never get a bride like you had, anyway. Nothing like your bride . . . going about these days. Like Jessie.

Pause.

SAM (*cont.*) After all, I escorted her once or twice, didn't I? Drove her round once or twice in my cab. She was a charming woman.

Pause.

SAM (*cont.*) All the same, she was your wife. But still . . . they were some of the most delightful evenings I've ever had. Used to just drive her about. It was my pleasure.

MAX (*softly, closing his eyes*) Christ.

SAM I used to pull up at a stall and buy her a cup of coffee. She was a very nice companion to be with.

Silence.

JOEY *comes in the front door. He walks into the room, takes his jacket off, throws it on a chair and stands.*

Silence.

JOEY   Feel a bit hungry.

SAM   Me, too.

MAX   Who do you think I am, your mother? Eh? Honest. They walk in here every time of the day and night like bloody animals. Go and find yourself a mother.

Lenny walks into the room, stands.

JOEY   I've been training down at the gym.

SAM   Yes, the boy's been working all day and training all night.

MAX   What do you want, you bitch? You spend all the day sitting on your arse at London Airport, buy yourself a jamroll. You expect me to sit here waiting to rush into the kitchen the moment you step in the door? You've been living sixty-three years, why don't you learn to cook?

SAM   I can cook.

MAX   Well, go and cook!

Pause.

LENNY   What the boys want, Dad, is your own special brand of cooking, Dad. That's what the boys look forward to. The special understanding of food, you know, that you've got.

MAX   Stop calling me Dad. Just stop all that calling me Dad, do you understand?

LENNY   But I'm your son. You used to tuck me up in bed every night. He tucked you up, too, didn't he, Joey?

Pause.

LENNY (*cont.*)   He used to like tucking up his sons.

Lenny turns and goes towards the front door.

MAX   Lenny.

LENNY (*turning*)   What?

MAX I'll give you a proper tuck up one of these nights, son. You mark my word.

They look at each other.

Lenny opens the front door and goes out.

Silence.

JOEY I've been training with Bobby Dodd.

Pause.

JOEY (*cont.*) And I had a good go at the bag as well.

Pause.

JOEY (*cont.*) I wasn't in bad trim.

MAX Boxing's a gentleman's game.

Pause.

MAX (*cont.*) I'll tell you what you've got to do. What you've got to do is you've got to learn how to defend yourself, and you've got to learn how to attack. That's your only trouble as a boxer. You don't know how to defend yourself, and you don't know how to attack.

Pause.

MAX (*cont.*) Once you've mastered those arts you can go straight to the top.

Pause.

JOEY I've got a pretty good idea . . . of how to do that.

Joey looks round for his jacket, picks it up, goes out of the room and up the stairs.

Pause.

MAX Sam . . . why don't you go, too, eh? Why don't you just go upstairs? Leave me quiet. Leave me alone.

SAM I want to make something clear about Jessie, Max. I want to. I do. When I took her out in the cab, round the town, I was taking care of her, for you. I was looking after her for you, when you were busy, wasn't I? I was showing her the West End.

Pause.

SAM (*cont.*)   You wouldn't have trusted any of your other brothers. You wouldn't have trusted Mac, would you? But you trusted me. I want to remind you.

Pause.

SAM (*cont.*)   Old Mac died a few years ago, didn't he? Isn't he dead?

Pause.

SAM (*cont.*)   He was a lousy stinking rotten loudmouth. A bastard uncouth sodding runt. Mind you, he was a good friend of yours.

Pause.

MAX   Eh, Sam . . .

SAM   What?

MAX   Why do I keep you here? You're just an old grub.

SAM   Am I?

MAX   You're a maggot.

SAM   Oh yes?

MAX   As soon as you stop paying your way here, I mean when you're too old to pay your way, you know what I'm going to do? I'm going to give you the boot.

SAM   You are, eh?

MAX   Sure. I mean, bring in the money and I'll put up with you. But when the firm gets rid of you—you can flake off.

SAM   This is my house as well, you know. This was our mother's house.

MAX   One lot after the other. One mess after the other.

SAM   Our father's house.

MAX   Look what I'm lumbered with. One cast-iron bunch of crap after another. One flow of stinking pus after another.

Pause.

MAX (*cont.*) Our father! I remember him. Don't worry. You kid your-self. He used to come over to me and look down at me. My old man did. He'd bend right over me, then he'd pick me up. I was only that big. Then he'd dandle me. Give me the bottle. Wipe me clean. Give me a smile. Pat me on the bum. Pass me around, pass me from hand to hand. Toss me up in the air. Catch me coming down. I remember my father.

Blackout.

Lights up.

Night.

TEDDY *and* RUTH *stand at the threshold of the room.*

They are both well dressed in light summer suits and light raincoats.

Two suitcases are by their side.

They look at the room. Teddy tosses the key in his hand, smiles.

TEDDY Well, the key worked.

Pause.

TEDDY (*cont.*) They haven't changed the lock.

Pause.

RUTH No one's here.

TEDDY (*looking up*) They're asleep.

Pause.

RUTH Can I sit down?

TEDDY Of course.

RUTH I'm tired.

Pause.

TEDDY Then sit down.

She does not move.

TEDDY (*cont.*) That's my father's chair.

RUTH That one?

TEDDY (*smiling*) Yes, that's it. Shall I go up and see if my room's still there?

RUTH It can't have moved.

TEDDY No, I mean if my bed's still there.

RUTH Someone might be in it.

TEDDY No. They've got their own beds.

Pause.

RUTH Shouldn't you wake someone up? Tell them you're here?

TEDDY Not at this time of night. It's too late.

Pause.

TEDDY (*cont.*) Shall I go up?

He goes into the hall, looks up the stairs, comes back.

TEDDY (*cont.*) Why don't you sit down?

Pause.

TEDDY (*cont.*) I'll just go up . . . have a look.

He goes up the stairs, stealthily.

Ruth stands, then slowly walks across the room.

Teddy returns.

TEDDY (*cont.*) It's still there. My room. Empty. The bed's there. What are you doing?

She looks at him.

TEDDY (*cont.*) Blankets, no sheets. I'll find some sheets. I could hear snores. Really. They're all still here, I think. They're all snoring up there. Are you cold?

RUTH No.

TEDDY I'll make something to drink, if you like. Something hot.

RUTH No, I don't want anything.

Teddy walks about.

TEDDY   What do you think of the room? Big, isn't it? It's a big house. I mean, it's a fine room, don't you think? Actually there was a wall, across there . . . with a door. We knocked it down . . . years ago . . . to make an open living area. The structure wasn't affected, you see. My mother was dead.

Ruth sits.

TEDDY *(cont.)*   Tired?

RUTH   Just a little.

TEDDY   We can go to bed if you like. No point in waking anyone up now. Just go to bed. See them all in the morning . . . see my father in the morning. . . .

Pause.

RUTH   Do you want to stay?

TEDDY   Stay?

Pause.

TEDDY *(cont.)*   We've come to stay. We're bound to stay . . . for a few days.

RUTH   I think . . . the children . . . might be missing us.

TEDDY   Don't be silly.

RUTH   They might.

TEDDY   Look, we'll be back in a few days, won't we?

He walks about the room.

TEDDY *(cont.)*   Nothing's changed. Still the same.

Pause.

TEDDY *(cont.)*   Still, he'll get a surprise in the morning, won't he? The old man. I think you'll like him very much. Honestly. He's a . . . well, he's old, of course. Getting on.

Pause.

TEDDY (*cont.*)   I was born here, do you realize that?

RUTH   I know.

Pause.

TEDDY   Why don't you go to bed? I'll find some sheets. I feel . . . wide awake, isn't it odd? I think I'll stay up for a bit. Are you tired?

RUTH   No.

TEDDY   Go to bed. I'll show you the room.

RUTH   No, I don't want to.

TEDDY   You'll be perfectly all right up there without me. Really you will. I mean, I won't be long. Look, it's just up there. It's the first door on the landing. The bathroom's right next door. You . . . need some rest, you know.

Pause.

TEDDY (*cont.*)   I just want to . . . walk about for a few minutes. Do you mind?

RUTH   Of course I don't.

TEDDY   Well . . . Shall I show you the room?

RUTH   No, I'm happy at the moment.

TEDDY   You don't have to go to bed. I'm not saying you have to. I mean, you can stay up with me. Perhaps I'll make a cup of tea or something. The only thing is we don't want to make too much noise, we don't want to wake anyone up.

RUTH   I'm not making any noise.

TEDDY   I know you're not.

He goes to her.

TEDDY (*cont.*) (*gently*)   Look, it's all right, really. I'm here. I mean . . . I'm with you. There's no need to be nervous. Are you nervous?

RUTH   No.

TEDDY   There's no need to be.

Pause.

TEDDY (*cont.*)   They're very warm people, really. Very warm. They're my family. They're not ogres.

Pause.

TEDDY (*cont.*)   Well, perhaps we should go to bed. After all, we have to be up early, see Dad. Wouldn't be quite right if he found us in bed, I think. (*He chuckles.*) Have to be up before six, come down, say hullo.

Pause.

RUTH   I think I'll have a breath of air.

TEDDY   Air?

Pause.

TEDDY (*cont.*)   What do you mean?

RUTH (*standing*)   Just a stroll.

TEDDY   At this time of night? But we've . . . only just got here. We've got to go to bed.

RUTH   I just feel like some air.

TEDDY   But I'm going to bed.

RUTH   That's all right

TEDDY   But what am I going to do?

Pause.

TEDDY (*cont.*)   The last thing I want is a breath of air. Why do you want a breath of air?

RUTH   I just do.

TEDDY   But it's late.

RUTH   I won't go far. I'll come back.

Pause.

TEDDY   I'll wait up for you.

RUTH   Why?

TEDDY   I'm not going to bed without you.

RUTH   Can I have the key?

He gives it to her.

RUTH (*cont.*)   Why don't you go to bed?

He puts his arms on her shoulders and kisses her.

They look at each other, briefly. She smiles.

RUTH (*cont.*)   I won't be long.

She goes out of the front door.

Teddy goes to the window, peers out after her, half turns from the window, stands, suddenly chews his knuckles. Lenny walks into the room front U.L. He stands. He wears pyjamas and dressing-gown. He watches Teddy.

Teddy turns and sees him.

Silence.

TEDDY   Hullo, Lenny.

LENNY   Hullo, Teddy.

Pause.

TEDDY   I didn't hear you come down the stairs.

LENNY   I didn't.

Pause.

LENNY (*cont.*)   I sleep down here now. Next door. I've got a kind of study, workroom cum bedroom next door now, you see.

TEDDY   Oh. Did I . . . wake you up?

LENNY   No. I just had an early night tonight. You know how it is. Can't sleep. Keep waking up.

Pause

TEDDY   How are you?

LENNY   Well, just sleeping a bit restlessly, that's all. Tonight, anyway.

TEDDY   Bad dreams?

LENNY   No, I wouldn't say I was dreaming. It's not exactly a dream. It's just that something keeps waking me up. Some kind of tick.

TEDDY   A tick?

LENNY   Yes.

TEDDY   Well, what is it?

LENNY   I don't know.

Pause.

TEDDY   Have you got a clock in your room?

LENNY   Yes.

TEDDY   Well, maybe it's the clock.

LENNY   Yes, could be, I suppose.

Pause.

LENNY *(cont.)*   Well, if it's the clock I'd better do something about it. Stifle it in some way, or something.

Pause.

TEDDY   I've . . . just come back for a few days

LENNY   Oh yes? Have you?

Pause.

TEDDY   How's the old man?

LENNY   He's in the pink.

Pause.

TEDDY   I've been keeping well.

LENNY   Oh, have you?

Pause.

LENNY *(cont.)*   Staying the night then, are you?

TEDDY   Yes.

LENNY   Well, you can sleep in your old room.

TEDDY   Yes, I've been up.

LENNY   Yes, you can sleep there.

Lenny yawns.

LENNY (*cont.*)   Oh well.

TEDDY   I'm going to bed.

LENNY   Are you?

TEDDY   Yes, I'll get some sleep.

LENNY   Yes, I'm going to bed, too.

Teddy picks up the cases.

LENNY (*cont.*)   I'll give you a hand.

TEDDY   No, they're not heavy.

Teddy goes into the hall with the cases.

Lenny turns out the light in the room.

The light in the hall remains on.

Lenny follows into the hall.

LENNY   Nothing you want?

TEDDY   Mmmm?

LENNY   Nothing you might want, for the night? Glass of water, anything like that?

TEDDY   Any sheets anywhere?

LENNY   In the sideboard in your room.

TEDDY   Oh, good.

LENNY   Friends of mine occasionally stay there, you know, in your room, when they're passing through this part of the world.

Lenny turns out the hall light and turns on the first landing light.

Teddy begins to walk up the stairs.

TEDDY   Well, I'll see you at breakfast, then.

LENNY   Yes, that's it. Ta-ta.

Teddy goes upstairs.

Lenny goes off L.

Silence.

The landing light goes out.

Slight night light in the hall and room.

Lenny comes back into the room, goes to the window and looks out.

He leaves the window and turns on a lamp.

He is holding a small clock.

He sits, places the clock in front of him, lights a cigarette and sits.

Ruth comes in the front door.

She stands still. Lenny turns his head, smiles. She walks slowly into the room.

LENNY   Good evening.

RUTH   Morning, I think.

LENNY   You're right there.

Pause.

LENNY (*cont.*)   My name's Lenny. What's yours?

RUTH   Ruth.

She sits, puts her coat collar around her.

LENNY   Cold?

RUTH   No.

LENNY   It's been a wonderful summer, hasn't it? Remarkable.

Pause.

LENNY (*cont.*)   Would you like something? Refreshment of some kind? An aperitif, anything like that?

RUTH   No, thanks.

LENNY I'm glad you said that. We haven't got a drink in the house. Mind you, I'd soon get some in, if we had a party or something like that. Some kind of celebration . . . you know.

Pause.

LENNY (*cont.*) You must be connected with my brother in some way. The one who's been abroad.

RUTH I'm his wife.

LENNY Eh listen, I wonder if you can advise me. I've been having a bit of a rough time with this clock. The tick's been keeping me up. The trouble is I'm not all that convinced it was the clock. I mean there are lots of things which tick in the night, don't you find that? All sorts of objects, which, in the day, you wouldn't call anything else but commonplace. They give you no trouble. But in the night any given one of a number of them is liable to start letting out a bit of a tick. Whereas you look at these objects in the day and they're just commonplace. They're as quiet as mice during the daytime. So . . . all things being equal . . . this question of me saying it was the clock that woke me up, well, that could very easily prove something of a false hypothesis.

He goes to the sideboard, pours from a jug into a glass, takes the glass to Ruth.

LENNY (*cont.*) Here you are. I bet you could do with this.

RUTH What is it?

LENNY Water.

She takes it, sips, places the glass on a small table by her chair.

Lenny watches her.

LENNY (*cont.*) Isn't it funny? I've got my pyjamas on and you're fully dressed.

He goes to the sideboard and pours another glass of water.

LENNY (*cont.*) Mind if I have one? Yes, it's funny seeing my old brother again after all these years. It's just the sort of tonic my Dad needs, you know. He'll be chuffed to his bollocks in the morning, when he sees his eldest son. I was surprised myself when I saw Teddy, you know. Old Ted. I thought he was in America.

RUTH We're on a visit to Europe.

LENNY What, both of you?

RUTH Yes.

LENNY What, you sort of live with him over there, do you?

RUTH We're married.

LENNY On a visit to Europe, eh? Seen much of it?

RUTH We've just come from Italy.

LENNY Oh, you went to Italy first, did you? And then he brought you over here to meet the family, did he? Well, the old man'll be pleased to see you, I can tell you.

RUTH Good.

LENNY What did you say?

RUTH Good.

Pause.

LENNY Where'd you go to in Italy?

RUTH Venice.

LENNY Not dear old Venice? Eh? That's funny. You know, I've always had a feeling that if I'd been a soldier in the last war—say in the Italian campaign—I'd probably have found myself in Venice. I've always had that feeling. The trouble was I was too young to serve, you see. I was only a child, I was too small, otherwise I've got a pretty shrewd idea I'd probably have gone through Venice. Yes, I'd almost certainly have gone through it with my battalion. Do you mind if I hold your hand?

RUTH Why?

LENNY Just a touch.

He stands and goes to her.

LENNY (*cont.*) Just a tickle.

RUTH Why?

He looks down at her.

LENNY   I'll tell you why.

Slight pause.

LENNY (*cont.*)   One night, not too long ago, one night down by the docks, I was standing alone under an arch, watching all the men jibbing the boom, out in the harbour, and playing about with a yardarm, when a certain lady came up to me and made me a certain proposal. This lady had been searching for me for days. She'd lost tracks of my whereabouts. However, the fact was she eventually caught up with me, and when she caught up with me she made me this certain proposal. Well, this proposal wasn't entirely out of order and normally I would have subscribed to it. I mean I would have subscribed to it in the normal course of events. The only trouble was she was falling apart with the pox. So I turned it down. Well, this lady was very insistent and started taking liberties with me down under this arch, liberties which by any criterion I couldn't be expected to tolerate, the facts being what they were, so I clumped her one. It was on my mind at the time to do away with her, you know, to kill her, and the fact is, that as killings go, it would have been a simple matter, nothing to it. Her chauffeur, who had located me for her, he'd popped round the corner to have a drink, which just left this lady and myself, you see, alone, standing underneath this arch, watching all the steamers steaming up, no one about, all quiet on the Western Front, and there she was up against this wall—well, just sliding down the wall, following the blow I'd given her. Well, to sum up, everything was in my favour, for a killing. Don't worry about the chauffeur. The chauffeur would never have spoken. He was an old friend of the family. But . . . in the end I thought . . . Aaah, why go to all the bother . . . you know, getting rid of the corpse and all that, getting yourself into a state of tension. So I just gave her another belt in the nose and a couple of turns of the boot and sort of left it at that.

RUTH   How did you know she was diseased?

LENNY   How did I know?

Pause.

LENNY (*cont.*)   I decided she was.

Silence.

LENNY (*cont.*)   You and my brother are newly-weds, are you?

RUTH   We've been married six years.

LENNY   He's always been my favourite brother, old Teddy. Do you
know that? And my goodness we are proud of him here, I can tell
you. Doctor of Philosophy and all that . . . leaves quite an impression.
Of course, he's a very sensitive man, isn't he? Ted. Very. I've often
wished I was as sensitive as he is.

RUTH   Have you?

LENNY   Oh yes. Oh yes, very much so. I mean, I'm not saying I'm not
sensitive. I am. I could just be a bit more so, that's all.

RUTH   Could you?

LENNY   Yes, just a bit more so, that's all.

Pause.

LENNY (*cont.*)   I mean, I am very sensitive to atmosphere, but I tend to
get desensitized, if you know what I mean, when people make
unreasonable demands on me. For instance, last Christmas I decided to
do a bit of snow-clearing for the Borough Council, because we had a
heavy snow over here that year in Europe. I didn't have to do this
snow-clearing—I mean I wasn't financially embarrassed in any way—
it just appealed to me, it appealed to something inside me. What I
anticipated with a good deal of pleasure was the brisk cold bite in the
air in the early morning. And I was right. I had to get my snowboots
on and I had to stand on a corner, at about five-thirty in the morning,
to wait for the lorry to pick me up, to take me to the allotted area.
Bloody freezing. Well, the lorry came, I jumped on the tailboard,
headlights on, dipped, and off we went. Got there, shovels up, fags
on, and off we went, deep into the December snow, hours before
cockcrow. Well, that morning, while I was having my midmorning
cup of tea in a neighbouring café, the shovel standing by my chair, an
old lady approached me and asked me if I would give her a hand with
her iron mangle. Her brother-in-law, she said, had left it for her, but
he'd left it in the wrong room, he'd left it in the front room. Well,
naturally, she wanted it in the back room. It was a present he'd given
her, you see, a mangle, to iron out the washing. But he'd left it in the
wrong room, he'd left it in the front room, well that was a silly place

to leave it, it couldn't stay there. So I took time off to give her a hand. She only lived up the road. Well, the only trouble was when I got there I couldn't move this mangle. It must have weighed about half a ton. How this brother-in-law got it up there in the first place I can't even begin to envisage. So there I was, doing a bit of shoulders on with the mangle, risking a rupture, and this old lady just standing there, waving me on, not even lifting a little finger to give me a helping hand. So after a few minutes I said to her, now look here, why don't you stuff this iron mangle up your arse? Anyway, I said, they're out of date, you want to get a spin drier. I had a good mind to give her a workover there and then, but as I was feeling jubilant with the snow-clearing I just gave her a short-arm jab to the belly and jumped on a bus outside. Excuse me, shall I take this ashtray out of your way?

RUTH It's not in my way.

LENNY It seems to be in the way of your glass. The glass was about to fall. Or the ashtray. I'm rather worried about the carpet. It's not me, it's my father. He's obsessed with order and clarity. He doesn't like mess. So, as I don't believe you're smoking at the moment, I'm sure you won't object if I move the ashtray.

He does so.

LENNY (*cont.*) And now perhaps I'll relieve you of your glass.

RUTH I haven't quite finished.

LENNY You've consumed quite enough, in my opinion.

RUTH No, I haven't.

LENNY Quite sufficient, in my own opinion.

RUTH Not in mine, Leonard.

Pause.

LENNY Don't call me that, please.

RUTH Why not?

LENNY That's the name my mother gave me.

Pause.

210

LENNY (*cont.*)   Just give me the glass.

RUTH   No.

Pause.

LENNY   I'll take it, then.

RUTH   If you take the glass . . . I'll take you.

Pause.

LENNY   How about me taking the glass without you taking me?

RUTH   Why don't I just take you?

Pause.

LENNY   You're joking.

Pause.

LENNY (*cont.*)   You're in love, anyway, with another man. You've had a secret liaison with another man. His family didn't even know. Then you come here without a word of warning and start to make trouble.

She picks up the glass and lifts it towards him.

RUTH   Have a sip. Go on. Have a sip from my glass.

He is still.

RUTH (*cont.*)   Sit on my lap. Take a long cool sip.

She pats her lap. Pause.

She stands, moves to him with the glass.

RUTH (*cont.*)   Put your head back and open your mouth.

LENNY   Take that glass away from me.

RUTH   Lie on the floor. Go on. I'll pour it down your throat.

LENNY   What are you doing, making me some kind of proposal?

She laughs shortly, drains the glass.

RUTH   Oh, I was thirsty.

She smiles as him, puts the glass down, goes into the hall and up the stairs.

He follows into the hall and shouts up the stairs.

LENNY   What was that supposed to be? Some kind of proposal?

Silence.

He comes back into the room, goes to his own glass, drains it.

A door slams upstairs.

The landing light goes on.

Max comes down the stairs, in pyjamas and cap. He comes into the room.

MAX   What's going on here? You drunk?

He stares at Lenny.

MAX (*cont.*)   What are you shouting about? You gone mad?

Lenny pours another glass of water.

MAX (*cont.*)   Prancing about in the middle of the night shouting your head off. What are you, a raving lunatic?

LENNY   I was thinking aloud.

MAX   Is Joey down here? You been shouting at Joey?

LENNY   Didn't you hear what I said, Dad? I said I was thinking aloud.

MAX   You were thinking so loud you got me out of bed.

LENNY   Look, why don't you just . . . pop off, eh?

MAX   Pop off? He wakes me up in the middle of the night, I think we got burglars here, I think he's got a knife stuck in him, I come down here, he tells me to pop off.

Lenny sits down.

MAX (*cont.*)   He was talking to someone. Who could he have been talking to? They're all asleep. He was having a conversation with someone. He won't tell me who it was. He pretends he was thinking aloud. What are you doing, hiding someone here?

LENNY   I was sleepwalking. Get out of it, leave me alone, will you?

MAX   I want an explanation, you understand? I asked you who you got hiding here.

Pause.

LENNY   I'll tell you what, Dad, since you're in the mood for a bit of a
. . . chat, I'll ask you a question. It's a question I've been meaning to
ask you for some time. That night . . . you know . . . the night you
got me . . . that night with Mum, what was it like? Eh? When I was
just a glint in your eye. What was it like? What was the background
to it? I mean, I want to know the real facts about my background. I
mean, for instance, is it a fact that you had me in mind all the time, or
is it a fact that I was the last thing you had in mind?

Pause.

LENNY (*cont.*)   I'm only asking this in a spirit of inquiry, you understand
that, don't you? I'm curious. And there's lots of people of my age
share that curiosity, you know that, Dad? They often ruminate,
sometimes singly, sometimes in groups, about the true facts of that
particular night—the night they were made in the image of those two
people *at it.* It's a question long overdue, from my point of view, but
as we happen to be passing the time of day here tonight I thought I'd
pop it to you.

Pause.

MAX   You'll drown in your own blood.

LENNY   If you prefer to answer the question in writing I've got no
objection.

Max stands.

LENNY (*cont.*)   I should have asked my dear mother. Why didn't I ask
my dear mother? Now it's too late. She's passed over to the other
side.

Max spits at him.

Lenny looks down at the carpet.

LENNY (*cont.*)   Now look what you've done. I'll have to Hoover that in
the morning, you know.

Max turns and walks up the stairs.

Lenny sits still.

Blackout.

Lights up.

Morning.

Joey in front of the mirror. He it doing some slow limbering-up exercises. He stops, combs his hair, carefully. He then shadowboxes, heavily, watching himself in the mirror.

Max comes in from U.L.

Both Max and Joey are dressed. Max watches Joey in silence. Joey stops shadowboxing, picks up a newspaper and sits.

Silence.

MAX   I hate this room.

Pause.

MAX (*cont.*)   It's the kitchen I like. It's nice in there. It's cosy.

Pause.

MAX (*cont.*)   But I can't stay in there. You know why? Because he's always washing up in there, scraping the plates, driving me out of the kitchen, that's why.

JOEY   Why don't you bring your tea in here?

MAX   I don't want to bring my tea in here. I hate it here. I want to drink my tea in there.

He goes into the hall and looks towards the kitchen.

MAX (*cont.*)   What's he doing in there?

He returns.

MAX (*cont.*)   What's the time?

JOEY   Half past six.

MAX   Half past six.

Pause.

MAX (*cont.*)   I'm going to see a game of football this afternoon. You want to come?

Pause.

MAX (*cont.*) I'm talking to you.

JOEY I'm training this afternoon. I'm doing six rounds with Blackie.

MAX That's not till five o'clock. You've got time to see a game of football before five o'clock. It's the first game of the season.

JOEY No, I'm not going.

MAX Why not?

Pause.

Max goes into the hall.

MAX (*cont.*) Sam! Come here!

Max comes back into the room.

Sam enters with a cloth.

SAM What?

MAX What are you doing in there?

SAM Washing up.

MAX What else?

SAM Getting rid of your leavings.

MAX Putting them in the bin, eh?

SAM Right in.

MAX What point you trying to prove?

SAM No point.

MAX Oh yes, you are. You resent making my breakfast, that's what it is, isn't it? That's why you bang round the kitchen like that, scraping the frying-pan, scraping all the leavings into the bin, scraping all the plates, scraping all the tea out of the teapot . . . that's why you do that, every single stinking morning. I know. Listen, Sam. I want to say something to you. From my heart.

He moves closer.

MAX (*cont.*) I want you to get rid of these feelings of resentment you've got towards me. I wish I could understand them. Honestly, have I ever given you cause? Never. When Dad died be said to me, Max, look after your brothers. That's exactly what he said to me.

SAM How could he say that when he was dead?

MAX What?

SAM How could he speak if he was dead?

Pause.

MAX Before he died, Sam. Just before. They were his last words. His last sacred words, Sammy. You think I'm joking? You think when my father spoke—on his deathbed—I wouldn't obey his words to the last letter? You hear that, Joey? He'll stop at nothing. He's even prepared to spit on the memory of our Dad. What kind of a son were you, you wet wick? You spent half your time doing crossword puzzles! We took you into the butcher's shop, you couldn't even sweep the dust off the floor. We took MacGregor into the shop, he could run the place by the end of a week. Well, I'll tell you one thing. I respected my father not only as a man but as a number one butcher! And to prove it I followed him into the shop. I learned to carve a carcass at his knee. I commemorated his name in blood. I gave birth to three grown men! All on my own bat. What have you done?

Pause.

MAX (*cont.*) What have you done? You tit!

SAM Do you want to finish the washing up? Look, here's the cloth.

MAX So try to get rid of these feelings of resentment, Sam. After all, we are brothers.

SAM Do you want the cloth? Here you are. Take it.

Teddy and Ruth come down the stairs. They walk across the hall and stop just inside the room.

The others turn and look at them. Joey stands.

Teddy and Ruth are wearing dressing-gowns.

Silence.

Teddy smiles.

TEDDY   Hullo . . . Dad . . . We overslept.

Pause.

TEDDY (*cont.*)   What's for breakfast?

Silence.

Teddy chuckles.

TEDDY (*cont.*)   Huh. We overslept.

Max turns to Sam.

MAX   Did you know he was here?

SAM   No.

Max turns to Joey.

MAX   Did you know he was here?

Pause.

MAX (*cont.*)   I asked you if you knew he was here.

JOEY   No.

MAX   Then who knew?

Pause.

MAX (*cont.*)   Who knew?

Pause.

MAX (*cont.*)   I didn't know.

TEDDY   I was going to come down, Dad, I was going to . . . be here, when you came down.

Pause.

TEDDY (*cont.*)   How are you?

Pause.

TEDDY (*cont.*)   Uh . . . look, I'd . . . like you to meet . . .

MAX   How long you been in this house?

TEDDY   All night.

MAX   All night? I'm a laughing-stock. How did you get in?

TEDDY   I had my key.

Max whistles and laughs.

MAX   Who's this?

TEDDY   I was just going to introduce you.

MAX   Who asked you to bring tarts in here?

TEDDY   Tarts?

MAX   Who asked you to bring dirty tarts into this house?

TEDDY   Listen, don't be silly—

MAX   You been here all night?

TEDDY   Yes, we arrived from Venice—

MAX   We've had a smelly scrubber in my house all night. We've had a
stinking pox-ridden slut in my house all night.

TEDDY   Stop it! What are you talking about?

MAX   I haven't seen the bitch for six years, he comes home without a
word, he brings a filthy scrubber off the street, he shacks up in my
house!

TEDDY   She's my wife! We're married!

Pause.

MAX   I've never had a whore under this roof before. Ever since your
mother died. My word of honour. (*to Joey*) Have you ever had a
whore here? Has Lenny ever had a whore here? They come back
from America, they bring the slopbucket with them. They bring the
bedpan with them. (*to Teddy*) Take that disease away from me. Get
her away from me.

TEDDY   She's my wife.

MAX (*to Joey*)   Chuck them out.

Pause.

MAX (*cont.*)   A Doctor of Philosophy, Sam, you want to meet a Doctor of Philosophy? (*to Joey*) I said chuck them out.

Pause.

MAX (*cont.*)   What's the matter? You deaf?

JOEY   You're an old man. (*to Teddy*) He's an old man.

Lenny walks into the room, in a dressing-gown.

He stops.

They all look round.

Max turns back, hits Joey in the stomach with all his might.

Joey contorts, staggers across the stage. Max, with the exertion of the blow, begins to collapse. His knees buckle. He clutches his stick.

Sam moves forward to help him.

Max hits him across the head with his stick, Sam sits, head in hands.

Joey, hands pressed to his stomach, sinks down at the feet of Ruth.

She looks down at him.

Lenny and Teddy are still.

Joey slowly stands. He is close to Ruth. He turns from Ruth, looks round at Max.

Sam clutches his head.

Max breathes heavily, very slowly gets to his feet.

Joey moves to him.

They look at each other.

Silence.

Max moves past Joey, walks towards Ruth. He gestures with his stick.

MAX   Miss.

Ruth walks towards him.

RUTH   Yes?

He looks as her.

MAX   You a mother?

RUTH   Yes.

MAX   How many you got?

RUTH   Three.

He turns to Teddy.

MAX   All yours, Ted?

Pause.

MAX (*cont.*)   Teddy, why don't we have a nice cuddle and kiss, eh? Like the old days? What about a nice cuddle and kiss, eh?

TEDDY   Come on, then.

Pause.

MAX   You want to kiss your old father? Want a cuddle with your old father?

TEDDY   Come on, then.

Teddy moves a step towards him.

TEDDY (*cont.*)   Come on.

Pause.

MAX   You still love your old Dad, eh?

They face each other.

TEDDY   Come on, Dad. I'm ready for the cuddle.

Max begins to chuckle, gurgling.

He turns to the family and addresses them.

MAX   He still loves his father!

Curtain

ACT TWO

Afternoon.

Max, Teddy, Lenny and Sam are about the stage, lighting cigars.

Joey comes in from U.L. with a coffee tray, followed by Ruth. He puts the tray down. Ruth hands coffee to all the men. She sits with her cup. Max smiles at her.

RUTH That was a very good lunch.

MAX I'm glad you liked it. (*to the others*) Did you hear that? (*to Ruth*) Well, I put my heart and soul into it, I can tell you. (*He sips.*) And this is a lovely cup of coffee.

RUTH I'm glad.

Pause.

MAX I've got the feeling you're a first-rate cook.

RUTH I'm not bad.

MAX No, I've got the feeling you're a number one cook. Am I right, Teddy?

TEDDY Yes, she's a very good cook.

Pause.

MAX Well, it's a long time since the whole family was together, eh? If only your mother was alive. Eh, what do you say, Sam? What would Jessie say if she was alive? Sitting here with her three sons. Three fine grown-up lads. And a lovely daughter-in-law. The only shame is her grandchildren aren't here. She'd have petted them and cooed over them, wouldn't she, Sam? She'd have fussed over them and played with them, told them stories, tickled them—I tell you she'd have been hysterical. (*to Ruth*) Mind you, she taught those boys everything they know. She taught them all the morality they know. I'm telling you. Every single bit of the moral code they live by—was taught to them by their mother. And she had a heart to go with it. What a heart. Eh, Sam? Listen, what's the use of beating round the bush? That woman was the backbone to this family. I mean, I was busy working twenty-four hours a day in the shop, I was going all over the country to find meat, I was making my way in the world, but I left a woman at home with a will of iron, a heart of gold and a mind. Right, Sam?

Pause.

MAX (*cont.*)   What a mind.

Pause.

MAX (*cont.*)   Mind you, I was a generous man to her. I never left her short of a few bob. I remember one year I entered into negotiations with a top-class group of butchers with continental connections. I was going into association with them. I remember the night I came home, I kept quiet. First of all I gave Lenny a bath, then Teddy a bath, then Joey a bath. What fun we used to have in the bath, eh, boys? Then I came downstairs and I made Jessie put her feet up on a pouffe—what happened to that pouffe, I haven't seen it for years—she put her feet up on the pouffe and I said to her, Jessie, I think our ship is going to come home, I'm going to treat you to a couple of items, I'm going to buy you a dress in pale corded blue silk, heavily encrusted in pearls, and for casual wear, a pair of pantaloons in lilac flowered taffeta. Then I gave her a drop of cherry brandy. I remember the boys came down, in their pyjamas, all their hair shining, their faces pink, it was before they started shaving, and they knelt down at our feet, Jessie's and mine. I tell you, it was like Christmas.

Pause.

RUTH   What happened to the group of butchers?

MAX   The group? They turned out to be a bunch of criminals like everyone else.

Pause.

MAX (*cont.*)   This is a lousy cigar.

He stubs is out.

He turns to Sam.

MAX (*cont.*)   What time you going to work?

SAM   Soon.

MAX   You've got a job on this afternoon, haven't you?

SAM   Yes, I know.

MAX   What do you mean, you know? You'll be late. You'll lose your job. What are you trying to do, humiliate me?

SAM   Don't worry about me.

MAX   It makes the bile come up in my mouth. The bile—you understand? (*to Ruth*) I worked as a butcher all my life, using the chopper and the slab, the slab, you know what I mean, the chopper and the slab! To keep my family in luxury. Two families! My mother was bedridden, my brothers were all invalids. I had to earn the money for the leading psychiatrists. I had to read books! I had to study the disease, so that I could cope with an emergency at every stage. A crippled family, three bastard sons, a slutbitch of a wife—don't talk to me about the pain of childbirth—I suffered the pain, I've still got the pangs—when I give a little cough my back collapses—and here I've got a lazy idle bugger of a brother won't even get to work on time. The best chauffeur in the world. All his life he's sat in the front seat giving lovely hand signals. You call that work? This man doesn't know his gearbox from his arse!

SAM   You go and ask my customers! I'm the only one they ever ask for.

MAX   What do the other drivers do, sleep all day?

SAM   I can only drive one car. They can't all have me at the same time.

MAX   Anyone could have you at the same time. You'd bend over for half a dollar on Blackfriars Bridge.

SAM   Me!

MAX   For two bob and a toffee apple.

SAM   He's insulting me. He's insulting his brother. I'm driving a man to Hampton Court at four forty-five.

MAX   Do you want to know who could drive? MacGregor! MacGregor was a driver.

SAM   Don't you believe it.

Max points his stick at Sam.

MAX   He didn't even fight in the war. This man didn't even fight in the bloody war!

SAM   I did!

MAX   Who did you kill?

Silence.

Sam gets up, goes to Ruth, shakes her hand and goes out of the front door.

Max turns to Teddy.

MAX (*cont.*)   Well, how you been keeping, son?

TEDDY   I've been keeping very well, Dad.

MAX   It's nice to have you with us, son.

TEDDY   It's nice to be back, Dad.

Pause.

MAX   You should have told me you were married, Teddy. I'd have sent you a present. Where was the wedding, in America?

TEDDY   No, Here. The day before we left.

MAX   Did you have a big function?

TEDDY   No, there was no one there.

MAX   You're mad. I'd have given you a white wedding. We'd have had the cream of the cream here. I'd have been only too glad to bear the expense, my word of honour.

Pause.

TEDDY   You were busy at the time. I didn't want to bother you.

MAX   But you're my own flesh and blood. You're my first born. I'd have dropped everything. Sam would have driven you to the reception in the Snipe, Lenny would have been your best man, and then we'd have all seen you off on the boat. I mean, you don't think I disapprove of marriage, do you? Don't be daft. (*to Ruth*) I've been begging my two youngsters for years to find a nice feminine girl with proper credentials—it makes life worth living. (*to Teddy*) Anyway, what's the difference, you did it, you made a wonderful choice, you've got a wonderful family, a marvellous career . . . so why don't we let bygones by bygones?

Pause.

MAX (*cont.*)   You know what I'm saying? I want you both to know that you have my blessing.

TEDDY   Thank you.

MAX   Don't mention it. How many other houses in the district have got a Doctor of Philosophy sitting down drinking a cup of coffee?

Pause.

RUTH   I'm sure Teddy's very happy . . . to know that you're pleased with me.

Pause.

RUTH (*cont.*)   I think he wondered whether you would be pleased with me.

MAX   But you're a charming woman.

Pause.

RUTH   I was . . .

MAX   What?

Pause.

MAX (*cont.*)   What she say?

They all look at her.

RUTH   I was . . . different . . . when I met Teddy . . . first.

TEDDY   No you weren't. You were the same.

RUTH   I wasn't

MAX   Who cares? Listen, live in the present, what are you worrying about? I mean, don't forget the earth's about five thousand million years old, at least. Who can afford to live in the past?

Pause.

TEDDY   She's a great help to me over there. She's a wonderful wife and mother. She's a very popular woman. She's got lots of friends. It's a great life, at the University . . . you know . . . it's a very good life. We've got a lovely house . . . we've got all . . . we've got everything we want. It's a very stimulating environment.

Pause.

TEDDY (*cont.*)   My department . . . is highly successful.

Pause.

TEDDY (*cont.*)   We've got three boys, you know.

MAX   All boys? Isn't that funny, eh? You've got three, I've got three. You've got three nephews, Joey. Joey! You're an uncle, do you hear? You could teach them how to box.

Pause.

JOEY (*to Ruth*)   I'm a boxer. In the evenings, after work. I'm in demolition in the daytime.

RUTH   Oh?

JOEY   Yes. I hope to be full time, when I get more bouts.

MAX (*to Lenny*)   He speaks so easily to his sister-in-law, do you notice? That's because she's an intelligent and sympathetic woman.

He leans to her.

MAX (*cont.*)   Eh, tell me, do you think the children are missing their mother?

She looks at him.

TEDDY   Of course they are. They love her. We'll be seeing them soon.

Pause.

LENNY (*to Teddy*)   Your cigar's gone out.

TEDDY   Oh, yes.

LENNY   Want a light?

TEDDY   No. No.

Pause.

TEDDY (*cont.*)   So has yours.

LENNY   Oh, yes.

Pause.

LENNY (*cont.*)   Eh, Teddy, you haven't told us much about your Doctorship of Philosophy. What do you teach?

TEDDY   Philosophy.

LENNY   Well, I want to ask you something. Do you detect a certain logical incoherence in the central affirmations of Christian theism?

TEDDY   That question doesn't fall within my province.

LENNY   Well, look at it this way . . . you don't mind my asking you some questions, do you?

TEDDY   If they're within my province.

LENNY   Well, look at it this way. How can the unknown merit reverence? In other words, how can you revere that of which you're ignorant? At the same time, it would be ridiculous to propose that what we *know* merits reverence. What we know merits any one of a number of things, but it stands to reason reverence isn't one of them. In other words, apart from the known and the unknown, what else is there?

Pause.

TEDDY   I'm afraid I'm the wrong person to ask.

LENNY   But you're a philosopher. Come on, be frank. What do you make of all this business of being and not-being?

TEDDY   What do you make of it?

LENNY   Well, for instance, take a table. Philosophically speaking. What is it?

TEDDY   A table.

LENNY   Ah. You mean it's nothing else but a table. Well, some people would envy your certainty, wouldn't they, Joey? For instance, I've got a couple of friends of mine, we often sit round the Ritz Bar having a few liqueurs, and they're always saying things like that, you know, things like: Take a table, take it. All right, I say, *take* it, *take* a table, but once you've taken it, what you going to do with it? Once you've got hold of it, where you going to take it?

MAX   You'd probably sell it.

LENNY   You wouldn't get much for it.

JOEY   Chop it up for firewood.

Lenny looks at him and laughs.

RUTH   Don't be too sure though. You've forgotten something. Look at me. I . . . move my leg. That's all it is. But I wear . . . underwear . . . which moves with me . . . it captures your attention. Perhaps you misinterpret. The action is simple. It's a leg . . . moving. My lips move. Why don't you restrict . . . your observations to that? Perhaps the fact that they move is more significant . . . than the words which come through them. You must bear that . . . possibility . . . in mind.

Silence

Teddy stands.

RUTH (*cont.*)   I was born quite near here.

Pause.

RUTH (*cont.*)   Then . . . six years ago, I went to America.

Pause.

RUTH (*cont.*)   It's all rock. And sand. It stretches . . . so far . . . everywhere you look. And there's lots of insects there.

Pause.

RUTH (*cont.*)   And there's lots of insects there.

Silence.

She is still.

Max stands.

MAX   Well, it's time to go to the gym. Time for your workout, Joey.

LENNY (*standing*)   I'll come with you.

Joey sits looking at Ruth.

MAX   Joe.

Joey stands. The three go out.

Teddy sits by Ruth, holds her hand.

She smiles at him.

Pause.

TEDDY   I think we'll go back. Mmnn?

Pause.

TEDDY (*cont.*)   Shall we go home?

RUTH   Why?

TEDDY   Well, we were only here for a few days, weren't we? We might as well . . . cut it short, I think.

RUTH   Why? Don't you like it here?

TEDDY   Of course I do. But I'd like to go back and see the boys now.

Pause.

RUTH   Don't you like your family?

TEDDY   Which family?

RUTH   Your family here.

TEDDY   Of course I like them. What are you talking about?

Pause.

RUTH   You don't like them as much as you thought you did?

TEDDY   Of course I do. Of course I . . . like them. I don't know what you're talking about.

Pause.

TEDDY (*cont.*)   Listen. You know what time of the day it is there now, do you?

RUTH   What?

TEDDY   It's morning. It's about eleven o'clock.

RUTH   Is it?

TEDDY   Yes, they're about six hours behind us . . . I mean . . . behind the time here. The boys'll be at the pool . . . now . . . swimming. Think of it. Morning over there. Sun. We'll go anyway, mmnn? It's so clean there.

RUTH   Clean.

TEDDY   Yes.

RUTH   Is it dirty here?

TEDDY   No, of course not. But it's cleaner there.

Pause.

TEDDY (*cont.*)   Look, I just brought you back to meet the family, didn't I? You've met them, we can go. The fall semester will be starting soon.

RUTH   You find it dirty here?

TEDDY   I didn't say I found it dirty here.

Pause.

TEDDY (*cont.*)   I didn't say that.

Pause.

TEDDY (*cont.*)   Look. I'll go and pack. You rest for a while. Will you? They won't be back for at least an hour. You can sleep. Rest. Please.

She looks at him.

TEDDY (*cont.*)   You can help me with my lectures when we get back. I'd love that. I'd be so grateful for it, really. We can bathe till October. You know that. Here, there's nowhere to bathe, except the swimming bath down the road. You know what it's like? It's like a urinal. A filthy urinal!

Pause.

TEDDY (*cont.*)   You liked Venice, didn't you? It was lovely, wasn't it? You had a good week. I mean . . . I took you there. I can speak Italian.

RUTH   But if I'd been a nurse in the Italian campaign I would have been there before.

Pause.

TEDDY   You just rest. I'll go and pack.

Teddy goes out and up the stairs.

She closes her eyes.

Lenny appears from U.L.

He walks into the room and sits near her.

She opens her eyes.

Silence.

LENNY   Well, the evenings are drawing in.

RUTH   Yes, it's getting dark.

Pause.

LENNY   Winter'll soon be upon us. Time to renew one's wardrobe.

Pause.

RUTH   That's a good thing to do.

LENNY   What?

Pause.

RUTH   I always . . .

Pause.

RUTH (*cont.*)   Do you like clothes?

LENNY   Oh, yes. Very fond of clothes.

Pause.

RUTH   I'm fond . . .

Pause.

RUTH (*cont.*)   What do you think of my shoes?

LENNY   They're very nice.

RUTH   No, I can't get the ones I want over there.

LENNY   Can't get them over there, eh?

RUTH   No . . . you don't get them there.

Pause.

RUTH (*cont.*)   I was a model before I went away.

LENNY   Hats?

Pause.

LENNY (*cont.*)   I bought a girl a hat once. We saw it in a glass case, in a shop. I tell you what it had. It had a bunch of daffodils on it, tied with a black satin bow, and then it was covered with a cloche of black veiling. A cloche. I'm telling you. She was made for it.

RUTH   No . . . I was a model for the body. A photographic model for the body.

LENNY   Indoor work?

RUTH   That was before I had . . . all my children.

Pause.

RUTH (*cont.*)   No, not always indoors.

Pause.

RUTH (*cont.*)   Once or twice we went to a place in the country, by train. Oh, six or seven times. We used to pass a . . . a large white water tower. This place . . . this house . . . was very big . . . the trees . . . there was a lake, you see . . . we used to change and walk down towards the lake . . . we went down a path . . . on stones . . . there were . . . on this path. Oh, just . . . wait . . . yes . . . when we changed in the house we had a drink. There was a cold buffet.

Pause.

RUTH (*cont.*)   Sometimes we stayed in the house but . . . most often . . . we walked down to the lake . . . and did our modelling there.

Pause.

RUTH (*cont.*)   Just before we went to America I went down there. I walked from the station to the gate and then I walked up the drive. There were lights on . . . I stood in the drive . . . the house was very light.

Teddy comes down the stairs with the cases. He puts them down, looks at Lenny.

TEDDY   What have you been saying to her?

He goes to Ruth.

TEDDY (*cont.*)   Here's your coat.

Lenny goes to the radiogram and puts on a record of slow jazz.

TEDDY (*cont.*)   Ruth. Come on. Put it on.

LENNY (*to Ruth*)   What about one dance before you go?

TEDDY   We're going.

LENNY   Just one.

TEDDY   No. We're going.

LENNY   Just one dance, with her brother-in-law, before she goes.

Lenny bends to her.

LENNY (*cont.*)   Madam?

Ruth stands. They dance, slowly.

Teddy stands, with Ruth's coat.

Max and Joey come in the front door and into the room.

They stand.

Lenny kisses Ruth. They stand, kissing.

JOEY   Christ, she's wide open.

Pause.

JOEY (*cont.*)   She's a tart.

Pause.

JOEY (*cont.*)   Old Lenny's got a tart in here.

Joey goes to them. He takes Ruth's arm. He smiles at Lenny. He sits with Ruth on the sofa, embraces and kisses her.

He looks up at Lenny.

JOEY (*cont.*)   Just up my street.

He leans her back until she lies beneath him. He kisses her. He looks up at Teddy and Max.

JOEY (*cont.*)   It's better than a rubdown, this.

Lenny sits on the arm of the sofa. He caresses Ruth's hair as Joey embraces her.

Max comes forward, looks at the cases.

MAX   You going, Teddy? Already?

Pause.

MAX (*cont.*)   Well, when you coming over again, eh? Look, next time you come over, don't forget to let us know beforehand whether you're married or not. I'll always be glad to meet the wife. Honest. I'm telling you.

Joey lies heavily on Ruth.

They are almost still.

Lenny caresses her hair.

MAX (*cont.*)   Listen, you think I don't know why you didn't tell me you were married? I know why. You were ashamed. You thought I'd be annoyed because you married a woman beneath you. You should have known me better. I'm broadminded. I'm a broadminded man.

He peers to see Ruth's face under Joey, turns back to Teddy.

MAX (*cont.*)   Mind you, she's a lovely girl. A beautiful woman. And a mother too. A mother of three. You've made a happy woman out of her. It's something to be proud of. I mean, we're talking about a woman of quality. We're talking about a woman of feeling.

Joey and Ruth roll off the sofa on to the floor.

Joey clasps her. Lenny moves to stand above them. He looks down on them. He touches Ruth gently with his foot.

Ruth suddenly pushes Joey away.

She stands up.

Joey gets to his feet, stares at her.

RUTH   I'd like something to eat. (*to Lenny*) I'd like a drink. Did you get any drink?

LENNY   We've got drink.

RUTH   I'd like one, please.

LENNY   What drink?

RUTH   Whisky.

LENNY   I've got it.

Pause.

RUTH   Well, get it.

Lenny goes to the sideboard, takes out bottle and glasses. Joey moves towards her.

RUTH (*cont.*)   Put the record off.

He looks at her, turns, puts the record off.

RUTH (*cont.*)   I want something to eat.

Pause.

JOEY   I can't cook. (*pointing to Max*) He's the cook.

Lenny brings her a glass of whisky.

LENNY   Soda on the side?

RUTH   What's this glass? I can't drink out of this. Haven't you got a tumbler?

LENNY   Yes.

RUTH   Well, put it in a tumbler.

He takes the glass back, pours whisky into a tumbler, brings it to her.

LENNY   On the rocks? Or as it comes?

RUTH   Rocks? What do you know about rocks?

LENNY   We've got rocks. But they're frozen stiff in the fridge.

Ruth drinks.

Lenny looks round at the others.

LENNY (*cont.*)   Drinks all round?

He goes to the sideboard and pours drinks.

Joey moves closer to Ruth.

JOEY   What food do you want?

Ruth walks round the room.

RUTH (*to Teddy*)   Has your family read your critical works?

MAX   That's one thing I've never done. I've never read one of his critical works.

TEDDY   You wouldn't understand them.

Lenny hands drinks all round.

JOEY   What sort of food do you want? I'm not the cook, anyway.

LENNY   Soda, Ted? Or as it comes?

TEDDY   You wouldn't understand my works. You wouldn't have the faintest idea of what they were about. You wouldn't appreciate the points of reference. You're way behind. All of you. There's no point in my sending you my works. You'd be lost. It's nothing to do with the question of intelligence. It's a way of being able to look at the world. It's a question of how far you can operate on things and not in things. I mean its a question of your capacity to ally the two, to relate the two, to balance the two. To see, to be able to *see*! I'm the one who can see. That's why I can write my critical works. Might do you good . . . have a look at them . . . see bow certain people can view. . . things . . . how certain people can maintain . . . intellectual equilibrium. Intellectual equilibrium. You're just objects. You just . . . move about. I can observe it. I can see what you do. It's the same as I do. But you're lost in it You won't get me being . . . I won't be lost in it.

Blackout.

Lights up.

Evening.

Teddy sitting, in his coat, the cases by him, Sam.

Pause.

SAM Do you remember MacGregor, Teddy?

TEDDY Mac?

SAM Yes.

TEDDY Of course I do.

SAM What did you think of him? Did you take to him?

TEDDY Yes. I liked him. Why?

Pause.

SAM You know, you were always my favourite, of the lads. Always.

Pause.

SAM (*cont.*) When you wrote to me from America I was very touched, you know. I mean you'd written to your father a few times but you'd never written to me. But then, when I got that letter from you . . . well, I was very touched. I never told him. I never told him I'd heard from you.

Pause.

SAM (*cont.*) (*whispering*) Teddy, shall I tell you something? You were always your mother's favourite. She told me. It's true. You were always the . . . you were always the main object of her love.

Pause.

SAM (*cont.*) Why don't you stay for a couple more weeks, eh? We could have a few laughs.

Lenny comes is the front door and into the room.

LENNY   Still here, Ted? You'll be late for your first seminar.

He goes to the sideboard, opens it, peers in it, to the right and the left, stands.

LENNY (*cont.*)   Where's my cheese-roll?

Pause.

LENNY (*cont.*)   Someone's taken my cheese-roll. I left it there. (*to Sam*) You been thieving?

TEDDY   I took your cheese-roll, Lenny.

Silence.

Sam looks as them, picks up his hat and goes out of the front door.

Silence.

LENNY   You took my cheese-roll?

TEDDY   Yes.

LENNY   I made that roll myself. I cut it and put the butter on. I sliced a piece of cheese and put it in between. I put it on a plate and I put it in the sideboard. I did all that before I went out. Now I come back and you've eaten it.

TEDDY   Well, what are you going to do about it?

LENNY   I'm waiting for you to apologise.

TEDDY   But I took it deliberately, Lenny.

LENNY   You mean you didn't stumble on it by mistake?

TEDDY   No, I saw you put it there. I was hungry, so I ate it.

Pause.

LENNY   Barefaced audacity.

Pause.

LENNY (*cont.*)   What led you to be so . . . vindictive against your own brother? I'm bowled over.

Pause.

LENNY (*cont.*)   Well, Ted, I would say this is something approaching the naked truth, isn't it? It's a real cards on the table stunt. I mean, we're in the land of no holds barred now. Well, how else can you interpret it? To pinch your younger brother's specially made cheese-roll when he's out doing a spot of work, that's not equivocal, it's unequivocal.

Pause.

LENNY (*cont.*)   Mind you, I will say you do seem to have grown a bit sulky during the last six years. A bit sulky. A bit inner. A bit less forthcoming. It's funny, because I'd have thought that in the United States of America, I mean with the sun and all that, the open spaces, on the old campus, in your position, lecturing, in the centre of all the intellectual life out there, on the old campus, all the social whirl, all the stimulation of it all, all your kids and all that, to have fun with, down by the pool, the Greyhound buses and all that, tons of iced water, all the comfort of those Bermuda shorts and all that, on the old campus, no time of the day or night you can't get a cup of coffee or a Dutch gin, I'd have thought you'd have grown more forthcoming, not less. Because I want you to know that you set a standard for us, Teddy. Your family looks up to you, boy, and you know what it does? It does its best to follow the example you set. Because you're a great source of pride to us. That's why we were so glad to see you come back, to welcome you back to your birthplace. That's why.

Pause.

LENNY (*cont.*)   No, listen, Ted, there's no question that we live a less rich life here than you do over there. We live a closer life. We're busy, of course. Joey's busy with his boxing, I'm busy with my occupation, Dad still plays a good game of poker, and he does the cooking as well, well up to his old standard, and Uncle Sam's the best chauffeur in the firm. But nevertheless we do make up a unit, Teddy, and you're an integral part of it. When we all sit round the backyard having a quiet gander at the night sky, there's always an empty chair standing in the circle, which is in fact yours. And so when you at length return to us, we do expect a bit of grace, a bit of je ne sais quoi, a bit of generosity of mind, a bit of liberality of spirit, to reassure us. We do expect that. But do we get it? Have we got it? Is that what you've given us?

Pause.

TEDDY Yes.

Joey comes down the stairs and into the room, with a newspaper.

LENNY (*to Joey*)   How'd you get on?

JOEY Er . . . not bad.

LENNY What do you mean?

Pause.

LENNY (*cont.*)   What do you mean?

JOEY Not bad.

LENNY I want to know what you *mean*—by not bad.

JOEY What's it got to do with you?

LENNY Joey, you tell your brother everything.

Pause.

JOEY I didn't get all the way.

LENNY You didn't get all the way?

Pause.

LENNY (*cont.*) (*with emphasis*)   You didn't get all the way? But you've had her up there for two hours.

JOEY Well?

LENNY You didn't get all the way and you've had her up there for two hours!

JOEY What about it?

Lenny moves closer to him.

LENNY What are you telling me?

JOEY What do you mean?

LENNY Are you telling me she's a tease?

Pause.

LENNY (*cont.*)   She's a tease!

Pause.

LENNY (*cont.*)   What do you think of that, Ted? Your wife turns out to be a tease. He's had her up there for two hours and he didn't go the whole hog.

JOEY   I didn't say she was a tease.

LENNY   Are you joking? It sounds like a tease to me, don't it to you, Ted?

TEDDY   Perhaps he hasn't got the right touch.

LENNY   Joey? Not the right touch? Don't be ridiculous. He's had more dolly than you've had cream cakes. He's irresistible. He's one of the few and far between. Tell him about the last bird you had, Joey.

Pause.

JOEY   What bird?

LENNY   The last bird! When we stopped the car . . .

JOEY   Oh, that . . . yes . . . well, we were in Lenny's car one night last week . . .

LENNY   The Alfa.

JOEY   And er . . . bowling down the road . . .

LENNY   Up near the Scrubs.

JOEY   Yes, up over by the Scrubs . . .

LENNY   We were doing a little survey of North Paddington.

JOEY   And er . . . it was pretty late, wasn't it?

LENNY   Yes, it was late. Well?

Pause.

JOEY   And then we . . . well, by the kerb, we saw this parked car . . . with a couple of girls in it.

LENNY   And their escorts.

JOEY Yes, there were two geezers in it. Anyway . . . we got out . . . and we told the . . . two escorts . . . to go away . . . which they did . . . and then we . . . got the girls out of the car. . . .

LENNY We didn't take them over the Scrubs.

JOEY Oh, no. Not over the Scrubs. Well, the police would have noticed us there . . . you see. We took them over a bombed site.

LENNY Rubble. In the rubble.

JOEY Yes, plenty of rubble.

Pause.

JOEY (*cont.*) Well . . . you know . . . then we had them.

LENNY You've missed out the best bit. He's missed out the best bit!

JOEY What bit?

LENNY (*to Teddy*) His bird says to him, I don't mind, she says, but I've got to have some protection. I've got to have some contraceptive protection. I haven't got any contraceptive protection, old Joey says to her. In that case I won't do it, she says. Yes you will, says Joey, never mind about the contraceptive protection.

Lenny laughs.

LENNY (*cont.*) Even my bird laughed when she heard that. Yes, even she gave out a bit of a laugh. So you can't say old Joey isn't a bit of a knockout when he gets going, can you? And here he is upstairs with your wife for two hours and he hasn't even been the whole hog. Well, your wife sounds like a bit of a tease to me, Ted. What do you make of it, Joey? You satisfied? Don't tell me you're satisfied without going the whole hog.

Pause.

JOEY I've been the whole hog plenty of times. Sometimes . . . you can be happy . . . and not go the whole hog. Now and again . . . you can be happy . . . without going any hog.

Lenny stares as him.

Max and Sam come in the front door and into the room.

MAX   Where's the whore? Still in bed? She'll make us all animals.

LENNY   The girl's a tease.

MAX   What?

LENNY   She's had Joey on a string.

MAX   What do you mean?

TEDDY   He had her up there for two hours and he didn't go the whole hog.

Pause.

MAX   My Joey? She did that to my boy?

Pause.

MAX (*cont.*)   To my youngest son? Tch, tch, tch, tch. How you feeling, son? Are you all right?

JOEY   Sure I'm all right.

MAX (*to Teddy*)   Does she do that to you, too?

TEDDY   No.

LENNY   He gets the gravy.

MAX   You think so?

JOEY   No he don't.

Pause.

SAM   He's her lawful husband. She's his lawful wife.

JOEY   No he don't! He don't get no gravy! I'm telling you. I'm telling all of you. I'll kill the next man who says he gets the gravy.

MAX   Joe . . . what are you getting so excited about? (*to Lenny*) It's because he's frustrated. You see what happens?

JOEY   Who is?

MAX   Joey. No one's saying you're wrong. In fact everyone's saying you're right.

Pause.

Max turns to the others.

MAX (*cont.*) You know something? Perhaps it's not a bad idea to have a woman in the house. Perhaps it's a good thing. Who knows? Maybe we should keep her.

Pause.

MAX (*cont.*) Maybe we'll ask her if she wants to stay.

Pause.

TEDDY I'm afraid not, Dad. She's not well, and we got to get home to the children.

MAX Not well? I told you, I'm used to looking after people who are not so well. Don't worry about that. Perhaps we'll keep her here.

Pause.

SAM Don't be silly.

MAX What's silly?

SAM You're talking rubbish.

MAX Me?

SAM She's got three children.

MAX She can have more! Here. If she's so keen.

TEDDY She doesn't want any more.

MAX What do you know about what she wants, eh, Ted?

TEDDY (*smiling*) The best thing for her is to come home with me, Dad. Really. We're married, you know.

Max walks about the room, clicks his fingers.

MAX We'd have to pay her, of course. You realize that? We can't leave her walking about without any pocket money. She'll have to have a little allowance.

JOEY Of course we'll pay her. She's got to have some money in her pocket.

MAX   That's what I'm saying. You can't expect a woman to walk about without a few bob to spend on a pair of stockings.

Pause.

LENNY   Where's the money going to come from?

MAX   Well, how much is she worth? What we talking about, three figures?

LENNY   I asked you where the money's going to come from. It'll be an extra mouth to feed. It'll be an extra body to clothe. You realize that?

JOEY   I'll buy her clothes.

LENNY   What with?

JOEY   I'll put in a certain amount out of my wages.

MAX   That's it. We'll pass the hat round. We'll make a donation. We're all grown-up people, we've got a sense of responsibility. We'll all put a little in the hat. It's democratic.

LENNY   It'll come to a few quid, Dad.

Pause.

LENNY (*cont.*)   I mean, she's not a woman who likes walking around in second-hand goods. She's up to the latest fashion. You wouldn't want her walking about in clothes which don't show her off at her best, would you?

MAX   Lenny, do you mind if I make a little comment? It's not meant to be critical. But I think you're concentrating too much on the economic considerations. There are other considerations. There are the human considerations. You understand what I mean? There are the human considerations. Don't forget them.

LENNY   I won't.

MAX   Well don't.

Pause.

MAX (*cont.*)   Listen, we're bound to treat her in something approximating, at least, to the manner in which she's accustomed. After all, she's not someone off the street, she's my daughter-in-law!

JOEY   That's right.

MAX   There you are, you see. Joey'll donate, Sam'll donate. . . .

Sam looks at him.

MAX (*cont.*)   I'll put a few bob out of my pension, Lenny'll cough up. We're laughing. What about you, Ted? How much you going to put in the kitty?

TEDDY   I'm not putting anything in the kitty.

MAX   What? You won't even help to support your own wife? You lousy stinkpig. Your mother would drop dead if she heard you take that attitude.

LENNY   Eh, Dad.

Lenny walks forward.

LENNY (*cont.*)   I've got a better idea.

MAX   What?

LENNY   There's no need for us to go to all this expense. I know these women. Once they get started they ruin your budget. I've got a better idea. Why don't I take her up with me to Greek Street?

Pause.

MAX   You mean put her on the game?

Pause.

MAX (*cont.*)   We'll put her on the game. That's a stroke of genius, that's a marvellous idea. You mean she can earn the money herself—on her back?

LENNY   Yes.

MAX   Wonderful. The only thing is, it'll have to be short hours. We don't want her out of the house all night.

LENNY   I can limit the hours.

MAX   How many?

LENNY   Four hours a night.

MAX (*dubiously*) Is that enough?

LENNY She'll bring in a good sum for four hours a night.

MAX Well, you should know. After all, it's true, the last thing we want to do is wear the girl out. She's going to have her obligations this end as well. Where you going to put her in Greek Street?

LENNY It doesn't have to be right in Greek Street, Dad. I've got a number of flats all around that area.

MAX You have? Well, what about me? Why don't you give me one?

LENNY You're sexless.

JOEY Eh, wait a minute, what's all this?

MAX I know what Lenny's saying. Lenny's saying she can pay her own way. What do you think, Teddy? That'll solve all our problems.

JOEY Eh, wait a minute. I don't want to share her.

MAX What did you say?

JOEY I don't want to share her with a lot of yobs!

MAX Yobs! You arrogant git! What arrogance. (*to Lenny*) Will you be supplying her with yobs?

LENNY I've got a very distinguished clientele, Joey. They're more distinguished than you'll ever be.

MAX So you can count yourself lucky we're including you in.

JOEY I didn't think I was going to have to share her!

MAX Well, you *are* going to have to share her! Otherwise she goes straight back to America. You understand?

Pause.

MAX (*cont.*) It's tricky enough as it is, without you shoving your oar in. But there's something worrying me. Perhaps she's not so up to the mark. Eh? Teddy, you're the best judge. Do you think she'd be up to the mark?

Pause.

MAX (*cont.*)   I mean what about all this teasing? Is she going to make a habit of it? That'll get us nowhere.

Pause.

TEDDY   It was just love play . . . I suppose . . . that's all I suppose it was.

MAX   Love play? Two bleeding hours? That's a bloody long time for love play!

LENNY   I don't think we've got anything to worry about on that score, Dad.

MAX   How do you know?

LENNY   I'm giving you a professional opinion.

Lenny goes to Teddy.

LENNY   Listen, Teddy, you could help us, actually. If I were to send you some cards, over to America . . . you know, very nice ones, with a name on, and a telephone number, very discreet, well, you could distribute them . . . to various parties, who might be making a trip over here. Of course, you'd get a little percentage out of it.

MAX   I mean, you needn't tell them she's your wife.

LENNY   No, we'd call her something else. Dolores, or something.

MAX   Or Spanish Jacky.

LENNY   No, you've got to be reserved about it, Dad. We could call her something nice . . . like Cynthia . . . or Gillian.

Pause.

JOEY   Gillian.

Pause.

LENNY   No, what I mean, Teddy, you must know lots of professors, heads of departments, men like that. They pop over here for a week at the Savoy, they need somewhere they can go to have a nice quiet poke. And of course you'd be in a position to give them inside information.

MAX Sure. You can give them proper data. I bet you before two months we'd have a waiting list.

LENNY You could be our representative in the States.

MAX Of course. We're talking in international terms! By the time we've finished Pan-American'll give us a discount.

Pause.

TEDDY She'd get old . . . very quickly.

MAX No . . . not in this day and age! With the health service? Old! How could she get old? She'll have the time of her life.

Ruth comes down the stairs, dressed.

She comes into the room.

She smiles at the gathering, and sits.

Silence.

TEDDY Ruth . . . the family have invited you to stay, for a little while longer. As a . . . as a kind of guest. If you like the idea I don't mind. We can manage very easily at home . . . until you come back.

RUTH How very nice of them.

Pause.

MAX It's an offer from our heart.

RUTH It's very sweet of you.

MAX Listen . . . it would be our pleasure.

Pause.

RUTH I think I'd be too much trouble.

MAX Trouble? What are you talking about? What trouble? Listen, I'll tell you something. Since poor Jessie died, eh, Sam? we haven't had a woman in the house. Not one. Inside this house. And I'll tell you why. Because their mother's image was so dear any other woman would have . . . tarnished it. But you . . . Ruth . . . you're not only lovely and beautiful, but you're kin. You're kith. You belong here.

Pause.

RUTH   I'm very touched.

MAX   Of course you're touched. I'm touched.

Pause.

TEDDY   But Ruth, I should tell you . . . that you'll have to pull your weight a little, if you stay. Financially. My father isn't very well off.

RUTH (*to Max*)   Oh, I'm sorry.

MAX   No, you'd just have to bring in a little, that's all. A few pennies. Nothing much. It's just that we're waiting for Joey to hit the top as a boxer. When Joey hits the top . . . well . . .

Pause.

TEDDY   Or you can come home with me.

LENNY   We'd get you a flat.

Pause.

RUTH   A flat?

LENNY   Yes.

RUTH   Where?

LENNY   In town.

Pause.

LENNY (*cont.*)   But you'd live here, with us.

MAX   Of course you would. This would be your home. In the bosom of the family.

LENNY   You'd just pop up to the flat a couple of hours a night, that's all.

MAX   Just a couple of hours, that's all. That's all.

LENNY   And you make enough money to keep you going here.

Pause.

RUTH   How many rooms would this flat have?

LENNY   Not many.

RUTH   I would want at least three rooms and a bathroom.

LENNY   You wouldn't need three rooms and a bathroom.

MAX   She'd need a bathroom.

LENNY   But not three rooms.

Pause.

RUTH   Oh, I would. Really.

LENNY   Two would do.

RUTH   No. Two wouldn't be enough.

Pause.

RUTH (*cont.*)   I'd want a dressing-room, a rest-room, and a bedroom.

Pause.

LENNY   All right, we'll get you a flat with three rooms and a bathroom.

RUTH   With what kind of conveniences?

LENNY   All conveniences.

RUTH   A personal maid?

LENNY   Of course.

Pause.

LENNY (*cont.*)   We'd finance you, to begin with, and then, when you were established, you could pay us back, in instalments.

RUTH   Oh, no, I wouldn't agree to that.

LENNY   Oh, why not?

RUTH   You would have to regard your original outlay simply as a capital investment.

Pause.

LENNY   I see. All right.

RUTH   You'd supply my wardrobe, of course?

LENNY   We'd supply everything. Everything you need.

RUTH   I'd need an awful lot. Otherwise I wouldn't be content.

LENNY   You'd have everything.

RUTH   I would naturally want to draw up an inventory of everything I would need, which would require your signatures in the presence of witnesses.

LENNY   Naturally.

RUTH   All aspects of the agreement and conditions of employment would have to be clarified to our mutual satisfaction before we finalized the contract.

LENNY   Of course.

Pause.

RUTH   Well, it might prove a workable arrangement.

LENNY   I think so.

MAX   And you'd have the whole of your daytime free, of course. You could do a bit of cooking here if you wanted to.

LENNY   Make the beds.

MAX   Scrub the place out a bit.

TEDDY   Keep everyone company.

Sam comes forward.

SAM (*in one breath*)   MacGregor had Jessie in the back of my cab as I drove them along.

He croaks and collapses.

He lies still.

They look at him.

MAX   What's he done? Dropped dead?

LENNY   Yes.

MAX   A corpse? A corpse on my floor? Get him out of here! Clear him out of here!

Joey bends over Sam.

JOEY He's not dead.

LENNY He probably was dead, for about thirty seconds.

MAX He's not even dead!

Lenny looks down at Sam.

LENNY Yes, there's still some breath there.

MAX (*pointing at Sam*) You know what that man had?

LENNY Has.

MAX Has! A diseased imagination.

Pause.

RUTH Yes, it sounds a very attractive idea.

MAX Do you want to shake on it now, or do you want to leave it till later?

RUTH Oh, we'll leave it till later.

Teddy stands.

He looks down at Sam.

TEDDY I was going to ask him to drive me to London Airport.

He goes to the cases, picks one up.

TEDDY (*cont.*) Well, I'll leave your case, Ruth. I'll just go up the road to the Underground.

MAX Listen, if you go the other way, first left, first right, you remember, you might find a cab passing there.

TEDDY Yes, I might do that.

MAX Or you can take the tube to Piccadilly Circus, won't take you ten minutes, and pick up a cab from there out to the Airport.

TEDDY Yes, I'll probably do that.

MAX Mind you, they'll charge you double fare. They'll charge you for the return trip. It's over the six-mile limit.

TEDDY   Yes. Well, bye-bye, Dad. Look after yourself.

They shake hands.

MAX   Thanks, son. Listen. I want to tell you something. It's been wonderful to see you.

Pause.

TEDDY   It's been wonderful to see you.

MAX   Do your boys know about me? Eh? Would they like to see a photo, do you think, of their grandfather?

TEDDY   I know they would.

Max brings out his wallet.

MAX   I've got one on me. I've got one here. Just a minute. Here you are. Will they like that one?

TEDDY   (*taking it*)   They'll be thrilled.

He turns to Lenny.

TEDDY   (*cont.*)   Good-bye, Lenny.

They shakes hands.

LENNY   Ta-ta, Ted. Good to see you. Have a good trip.

TEDDY   Bye-bye, Joey.

Joey does not move.

JOEY   Ta-ta.

Teddy goes to the front door.

RUTH   Eddie.

Teddy turns.

Pause.

RUTH   (*cont.*)   Don't become a stranger.

Teddy goes, shuts the front door.

Silence.

The three men stand.

Ruth sits relaxed in her chair.

Sam lies still.

Joey walks slowly across the room.

He kneels at her chair.

She touches his head, lightly.

He puts his head in her lap.

Max begins to move above them, backwards and forwards.

Lenny stands still.

Max turns to Lenny.

MAX   I'm too old, I suppose. She thinks I'm an old man.

Pause.

MAX (*cont.*)   I'm not such an old man.

Pause.

MAX (*cont.*) (*to Ruth*)   You think I'm too old for you?

Pause.

MAX (*cont.*)   Listen. You think you're just going to get that big slag all the time? You think you're just going to have him . . . you're going to just have him all the time? You're going to have to work! You'll have to take them on, you understand?

Pause.

MAX (*cont.*)   Does she realize that?

Pause.

MAX (*cont.*)   Lenny, do you think she understands . . .

He begins to stammer.

MAX (*cont.*)   What . . . what . . . what . . . we're getting at? What . . . we've got in mind? Do you think she's got it clear?

Pause.

MAX (*cont.*)   I don't think she's got it clear.

Pause.

MAX (*cont.*)   You understand what I mean? Listen, I've got a funny idea she'll do the dirty on us, you want to bet? She'll use us, make use of us, I can tell you! I can smell it! You want to bet?

Pause.

MAX (*cont.*)   She won't . . . be adaptable!

He begins to groan, clutches his stick, falls on to his knees by the side of her chair. His body sags. The groaning stops. His body straightens. He looks at her, still kneeling.

MAX (*cont.*)   I'm not an old man.

Pause.

MAX (*cont.*)   Do you hear me?

He raises his face to her.

MAX (*cont.*)   Kiss me.

She continues to touch Joey's head, lightly.

Lenny stands, watching.

Curtain.

LANDSCAPE

Landscape was first presented on radio by the BBC on April 25, 1968, with the following cast:

BETH   Peggy Ashcroft
DUFF   Eric Porter

Directed by Guy Vaesen

The play was first presented on the stage by the Royal Shakespeare Company at the Aldwych Theatre on July 2, 1969, with the following cast:

BETH   Peggy Ashcroft
DUFF   David Waller

Directed by Peter Hall

DUFF, *a man in his early fifties*
BETH, *a woman in her late forties*
The kitchen of a country house.
A long kitchen table.
BETH sits in an armchair, which stands away from the table, to its left.
DUFF sits in a chair at the right corner of the table. The background, of a
   sink, stove, etc., and a window, is dim. Evening.

NOTE:
Duff refers normally to Beth, but does not appear to hear her voice.
Beth never looks at Duff, and does not appear to hear his voice.
Both characters are relaxed, in no sense rigid.

Landscape received its American premiere by the Repertory Theater of Lincoln Center (under the direction of Jules Irving) in a double bill with *Silence,* at The Forum of the Vivian Beaumont Theater, New York, on April 2, 1970, with the following cast:

BETH   Mildred Natwick
DUFF   Robert Symonds

Directed by Peter Gill

BETH   I would like to stand by the sea. It is there.

Pause.

BETH (*cont.*)   I have. Many times. It's something I cared for. I've done it.

Pause.

BETH (*cont.*)   I'll stand on the beach. On the beach. Well . . . it was very fresh. But it was hot, in the dunes. But it was so fresh, on the shore. I loved it very much.

Pause.

BETH (*cont.*)   Lots of people . . .

Pause.

BETH (*cont.*)   People move so easily. Men. Men move.

Pause.

BETH (*cont.*)   I walked from the dune to the shore. My man slept in the dune. He turned over as I stood. His eyelids. Belly button. Snoozing how lovely.

Pause.

BETH (*cont.*)   Would you like a baby? I said. Children? Babies? Of our own? Would be nice.

Pause.

BETH (*cont.*)   Women turn, look at me.

Pause.

BETH (*cont.*)   Our own child? Would you like that?

Pause.

BETH (*cont.*)   Two women looked at me, turned and stared. No. I was walking, they were still. I turned.

Pause.

BETH (*cont.*)   Why do you look?

Pause.

BETH (*cont.*)   I didn't say that, I stared. Then I was looking at them.

Pause.

BETH (*cont.*)   I am beautiful.

Pause.

BETH (*cont.*)   I walked back over the sand. He had turned. Toes under sand, head buried in his arms.

DUFF   The dog's gone. I didn't tell you.

Pause.

DUFF (*cont.*)   I had to shelter under a tree for twenty minutes yesterday. Because of the rain. I meant to tell you. With some youngsters. I didn't know them.

Pause.

DUFF (*cont.*)   Then it eased. A downfall. I walked up as far as the pond. Then I felt a couple of big drops. Luckily I was only a few yards from the shelter. I sat down in there. I meant to tell you.

Pause.

DUFF (*cont.*)   Do you remember the weather yesterday? That downfall?

BETH   He felt my shadow. He looked up at me standing above him.

DUFF   I should have had some bread with me. I could have fed the birds.

BETH   Sand on his arms.

DUFF   They were hopping about. Making a racket.

BETH   I lay down by him, not touching.

DUFF   There wasn't anyone else in the shelter. There was a man and woman, under the trees, on the other side of the pond. I didn't feel like getting wet. I stayed where I was.

Pause.

DUFF (*cont.*)   Yes, I've forgotten something. The dog was with me.

Pause.

BETH   Did those women know me? I didn't remember their faces. I'd never seen their faces before. I'd never seen those women before. I'm certain of it. Why were they looking at me? There's nothing strange about me. There's nothing strange about the way I look. I look like anyone.

DUFF   The dog wouldn't have minded me feeding the birds. Anyway, as soon as we got in the shelter he fell asleep. But even if he'd been awake . . .

Pause.

BETH   They all held my arm lightly, as I stepped out of the car, or out of the door, or down the steps. Without exception. If they touched the back of my neck, or my hand, it was done so lightly. Without exception. With one exception.

DUFF   Mind you, there was a lot of shit all over the place, all along the paths, by the pond. Dogshit, duckshit . . . all kinds of shit . . . all over the paths. The rain didn't clean it up. It made it even more treacherous.

Pause.

DUFF *(cont.)*   The ducks were well away, right over on their island. But I wouldn't have fed them, anyway. I would have fed the sparrows.

BETH   I could stand now. I could be the same. I dress differently, but I am beautiful.

Silence.

DUFF   You should have a walk with me one day down to the pond, bring some bread. There's nothing to stop you.

Pause.

DUFF *(cont.)*   I sometimes run into one or two people I know. You might remember them.

Pause.

BETH   When I watered the flowers he stood, watching me, and watched me arrange them. My gravity, he said. I was so grave, attending to the flowers, I'm going to water and arrange the flowers, I said. He followed me and watched, standing at a distance from me. When the arrangement was done I stayed still. I heard him moving. He didn't touch me. I listened. I looked at the flowers, blue and white, in the bowl.

Pause.

BETH (*cont.*)   Then he touched me.

Pause.

BETH (*cont.*)   He touched the back of my neck. His fingers, lightly, touching, lightly, touching, the back, of my neck.

DUFF   The funny thing was, when I looked, when the shower was over, the man and woman under the trees on the other side of the pond had gone. There wasn't a soul in the park.

BETH   I wore a white beach robe. Underneath I was naked.

Pause.

BETH (*cont.*)   There wasn't a soul on the beach. Very far away a man was sitting, on a breakwater. But even so he was only a pinpoint, in the sun. And even so I could only see him when I was standing, or on my way from the shore to the dune. When I lay down I could no longer see him, therefore he couldn't see me.

Pause.

BETH (*cont.*)   I may have been mistaken. Perhaps the beach was empty. Perhaps there was no-one there.

Pause.

BETH (*cont.*)   He couldn't see . . . my man . . . anyway. He never stood up.

Pause.

BETH (*cont.*)   Snoozing how lovely I said to him. But I wasn't a fool, on that occasion. I lay quiet, by his side.

Silence.

DUFF   Anyway . . .

BETH My skin . . .

DUFF I'm sleeping all right these days.

BETH Was stinging.

DUFF Right through the night, every night.

BETH I'd been in the sea.

DUFF Maybe it's something to do with the fishing. Getting to learn more about fish.

BETH Stinging in the sea by myself.

DUFF They're very shy creatures. You've got to woo them. You must never get excited with them. Or flurried. Never.

BETH I knew there must be a hotel near, where we could get some tea.

Silence.

DUFF Anyway . . . luck was on my side for a change. By the time I got out of the park the pubs were open.

Pause.

DUFF (*cont.*) So I thought I might as well pop in and have a pint. I wanted to tell you. I met some nut in there. First of all I had a word with the landlord. He knows me. Then this nut came in. He ordered a pint and he made a criticism of the beer. I had no patience with it.

BETH But then I thought perhaps the hotel bar will be open. We'll sit in the bar. He'll buy me a drink. What will I order? But what will he order? What will he want? I shall hear him say it. I shall hear his voice. He will ask me what I would like first. Then he'll order the two drinks. I shall hear him do it.

DUFF This beer is piss, he said. Undrinkable. There's nothing wrong with the beer, I said. Yes there is, he said, I just told you what was wrong with it. It's the best beer in the area, I said. No it isn't, this chap said, it's piss. The landlord picked up the mug and had a sip. Good beer, he said. Someone's made a mistake, this fellow said, someone's used this pintpot instead of the boghole.

Pause.

DUFF (*cont.*)   The landlord threw a half a crown on the bar and told him to take it. The pint's only two and three, the man said, I owe you three pence, but I haven't got any change. Give the threepence to your son, the landlord said, with my compliments. I haven't got a son, the man said, I've never had any children. I bet you're not even married, the landlord said. This man said: I'm not married. No-one'll marry me.

Pause.

DUFF (*cont.*)   Then the man asked the landlord and me if we would have a drink with him. The landlord said he'd have a pint. I didn't answer at first, but the man came over to me and said: Have one with *me*. Have one with *me*.

Pause.

DUFF (*cont.*)   He put down a ten bob note and said he'd have a pint as well.

Silence.

BETH   Suddenly I stood. I walked to the shore and into the water. I didn't swim. I don't swim. I let the water billow me. I rested in the water. The waves were very light, delicate. They touched the back of my neck.

Silence.

DUFF   One day when the weather's good you could go out into the garden and sit down. You'd like that. The open air. I'm often out there. The dog liked it.

Pause.

DUFF (*cont.*)   I've put in some flowers. You'd find it pleasant. Looking at the flowers. You could cut a few if you liked. Bring them in. No-one would see you. There's no-one there.

Pause.

DUFF (*cont.*)   That's where we're lucky, in my opinion. To live in Mr Sykes' house in peace, no-one to bother us. I've thought of inviting one or two people I know from the village in here for a bit of a drink once or twice but I decided against it. It's not necessary.

Pause.

DUFF (*cont.*)   You know what you get quite a lot of out in the garden? Butterflies.

BETH   I slipped out of my costume and put on my beachrobe. Underneath I was naked. There wasn't a soul on the beach. Except for an elderly man, far away on a breakwater. I lay down beside him and whispered. Would you like a baby? A child? Of our own? Would be nice.

Pause.

DUFF   Yes, it was funny. Suddenly I realized there wasn't a soul in the park. The rain had stopped.

Pause.

DUFF (*cont.*)   What did you think of that downfall?

Pause.

DUFF (*cont.*)   Of course the youngsters I met under the first tree, during the first shower, they were larking about and laughing. I tried to listen, to find out what they were laughing about, but I couldn't work it out. They were whispering. I tried to listen, to find out what the joke was.

Pause.

DUFF (*cont.*)   Anyway I didn't find out.

Pause.

DUFF (*cont.*)   I was thinking . . . when you were young . . . you didn't laugh much. You were . . . grave.

Silence.

BETH   That's why he'd picked such a desolate place. So that I could draw in peace. I had my sketch book with me. I took it out. I took my drawing pencil out. But there was nothing to draw. Only the beach, the sea.

Pause.

BETH (*cont.*)   Could have drawn him. He didn't want it. He laughed.

Pause.

BETH (*cont.*) I laughed, with him.

Pause.

BETH (*cont.*) I waited for him to laugh, then I would smile, turn away, he would touch my back, turn me, to him. My nose . . . creased. I would laugh with him, a little.

Pause.

BETH (*cont.*) He laughed. I'm sure of it. So I didn't draw him.

Silence.

DUFF You were a first-rate housekeeper when you were young. Weren't you? I was very proud. You never made a fuss, you never got into a state, you went about your work. He could rely on you. He did. He trusted you, to run his house, to keep the house up to the mark, no panic.

Pause.

DUFF (*cont.*) Do you remember when I took him on that trip to the north? That long trip. When we got back he thanked you for looking after the place so well, everything running like clockwork.

Pause.

DUFF (*cont.*) You'd missed me. When I came into this room you stopped still. I had to walk all the way over the floor towards you.

Pause.

DUFF (*cont.*) I touched you.

Pause.

DUFF (*cont.*) But I had something to say to you, didn't I? I waited, I didn't say it then, but I'd made up my mind to say it, I'd decided I would say it, and I did say it, the next morning. Didn't I?

Pause.

DUFF (*cont.*) I told you that I'd let you down. I'd been unfaithful to you.

Pause.

DUFF (*cont.*) You didn't cry. We had a few hours off. We walked up to the pond, with the dog. We stood under the trees for a bit. I didn't know why you'd brought that carrier bag with you. I asked you. I said what's in that bag? It turned out to be bread. You fed the ducks. Then we stood under the trees and looked across the pond.

Pause.

DUFF (*cont.*) When we got back into this room you put your hands on my face and you kissed me.

BETH But I didn't really want a drink.

Pause.

BETH (*cont.*) I drew a face in the sand, then a body. The body of a woman. Then the body of a man, close to her, not touching. But they didn't look like anything. They didn't look like human figures. The sand kept on slipping, mixing the contours. I crept close to him and put my head on his arm, and closed my eyes. All those darting red and black flecks, under my eyelid. I moved my cheek on his skin. And all those darting red and black flecks, moving about under my eyelid. I buried my face in his side and shut the light out.

Silence.

DUFF Mr Sykes took to us from the very first interview, didn't he?

Pause.

DUFF (*cont.*) He said I've got the feeling you'll make a very good team. Do you remember? And that's what we proved to be. No question. I could drive well, I could polish his shoes well, I earned my keep. Turn my hand to anything. He never lacked for anything, in the way of being looked after. Mind you, he was a gloomy bugger.

Pause.

DUFF (*cont.*) I was never sorry for him, at any time, for his lonely life.

Pause.

DUFF (*cont.*) That nice blue dress he chose for you, for the house, that was very nice of him. Of course it was in his own interests for you to look good about the house, for guests.

BETH   He moved in the sand and put his arm around me.

Silence.

DUFF   Do you like me to talk to you?

Pause.

DUFF (*cont.*)   Do you like me to tell you about all the things I've been doing?

Pause.

DUFF (*cont.*)   About all the things I've been thinking?

Pause.

DUFF (*cont.*)   Mmmnn?

Pause.

DUFF (*cont.*)   I think you do.

BETH   And cuddled me.

Silence.

DUFF   Of course it was in his own interests to see that you were attractively dressed about the house, to give a good impression to his guests.

BETH   I caught a bus to the crossroads and then walked down the lane by the old church. It was very quiet, except for birds. There was an old man fiddling about on the cricket pitch, bending. I stood out of the sun, under a tree.

Pause.

BETH (*cont.*)   I heard the car. He saw me and stopped me. I stayed still. Then the car moved again, came towards me slowly. I moved round the front of it, in the dust. I couldn't see him for the sun, but he was watching me. When I got to the door it was locked. I looked through at him. He leaned over and opened the door. I got in and sat beside him. He smiled at me. Then he reversed, all in one movement, very quickly, quite straight, up the lane to the crossroads, and we drove to the sea.

Pause.

DUFF We're the envy of a lot of people, you know, living in this
house, having this house all to ourselves. It's too big for two people.

BETH He said he knew a very desolate beach, that no-one else in the
world knew, and that's where we are going.

DUFF I was very gentle to you. I was kind to you, that day. I knew
you'd had a shock, so I was gentle with you. I held your arm on
the way back from the pond. You put your hands on my face and
kissed me.

BETH All the food I had in my bag I had cooked myself, or prepared
myself. I had baked the bread myself.

DUFF The girl herself I considered unimportant. I didn't think it
necessary to go into details. I decided against it.

BETH The windows were open but we kept the hood up.

Pause.

DUFF Mr Sykes gave a little dinner party that Friday. He complimented
you on your cooking and the service.

Pause.

DUFF *(cont.)* Two women. That was all. Never seen them before.
Probably his mother and sister.

Pause.

DUFF *(cont.)* They wanted coffee late. I was in bed. I fell asleep. I
would have come down to the kitchen to give you a hand but I was
too tired.

Pause.

DUFF *(cont.)* But I woke up when you got into bed. You were out on
your feet. You were asleep as soon as you hit the pillow. Your
body . . . just fell back.

BETH He was right. It was desolate. There wasn't a soul on the beach.

Silence.

DUFF I had a look over the house the other day. I meant to tell you. The dust is bad. We'll have to polish it up.

Pause.

DUFF (*cont.*) We could go up to the drawing-room, open the windows. I could wash the old decanters. We could have a drink up there one evening, if it's a pleasant evening.

Pause.

DUFF (*cont.*) I think there's moths. I moved the curtain and they flew out.

Pause.

BETH Of course when I'm older I won't be the same as I am, I won't be what I am, my skirts, my long legs, I'll be older, I won't be the same.

DUFF At least now . . . at least now, I can walk down to the pub in peace and up to the pond in peace, with no-one to nag the shit out of me.

Silence.

BETH All it is, you see . . . I said . . . is the lightness of your touch, the lightness of your look, my neck, your eyes, the silence, that is my meaning, the loveliness of my flowers, my hands touching my flowers, that is my meaning.

Pause.

BETH (*cont.*) I've watched other people. I've seen them.

Pause.

BETH (*cont.*) All the cars zooming by. Men with girls at their sides. Bouncing up and down. They're dolls. They squeak.

Pause.

BETH (*cont.*) All the people were squeaking in the hotel bar. The girls had long hair. They were smiling.

DUFF That's what matters, anyway. We're together. That's what matters.

Silence.

BETH But I was up early. There was still plenty to be done and cleared up. I had put the plates in the sink to soak. They had soaked overnight. They were easy to wash. The dog was up. He followed me. Misty morning. Comes from the river.

DUFF This fellow knew bugger all about beer. He didn't know I'd been trained as a cellarman. That's why I could speak with authority.

BETH I opened the door and went out. There was no-one about. The sun was shining. Wet, I mean wetness, all over the ground.

DUFF A cellarman is the man responsible. He's the earliest up in the morning. Give the drayman a hand with the barrels. Down the slide through the cellarflaps. Lower them by rope to the racks. Rock them on the belly, put a rim up them, use balance and leverage, hike them up onto the racks.

BETH Still misty, but thinner, thinning.

DUFF The bung is on the vertical, in the bunghole. Spile the bang. Hammer the spile through the centre of the bung. That lets the air through the bung, down the bunghole, lets the beer breathe.

BETH Wetness all over the air. Sunny. Trees like feathers.

DUFF Then you hammer the tap in.

BETH I wore my blue dress.

DUFF Let it stand for three days. Keep wet sacks over the barrels. Hose the cellar floor daily. Hose the barrels daily.

BETH It was a beautiful autumn morning.

DUFF Run water through the pipes to the bar pumps daily.

BETH I stood in the mist.

DUFF Pull off. Pull off. Stop pulling just before you get to the dregs. The dregs'll give you the shits. You've got an ullage barrel. Feed the slops back to the ullage barrel, send them back to the brewery.

BETH In the sun.

DUFF Dip the barrels daily with a brass rod. Know your gallonage. Chalk it up. Then you're tidy. Then you never get caught short.

BETH Then I went back to the kitchen and sat down.

Pause.

DUFF This chap in the pub said he was surprised to hear it. He said he was surprised to hear about hosing the cellar floor. He said he thought most cellars had a thermostatically controlled cooling system. He said he thought keg beer was fed with oxygen through a cylinder. I said I wasn't talking about keg beer, I was talking about normal draught beer. He said he thought they piped the beer from a tanker into metal containers. I said they may do, but he wasn't talking about the quality of beer I was. He accepted that point.

Pause.

BETH The dog sat down by me. I stroked him. Through the window I could see down into the valley. I saw children in the valley. They were running through the grass. They ran up the hill.

Long silence.

DUFF I never saw your face. You were standing by the windows. One of those black nights. A downfall. All I could hear was the rain on the glass, smacking on the glass. You knew I'd come in but you didn't move. I stood close to you. What were you looking at? It was black outside. I could just see your shape in the window, your reflection. There must have been some kind of light somewhere. Perhaps just your face reflected, lighter than all the rest. I stood close to you. Perhaps you were just thinking, in a dream. Without touching you, I could feel your bottom.

Silence.

BETH I remembered always, in drawing, the basic principles of shadow and light. Objects intercepting the light cast shadows. Shadow is deprivation of light. The shape of the shadow is determined by that of the object. But not always. Not always directly. Sometimes it is only indirectly affected by it. Sometimes the cause of the shadow cannot be found.

Pause.

BETH (*cont.*) But I always bore in mind the basic principles of drawing.

Pause.

BETH (*cont.*)   So that I never lost track. Or heart.

Pause.

DUFF   You used to wear a chain round your waist. On the chain you carried your keys, your thimble, your notebook, your pencil, your scissors.

Pause.

DUFF (*cont.*)   You stood in the hall and banged the gong.

Pause.

DUFF (*cont.*)   What the bloody hell are you doing banging that bloody gong?

Pause.

DUFF (*cont.*)   It's bullshit. Standing in an empty hall banging a bloody gong. There's no one to listen. No one'll hear. There's not a soul in the house. Except me. There's nothing for lunch. There's nothing cooked. No stew. No pie. No greens. No joint. Fuck all.

Pause.

BETH   So that I never lost track. Even though, even when, I asked him to turn, to look at me, but he turned to look at me but I couldn't see his look.

Pause.

BETH (*cont.*)   I couldn't see whether he was looking at me.

Pause.

BETH (*cont.*)   Although he had turned. And appeared to be looking at me.

DUFF   I took the chain off and the thimble, the keys, the scissors slid off it and clattered down. I booted the gong down the hall. The dog came in. I thought you would come to me, I thought you would come into my arms and kiss me, even . . . offer yourself to me. I would have had you in front of the dog, like a man, in the hall, on the stone, banging the gong, mind you don't get the scissors up your arse, or the thimble, don't worry, I'll throw them for the dog to chase, the thimble will keep the dog happy, he'll play with it with his paws, you'll plead with me like a woman, I'll bang the gong on the floor, if the sound is too flat, lacks resonance, I'll hang it back on its hook, bang you against it swinging, gonging, waking the place up, calling them all for dinner, lunch is up, bring out the bacon, bang your lovely head, mind the dog doesn't swallow the thimble, slam—

Silence.

BETH He lay above me and looked down at me. He supported my shoulder.

Pause.

BETH (*cont.*) So tender his touch on my neck. So softly his kiss on my cheek.

Pause.

BETH (*cont.*) My hand on his rib.

Pause.

BETH (*cont.*) So sweetly the sand over me. Tiny the sand on my skin.

Pause.

BETH (*cont.*) So silent the sky in my eyes. Gently the sound of the tide.

Pause.

BETH (*cont.*) Oh my true love I said.

OLD TIMES

Old Times was first presented by the Royal Shakespeare Company at the Aldwych Theatre, London, on June 1, 1971, with the following cast:

DEELEY   Colin Blakely
KATE   Dorothy Tutin
ANNA   Vivien Merchant
All in their early forties

Directed by Peter Hall

Old Times received its Broadway premiere at the Billy Rose Theatre, New York, in association with the Royal Shakespeare Company, on November 16, 1971, with the following cast:

DEELEY   Robert Shaw
KATE   Mary Ure
ANNA   Rosemary Harris

Directed by Peter Hall

A converted farmhouse

A long window up centre. Bedroom door up left.
Front door up right.

Spare modern furniture.
Two sofas. An armchair.

Autumn. Night.

ACT ONE

Light dim. Three figures discerned.

DEELEY *slumped in armchair, still.*

KATE *curled on a sofa, still.*

ANNA *standing at the window, looking out.*

Silence.

Lights up on Deeley and Kate, smoking cigarettes.

Anna's figure remains still in dim light at the window.

KATE (*reflectively*) Dark.

Pause.

DEELEY Fat or thin?

KATE Fuller than me. I think.

Pause.

DEELEY She was then?

KATE I think so.

DEELEY She may not be now.

Pause.

DEELEY (*cont.*) Was she your best friend?

KATE Oh, what does that mean?

DEELEY What?

KATE The word friend . . . when you look back . . . all that time.

DEELEY Can't you remember what you felt?

Pause.

KATE It is a very long time.

DEELEY But you remember her. She remembers you. Or why would she be coming here tonight?

KATE I suppose because she remembers me.

Pause.

DEELEY Did you *think* of her as your best friend?

KATE She was my only friend.

DEELEY Your best and only.

KATE My one and only.

Pause

KATE (*cont.*) If you have only one of something you can't say it's the best of anything.

DEELEY Because you have nothing to compare it with?

KATE Mmnn.

Pause.

DEELEY (*smiling*) She was incomparable.

KATE Oh, I'm sure she wasn't.

Pause.

DEELEY I didn't know you had so few friends.

KATE I had none. None at all. Except her.

DEELEY Why her?

KATE I don't know.

Pause.

KATE (*cont.*) She was a thief. She used to steal things.

DEELEY Who from?

KATE Me.

DEELEY What things?

KATE Bits and pieces. Underwear.

Deeley chuckles.

DEELEY Will you remind her?

KATE Oh . . . I don't think so.

Pause.

DEELEY Is that what attracted you to her?

KATE What?

DEELEY The fact that she was a thief.

KATE No.

Pause

DEELEY Are you looking forward to seeing her?

KATE No.

DEELEY I am. I shall be very interested.

KATE In what?

DEELEY In you. I'll be watching you.

KATE Me? Why?

DEELEY To see if she's the same person.

KATE You think you'll find that out through me?

DEELEY Definitely.

Pause.

KATE I hardly remember her. I've almost totally forgotten her.

Pause.

DEELEY Any idea what she drinks?

KATE None.

DEELEY She may be a vegetarian.

KATE Ask her.

DEELEY It's too late. You've cooked your casserole.

Pause.

DEELEY (*cont.*) Why isn't she married? I mean, why isn't she bringing her husband?

KATE Ask her.

DEELEY Do I have to ask her everything?

KATE Do you want me to ask your questions for you?

DEELEY No. Not at all.

Pause.

KATE Of course she's married.

DEELEY How do you know?

KATE Everyone's married.

DEELEY Then why isn't she bringing her husband?

KATE Isn't she?

Pause.

DEELEY Did she mention a husband in her letter?

KATE No.

DEELEY What do you think he'd be like? I mean, what sort of man would she have married? After all, she was your best—your only—friend. You must have some idea. What kind of man would he be?

KATE I have no idea.

DEELEY Haven't you any curiosity?

KATE You forget. I know her.

DEELEY You haven't seen her for twenty years.

KATE You've never seen her. There's a difference.

Pause.

DEELEY At least the casserole is big enough for four.

KATE You said she was a vegetarian.

Pause.

DEELEY Did *she* have many friends?

KATE Oh . . . the normal amount, I suppose.

DEELEY Normal? What's normal? You had none.

KATE One.

DEELEY Is that normal?

Pause.

DEELEY (*cont.*) She . . . had quite a lot of friends, did she?

KATE Hundreds.

DEELEY You met them?

KATE Not all, I think. But after all, we were living together. There were visitors, from time to time. I met them.

DEELEY Her visitors?

KATE What?

DEELEY Her visitors. Her friends. You had no friends.

KATE Her friends, yes.

DEELEY You met them.

Pause.

DEELEY (*cont.*) (*abruptly*) You lived together?

KATE Mmmnn?

DEELEY You lived together?

KATE Of course.

DEELEY I didn't know that.

KATE Didn't you?

DEELEY You never told me that. I thought you just knew each other.

KATE We did.

DEELEY But in fact you lived with each other.

ould she steal my underwear from

h someone at one time . . .

it was her.

DEELEY   Anyway, none of this matters.

Anna turns from the window, speaking, and moves down to them, eventually sitting on the second sofa.

ANNA   Queuing all night, the rain, do you remember? my goodness, the Albert Hall, Covent Garden, what did we eat? to look back, half the night, to do things we loved, we were young then of course, but what stamina, and to work in the morning, and to a concert, or the opera, or the ballet, that night, you haven't forgotten? and then riding on top of the bus down Kensington High Street, and the bus conductors, and then dashing for the matches for the gasfire and then I suppose scrambled eggs, or did we? who cooked? both giggling and chattering, both huddling to the heat, then bed and sleeping, and all the hustle and bustle in the morning, rushing for the bus again for work, lunchtimes in Green Park, exchanging all our news, with our very own sandwiches, innocent girls, innocent secretaries, and then the night to come, and goodness knows what excitement in store, I mean the sheer expectation of it all, the looking-forwardness of it all, and so poor, but to be poor and young, and a girl, in London then . . . and the cafés we found, almost private ones, weren't they? where artists and writers and sometimes actors collected, and others with dancers, we sat hardly breathing with our coffee, heads bent, so as not to be seen, so as not to disturb, so as not to distract, and listened and listened to all those words, all those cafés and all those people, creative undoubtedly, and does it still exist I wonder? do you know? can you tell me?

Slight pause.

DEELEY We rarely get to London.

Kate stands, goes to a small table and pours coffee from a pot.

KATE Yes, I remember.

She adds milk and sugar to one cup and takes it to Anna. She takes a black coffee to Deeley and then sits with her own.

DEELEY (*to Anna*) Do you drink brandy?

ANNA I would love some brandy.

Deeley pours brandy for all and hands the glasses. He remains standing with his own.

ANNA Listen. What silence. Is it always as silent?

DEELEY It's quite silent here, yes. Normally.

Pause

DEELEY (*cont.*) You can hear the sea sometimes if you listen very carefully.

ANNA How wise you were to choose this part of the world, and how sensible and courageous of you both to stay permanently in such a silence.

DEELEY My work takes me away quite often, of course. But Kate stays here.

ANNA No one who lived here would want to go far. I would not want to go far, I would be afraid of going far, lest when I returned the house would be gone.

DEELEY Lest?

ANNA What?

DEELEY The word lest. Haven't heard it for a long time.

Pause.

KATE Sometimes I walk to the sea. There aren't many people. It's a long beach.

Pause.

ANNA   But I would miss London, nevertheless. But of course I was a girl in London. We were girls together.

DEELEY   I wish I had known you both then.

ANNA   Do you?

DEELEY   Yes.

Deeley pours more brandy for himself.

ANNA   You have a wonderful casserole.

DEELEY   What?

ANNA   I mean wife. So sorry. A wonderful wife.

DEELEY   Ah.

ANNA   I was referring to the casserole. I was referring to your wife's cooking.

DEELEY   You're not a vegetarian, then?

ANNA   No. Oh no.

DEELEY   Yes, you need good food in the country, substantial food, to keep you going, all the air . . . you know.

Pause.

KATE   Yes, I quite like those kind of things, doing it.

ANNA   What kind of things?

KATE   Oh, you know, that sort of thing.

Pause.

DEELEY   Do you mean cooking?

KATE   All that thing.

ANNA   We weren't terribly elaborate in cooking, didn't have the time, but every so often dished up an incredibly enormous stew, guzzled the lot, and then more often than not sat up half the night reading Yeats.

Pause.

ANNA   (*cont.*) (*to herself*)   Yes. Every so often. More often than not.

Anna stands, walks to the window.

ANNA (*cont.*)   And the sky is so still.

Pause.

ANNA (*cont.*)   Can you see that tiny ribbon of light? Is that the sea? Is that the horizon?

DEELEY   You live on a very different coast.

ANNA   Oh, very different. I live on a volcanic island.

DEELEY   I know it.

ANNA   Oh, do you?

DEELEY   I've been there.

Pause.

ANNA   I'm so delighted to be here.

DEELEY   It's nice I know for Katey to see you. She hasn't many friends.

ANNA   She has you.

DEELEY   She hasn't made many friends, although there's been every opportunity for her to do so.

ANNA   Perhaps she has all she wants.

DEELEY   She lacks curiosity.

ANNA   Perhaps she's happy.

Pause.

KATE   Are you talking about me?

DEELEY   Yes.

ANNA   She was always a dreamer.

DEELEY   She likes taking long walks. All that. You know. Raincoat on. Off down the lane, hands deep in pockets. All that kind of thing.

Anna turns to look at Kate.

ANNA   Yes.

DEELEY Sometimes I take her face in my hands and look at it.

ANNA Really?

DEELEY Yes, I look at it, holding it in my hands. Then I kind of let it go, take my hands away, leave it floating.

KATE My head is quite fixed. I have it on.

DEELEY (*to Anna*) It just floats away.

ANNA She was always a dreamer.

Anna sits.

ANNA (*cont.*) Sometimes, walking, in the park, I'd say to her, you're dreaming, you're dreaming, wake up, what are you dreaming? and she'd look round at me, flicking her hair, and look at me as if I were part of her dream.

Pause.

ANNA (*cont.*) One day she said to me, I've slept through Friday. No you haven't, I said, what do you mean? I've slept right through Friday, she said. But today is Friday, I said, it's been Friday all day, it's now Friday night, you haven't slept through Friday. Yes I have, she said, I've slept right through it, today is Saturday.

DEELEY You mean she literally didn't know what day it was?

ANNA No.

KATE Yes I did. It was Saturday.

Pause.

DEELEY What month are we in?

KATE September.

Pause.

DEELEY We're forcing her to think. We must see you more often. You're a healthy influence.

ANNA But she was always a charming companion.

DEELEY Fun to live with?

ANNA Delightful.

DEELEY Lovely to look at, delightful to know.

ANNA Ah, those songs. We used to play them, all of them, all the time, late at night, lying on the floor, lovely old things. Sometimes I'd look at her face, but she was quite unaware of my gaze.

DEELEY Gaze?

ANNA What?

DEELEY The word gaze. Don't hear it very often.

ANNA Yes, quite unaware of it. She was totally absorbed.

DEELEY In Lovely to look at, delightful to know?

KATE (*to Anna*) I don't know that song. Did we have it?

DEELEY (*singing, to Kate*) You're lovely to look at, delightful to know . . .

ANNA Oh we did. Yes, of course. We had them all.

DEELEY (*singing*) Blue moon, I see you standing alone . . .

ANNA (*singing*) The way you comb your hair . . .

DEELEY (*singing*) Oh no they can't take that away from me . . .

ANNA (*singing*) Oh but you're lovely, with your smile so warm . . .

DEELEY (*singing*) I've got a woman crazy for me. She's funny that way.

Slight pause.

ANNA (*singing*) You are the promised kiss of springtime . . .

DEELEY (*singing*) And someday I'll know that moment divine,
When all the things you are, are mine!

Slight pause.

ANNA (*singing*) I get no kick from champagne,
Mere alcohol doesn't thrill me at all,
So tell me why should it be true—

DEELEY (*singing*) That I get a kick out of you?

Pause.

ANNA (*singing*)   They asked me how I knew
My true love was true,
I of course replied,
Something here inside
Cannot be denied.

DEELEY (*singing*)   When a lovely flame dies . . .

ANNA (*singing*)   Smoke gets in your eyes.

Pause.

DEELEY (*singing*)   The sigh of midnight trains in empty stations . . .

Pause.

ANNA (*singing*)   The park at evening when the bell has sounded . . .

Pause.

DEELEY (*singing*)   The smile of Garbo and the scent of roses . . .

ANNA (*singing*)   The waiters whistling as the last bar closes . . .

DEELEY (*singing*)   Oh, how the ghost of you clings . . .

Pause.

DEELEY (*cont.*)   They don't make them like that any more.

Silence.

DEELEY (*cont.*)   What happened to me was this. I popped into a fleapit to see Odd Man Out. Some bloody awful summer afternoon, walking in no direction. I remember thinking there was something familiar about the neighbourhood and suddenly recalled that it was in this very neighbourhood that my father bought me my first tricycle, the only tricycle in fact I ever possessed. Anyway, there was the bicycle shop and there was this fleapit showing Odd Man Out and there were two usherettes standing in the foyer and one of them was stroking her breasts and the other one was saying "dirty bitch" and the one stroking her breasts was saying "mmnnn" with a very sensual relish and smiling at her fellow usherette, so I marched in on this excruciatingly hot summer afternoon in the middle of nowhere and watched Odd Man

Out and thought Robert Newton was fantastic. And I still think he was fantastic. And I would commit murder for him, even now. And there was only one other person in the cinema, one other person in the whole of the whole cinema, and there she is. And there she was, very dim, very still, placed more or less I would say at the dead centre of the auditorium. I was off centre and have remained so. And I left when the film was over, noticing, even though James Mason was dead, that the first usherette appeared to be utterly exhausted, and I stood for a moment in the sun, thinking I suppose about something and then this girl came out and I think looked about her and I said wasn't Robert Newton fantastic, and she said something or other, Christ knows what, but looked at me, and I thought Jesus this is it, I've made a catch, this is a trueblue pickup, and when we had sat down in the café with tea she looked into her cup and then up at me and told me she thought Robert Newton was remarkable. So it was Robert Newton who brought us together and it is only Robert Newton who can tear us apart.

Pause.

ANNA   F. J. McCormick was good too.

DEELEY   I know F. J. McCormick was good too. But he didn't bring us together.

Pause.

DEELEY (*cont.*)   You've seen the film then?

ANNA   Yes.

DEELEY   When?

ANNA   Oh . . . long ago.

Pause.

DEELEY (*to Kate*)   Remember that film?

KATE   Oh yes. Very well.

Pause.

DEELEY   I think I am right in saying the next time we met we held hands. I held her cool hand, as she walked by me, and I said

293

something which made her smile, and she looked at me, didn't you, flicking her hair back, and I thought she was even more fantastic than Robert Newton.

Pause.

DEELEY (*cont.*)   And then at a slightly later stage our naked bodies met, hers cool, warm, highly agreeable, and I wondered what Robert Newton would think of this. What would he think of this I wondered as I touched her profoundly all over. (*to Anna*) What do you think he'd think?

ANNA   I never met Robert Newton but I do know I know what you mean. There are some things one remembers even though they may never have happened. There are things I remember which may never have happened but as I recall them so they take place.

DEELEY   *What?*

ANNA   This man crying in our room. One night late I returned and found him sobbing, his hand over his face, sitting in the armchair, all crumpled in the armchair and Katey sitting on the bed with a mug of coffee and no one spoke to me, no one spoke, no one looked up. There was nothing I could do. I undressed and switched out the light and got into my bed, the curtains were thin, the light from the street came in, Katey still, on her bed, the man sobbed, the light came in, it flicked the wall, there was a slight breeze, the curtains occasionally shook, there was nothing but sobbing, suddenly it stopped. The man came over to me, quickly, looked down at me, but I would have absolutely nothing to do with him, nothing.

Pause.

ANNA (*cont.*)   No, no, I'm quite wrong . . . he didn't move quickly . . . that's quite wrong . . . he moved . . . very slowly, the light was bad, and stopped. He stood in the centre of the room. He looked at us both, at our beds. Then he turned towards me. He approached my bed. He bent down over me. But I would have nothing to do with him, absolutely nothing.

Pause.

DEELEY   What kind of man was he?

ANNA   But after a while I heard him go out. I heard the front door close, and footsteps in the street, then silence, then the footsteps fade away, and then silence.

Pause.

ANNA (*cont.*)   But then sometime later in the night I woke up and looked across the room to her bed and saw two shapes.

DEELEY   He'd come back!

ANNA   He was lying across her lap on her bed.

DEELEY   A man in the dark across my wife's lap?

Pause.

ANNA   But then in the early morning . . . he had gone.

DEELEY   Thank Christ for that.

ANNA   It was as if he had never been.

DEELEY   Of course he'd been. He went twice and came once.

Pause.

DEELEY (*cont.*)   Well, what an exciting story that was.

Pause.

DEELEY (*cont.*)   What did he look like, this fellow?

ANNA   Oh, I never saw his face clearly. I don't know.

DEELEY   But was he—?

Kate stands. She goes to a small table, takes a cigarette from a box and lights it. She looks down at Anna.

KATE   You talk of me as if I were dead.

ANNA   No, no, you weren't dead, you were so lively, so animated, you used to laugh—

DEELEY   Of course you did. I made you smile myself, didn't I? walking along the street, holding hands. You smiled fit to bust.

ANNA   Yes, she could be so . . . animated.

DEELEY   Animated is no word for it. When she smiled . . . how can I describe it?

ANNA   Her eyes lit up.

DEELEY   I couldn't have put it better myself.

Deeley stands, goes to cigarette box, picks it up, smiles at Kate. Kate looks at him, watches him light a cigarette, takes the box from him, crosses to Anna, offers her a cigarette. Anna takes one.

ANNA   You weren't dead. Ever. In any way.

KATE   I said you talk about me as if I *am* dead. Now.

ANNA   How can you say that? How cast you say that, when I'm looking at you now, seeing you so shyly poised over me, looking down at me—

DEELEY   Stop that!

Pause.

Kate sits.

Deeley pours a drink.

DEELEY (*cont.*)   Myself I was a student then, juggling with my future, wondering should I bejasus saddle myself with a slip of a girl not long out of her swaddling clothes whose only claim to virtue was silence but who lacked any sense of fixedness, any sense of decisiveness, but was compliant only to the shifting winds, with which she went, but not *the* winds, and certainly not my winds, such as they are, but I suppose winds that only she understood, and that of course with no understanding whatsoever, at least as I understand the word, at least that's the way I figured it. A classic female figure, I said to myself, or is it a classic female posture, one way or the other long outworn.

Pause.

DEELEY (*cont.*)   That's the position as I saw it then. I mean, that is my categorical pronouncement on the position as I saw it then. Twenty years ago.

Silence.

ANNA   When I heard that Katey was married my heart leapt with joy.

DEELEY   How did the news reach you?

ANNA   From a friend.

Pause.

ANNA *(cont.)*   Yes, it leapt with joy. Because you see I knew she never did things loosely or carelessly, recklessly. Some people throw a stone into a river to see if the water's too cold for jumping, others, a few others, will always wait for the ripples before they will jump.

DEELEY   Some people do *what*? *(to Kate)* What did she say?

ANNA   And I knew that Katey would always wait not just for the first emergence of ripple but for the ripples to pervade and pervade the surface, for of course as you know ripples on the surface indicate a shimmering in depth down through every particle of water down to the river bed, but even when she felt that happen, when she was assured it was happening, she still might not jump. But in this case she did jump and I knew therefore she had fallen in love truly and was glad. And I deduced it must also have happened to you.

DEELEY   You mean the ripples?

ANNA   If you like.

DEELEY   Do men ripple too?

ANNA   Some, I would say.

DEELEY   I see.

Pause.

ANNA   And later when I found out the kind of man you were I was doubly delighted because I knew Katey had always been interested in the arts.

KATE   I was interested once in the arts, but I can't remember now which ones they were.

ANNA   Don't tell me you've forgotten our days at the Tate? and how we explored London and all the old churches and all the old buildings, I mean those that were left from the bombing, in the City and south of the river in Lambeth and Greenwich? Oh my goodness. Oh yes. And the Sunday papers! I could never get her away from the review pages. She ravished them, and then insisted we visit that gallery, or this theatre, or that chamber concert, but of course there was so much, so much to see and to hear, in lovely London then, that sometimes we missed things, or had no more money, and so missed some things. For example, I remember one Sunday she said to me, looking up from the paper, come quick, quick, come with me quickly, and we seized our handbags and went, on a bus, to some totally obscure, some totally unfamiliar district and, almost alone, saw a wonderful film called Odd Man Out.

Silence.

DEELEY   Yes, I do quite a bit of travelling in my job.

ANNA   Do you enjoy it?

DEELEY   Enormously. Enormously.

ANNA   Do you go far?

DEELEY   I travel the globe in my job.

ANNA   And poor Katey when you're away? What does she do?

Anna looks at Kate.

KATE   Oh, I continue.

ANNA   Is he away for long periods?

KATE   I think, sometimes. Are you?

ANNA   You leave your wife for such long periods? How can you?

DEELEY   I have to do a lot of travelling in my job.

ANNA (*to Kate*)   I think I must come and keep you company when he's away.

DEELEY   Won't your husband miss you?

ANNA   Of course. But he would understand.

DEELEY   Does he understand now?

ANNA   Of course.

DEELEY   We had a vegetarian dish prepared for him.

ANNA He's not a vegetarian. In fact he's something of a gourmet. We live in a rather fine villa and have done so for many years. It's very high up, on the cliffs.

DEELEY You eat well up there, eh?

ANNA I would say so, yes.

DEELEY Yes, I know Sicily slightly. Just slightly. Taormina. Do you live in Taormina?

ANNA Just outside.

DEELEY Just outside, yes. Very high up. Yes, I've probably caught a glimpse of your villa.

Pause.

DEELEY (*cont.*) My work took me to Sicily. My work concerns itself with life all over, you see, in every part of the globe. With people all over the globe. I use the word globe because the word world possesses emotional political sociological and psychological pretensions and resonances which I prefer as a matter of choice to do without, or shall I say to steer clear of, or if you like to reject. How's the yacht?

ANNA Oh, very well.

DEELEY Captain steer a straight course?

ANNA As straight as we wish, when we wish it.

DEELEY Don't you find England damp, returning?

ANNA Rather beguilingly so.

DEELEY Rather beguilingly so? (*to himself*) What the hell does she mean by that?

Pause.

DEELEY (*cont.*) Well, any time your husband finds himself in this direction my little wife will be only too glad to put the old pot on the old gas stove and dish him up something luscious if not voluptuous. No trouble.

Pause.

DEELEY (*cont.*)   I suppose his business interests kept him from making the trip. What's his name? Gian Carlo or Per Paulo?

KATE (*to Anna*)   Do you have marble floors?

ANNA   Yes.

KATE   Do you walk in bare feet on them?

ANNA   Yes. But I wear sandals on the terrace, because it can be rather severe on the soles.

KATE   The sun, you mean? The heat.

ANNA   Yes.

DEELEY   I had a great crew in Sicily. A marvellous cameraman. Irving Shultz. Best in the business. We took a pretty austere look at the women in black. The little old women in black. I wrote the film and directed it. My name is Orson Welles.

KATE (*to Anna*)   Do you drink orange juice on your terrace in the morning, and bullshots at sunset, and look down at the sea?

ANNA   Sometimes, yes.

DEELEY   As a matter of fact I am at the top of my profession, as a matter of fact, and I have indeed been associated with substantial numbers of articulate and sensitive people, mainly prostitutes of all kinds.

KATE (*to Anna*)   And do you like the Sicilian people?

DEELEY   I've been there. There's nothing more to see, there's nothing more to investigate, nothing. There's nothing more in Sicily to investigate.

KATE (*to Anna*)   Do you like the Sicilian people?

Anna stares at her.

Silence.

ANNA (*quietly*)   Don't let's go out tonight, don't let's go anywhere tonight, let's stay in. I'll cook something, you can wash your hair, you can relax, we'll put on some records.

KATE   Oh, I don't know. We could go out.

ANNA   Why do you want to go out?

KATE   We could walk across the park.

ANNA   The park is dirty at night, all sorts of horrible people, men hiding behind trees and women with terrible voices, they scream at you as you go past, and people come out suddenly from behind trees and bushes and there are shadows everywhere and there are policemen, and you'll have a horrible walk, and you'll see all the traffic and the noise of the traffic and you'll see all the hotels, and you know you hate looking through all those swing doors, you hate it, to see all that, all those people in the lights in the lobbies all talking and moving . . . and all the chandeliers . . .

Pause.

ANNA (*cont.*)   You'll only want to come home if you go out. You'll want to run home . . . and into your room. . . .

Pause.

KATE   What shall we do then?

ANNA   Stay in. Shall I read to you? Would you like that?

KATE   I don't know.

Pause.

ANNA   Are you hungry?

KATE   No.

DEELEY   Hungry? After that casserole?

Pause.

KATE   What shall I wear tomorrow? I can't make up my mind.

ANNA   Wear your green.

KATE   I haven't got the right top.

ANNA   You have. You have your turquoise blouse.

KATE   Do they go?

ANNA   Yes, they do go. Of course they go.

KATE I'll try it.

Pause.

ANNA Would you like me to ask someone over?

KATE Who?

ANNA Charley . . . or Jake?

KATE I don't like Jake.

ANNA Well, Charley. . . . or . . .

KATE Who?

ANNA McCabe.

Pause.

KATE I'll think about it in the bath.

ANNA Shall I run your bath for you?

KATE (*standing*) No. I'll run it myself tonight.

Kate slowly walks to the bedroom door, goes out, closes it.

Deeley stands looking at Anna.

Anna turns her head towards him.

They look at each other.

Fade

ACT TWO

The bedroom.

A long window up centre. Door to bathroom up left. Door to sitting-room up right.

Two divans. An armchair.

The divans and armchair are disposed in precisely the same relation to each other as the furniture in the first act, but in reversed positions.

Lights dim. Anna discerned sitting on divan. Faint glow from glass panel in bathroom door.

Silence.

Lights up. The other door opens. Deeley comes in with tray.

Deeley comes into the room, places the tray on a table.

DEELEY Here we are. Good and hot. Good and strong and hot. You prefer it white with sugar, I believe?

ANNA Please.

DEELEY (*pouring*) Good and strong and hot with white and sugar.

He hands her the cup.

DEELEY (*cont.*) Like the room?

ANNA Yes.

DEELEY We sleep here. These are beds. The great thing about these beds is that they are susceptible to any amount of permutation. They can be separated as they are now. Or placed at right angles, or one can bisect the other, or you can sleep feet to feet, or head to head, or side by side. It's the castors that make all this possible.

He sits with coffee.

DEELEY (*cont.*) Yes, I remember you quite clearly from The Wayfarers.

ANNA The what?

DEELEY The Wayfarers Tavern, just off the Brompton Road.

ANNA   When was that?

DEELEY   Years ago.

ANNA   I don't think so.

DEELEY   Oh yes, it was you, no question. I never forget a face. You sat in the corner, quite often, sometimes alone, sometimes with others. And here you are, sitting in my house in the country. The same woman. Incredible. Fellow called Luke used to go in there. You knew him.

ANNA   Luke?

DEELEY   Big chap. Ginger hair. Ginger beard.

ANNA   I don't honestly think so.

DEELEY   Yes, a whole crowd of them, poets, stunt men, jockeys, stand-up comedians, that kind of setup. You used to wear a scarf, that's right, a black scarf, and a black sweater, and a skirt.

ANNA   Me?

DEELEY   And black stockings. Don't tell me you've forgotten The Wayfarers Tavern? You might have forgotten the name but you must remember the pub. You were the darling of the saloon bar.

ANNA   I wasn't rich, you know. I didn't have money for alcohol.

DEELEY   You had escorts. You didn't have to pay. You were looked after. I bought you a few drinks myself.

ANNA   You?

DEELEY   Sure.

ANNA   Never.

DEELEY   It's the truth. I remember clearly.

Pause.

ANNA   You?

DEELEY   I've bought you drinks.

Pause.

DEELEY (*cont.*)   Twenty years ago . . . or so.

ANNA You're saying we've met before?

DEELEY Of course we've met before.

Pause.

DEELEY (*cont.*) We've talked before. In that pub, for example. In the corner. Luke didn't like it much but we ignored him. Later we all went to a party. Someone's flat, somewhere in Westbourne Grove. You sat on a very low sofa, I sat opposite and looked up your skirt. Your black stockings were very black because your thighs were so white. That's something that's all over now, of course, isn't it, nothing like the same palpable profit in it now, it's all over. But it was worthwhile then. It was worthwhile that night. I simply sat sipping my light ale and gazed . . . gazed up your skirt. You didn't object, you found my gaze perfectly acceptable.

ANNA I was aware of your gaze, was I?

DEELEY There was a great argument going on, about China or something, or death, or China *and* death, I can't remember which, but nobody but I had a thigh-kissing view, nobody but you had the thighs which kissed. And here you are. Same woman. Same thighs.

Pause.

DEELEY (*cont.*) Yes. Then a friend of yours came in, a girl, a girl friend. She sat on the sofa with you, you both chatted and chuckled, sitting together, and I settled lower to gaze at you both, at both your thighs, squealing and hissing, you aware, she unaware, but then a great multitude of men surrounded me, and demanded my opinion about death, or about China, or whatever it was, and they would not let me be but bent down over me, so that what with their stinking breath and their broken teeth and the hair in their noses and China and death and their arses on the arms of my chair I was forced to get up and plunge my way through them, followed by them with ferocity, as if I were the cause of their argument, looking back through smoke, rushing to the table with the linoleum cover to look for one more full bottle of light ale, looking back through smoke, glimpsing two girls on the sofa, one of them you, heads close, whispering, no longer able to see anything, no longer able to see stocking or thigh, and then you were gone. I wandered over to the sofa. There was no one on it. I gazed at the indentations of four buttocks. Two of which were yours.

Pause.

ANNA I've rarely heard a sadder story.

DEELEY I agree.

ANNA I'm terribly sorry.

DEELEY That's all right.

Pause.

DEELEY (*cont.*) I never saw you again. You disappeared from the area. Perhaps you moved out.

ANNA No. I didn't.

DEELEY I never saw you in The Wayfarers Tavern again. Where were you?

ANNA Oh, at concerts, I should think, or the ballet.

Silence.

ANNA (*cont.*) Katey's taking a long time over her bath.

DEELEY Well, you know what she's like when she gets in the bath.

ANNA Yes.

DEELEY Enjoys it. Takes a long time over it.

ANNA She does, yes.

DEELEY A hell of a long time. Luxuriates in it. Gives herself a great soaping all over.

Pause.

DEELEY (*cont.*) Really soaps herself all over, and then washes the soap off, sud by sud. Meticulously. She's both thorough and, I must say it, sensuous. Gives herself a comprehensive going over, and apart from everything else she does emerge as clean as a new pin. Don't you think?

ANNA Very clean.

DEELEY Truly so. Not a speck. Not a tidemark. Shiny as a balloon.

ANNA Yes, a kind of floating.

DEELEY What?

ANNA She floats from the bath. Like a dream. Unaware of anyone standing, with her towel, waiting for her, waiting to wrap it round her. Quite absorbed.

Pause.

ANNA (*cont.*) Until the towel is placed on her shoulders.

Pause.

DEELEY Of course she's so totally incompetent at drying herself properly, did you find that? She gives herself a really good *scrub,* but can she with the same efficiency give herself an equally good *rub*? I have found, in my experience of her, that this is not in fact the case. You'll always find a few odd unexpected unwanted cheeky globules dripping about.

ANNA Why don't you dry her yourself?

DEELEY Would you recommend that?

ANNA You'd do it properly.

DEELEY In her bath towel?

ANNA How out?

DEELEY How out?

ANNA How could you dry her out? Out of her bath towel?

DEELEY I don't know.

ANNA Well, dry her yourself, in her bath towel.

Pause.

DEELEY Why don't *you* dry her in her bath towel?

ANNA Me?

DEELEY You'd do it properly.

ANNA No, no.

DEELEY   Surely? I mean, you're a woman, you know how and where and in what density moisture collects on women's bodies.

ANNA   No two women are the same.

DEELEY   Well, that's true enough.

Pause.

DEELEY (*cont.*)   I've got a brilliant idea. Why don't we do it with powder?

ANNA   Is that a brilliant idea?

DEELEY   Isn't it?

ANNA   It's quite common to powder yourself after a bath.

DEELEY   It's quite common to powder yourself after a bath but it's quite uncommon to be powdered. Or is it? It's not common where I come from, I can tell you. My mother would have a fit.

Pause.

DEELEY (*cont.*)   Listen. I'll tell you what. I'll do it. I'll do the whole lot. The towel and the powder. After all, I am her husband. But you can supervise the whole thing. And give me some hot tips while you're at it. That'll kill two birds with one stone.

Pause.

DEELEY (*cont.*) (*to himself*)   Christ.

He looks at her slowly.

DEELEY (*cont.*)   You must be about forty, I should think, by now.

Pause.

DEELEY (*cont.*)   If I walked into The Wayfarers Tavern now, and saw you sitting in the corner, I wouldn't recognise you.

The bathroom door opens. Kate comes into the bedroom. She wears a bathrobe.

She smiles at Deeley and Anna.

KATE (*with pleasure*)   Aaahh.

She walks to the window and looks out into the night. Deeley and Anna watch her.

Deeley begins to sing softly.

DEELEY (*singing*)   The way you wear your hat . . .

ANNA (*singing, softly*)   The way you sip your tea . . .

DEELEY (*singing*)   The memory of all that . . .

ANNA (*singing*)   No, no, they can't take that away from me . . .

Kate turns from the window to look at them.

ANNA (*singing*)   The way your smile just beams . . .

DEELEY (*singing*)   The way you sing off key . . .

ANNA (*singing*)   The way you haunt my dreams . . .

DEELEY (*singing*)   No, no, they can't take that away from me . . .

Kate walks down towards them and stands, smiling. Anna and Deeley sing again, faster on cue, and more perfunctorily.

ANNA (*singing*)   The way you hold your knife—

DEELEY (*singing*)   The way we danced till three—

ANNA (*singing*)   The way you've changed my life—

DEELEY   No, no, they can't take that away from me.

Kate sits on a divan.

ANNA (*to Deeley*)   Doesn't she look beautiful?

DEELEY   Doesn't she?

KATE   Thank you. I feel fresh. The water's very soft here. Much softer than London. I always find the water very hard in London. That's one reason I like living in the country. Everything's softer. The water, the light, the shapes, the sounds. There aren't such edges here. And living close to the sea too. You can't say where it begins or ends. That appeals to me. I don't care for harsh lines. I deplore that kind of urgency. I'd like to go to the East, or somewhere like that, somewhere very hot, where you can lie under a mosquito net and breathe quite slowly. You know . . . somewhere where you can look through the flap of a tent and see sand, that kind of thing. The only nice thing about a big city is that when it rains it blurs everything, and it blurs the lights from the cars, doesn't it, and blurs your eyes, and you have rain on your lashes. That's the only nice thing about a big city.

ANNA   That's not the only nice thing. You can have a nice room and a nice gasfire and a warm dressing-gown and a nice hot drink, all waiting for you for when you come in.

Pause.

KATE   Is it raining?

ANNA   No.

KATE   Well, I've decided I will stay in tonight anyway.

ANNA   Oh good. I am glad. Now you can have a good strong cup of coffee after your bath.

Anna stands, goes to coffee, pours.

ANNA (*cont.*)   I could do the hem on your black dress. I could finish it and you could try it on.

KATE   Mmmnn.

Anna hands her her coffee.

ANNA   Or I could read to you.

DEELEY   Have you dried yourself properly, Kate?

KATE   I think so.

DEELEY   Are you sure? All over?

KATE   I think so. I feel quite dry.

DEELEY   Are you quite sure? I don't want you sitting here damply all over the place.

Kate smiles.

DEELEY (*cont.*)   See that smile? That's the same smile she smiled when I was walking down the street with her, after Odd Man Out, well, quite some time after. What did you think of it?

ANNA   It is a very beautiful smile.

DEELEY   Do it again.

KATE I'm still smiling.

DEELEY You're not. Not like you were a moment ago, not like you did then. (*to Anna*) You know the smile I'm talking about?

KATE This coffee's cold.

Pause

ANNA Oh, I'm sorry. I'll make some fresh.

KATE No, I don't want any, thank you.

Pause.

KATE (*cont.*) Is Charley coming?

ANNA I can ring him if you like.

KATE What about McCabe?

ANNA Do you really want to see anyone?

KATE I don't think I like McCabe.

ANNA Nor do I.

KATE He's strange. He says some very strange things to me.

ANNA What things?

KATE Oh, all sorts of funny things.

ANNA I've never liked him.

KATE Duncan's nice though, isn't he?

ANNA Oh yes.

KATE I like his poetry so much.

Pause.

KATE (*cont.*) But you know who I like best?

ANNA Who?

KATE Christy.

ANNA He's lovely.

KATE He's so gentle, isn't he? And his humour. Hasn't he got a lovely sense of humour? And I think he's . . . so sensitive. Why don't you ask him round?

DEELEY He can't make it. He's out of town.

KATE Oh, what a pity.

Silence.

DEELEY (*to Anna*) Are you intending to visit anyone else while you're in England? Relations? Cousins? Brothers?

ANNA No. I know no one. Except Kate.

Pause.

DEELEY Do you find her changed?

ANNA Oh, just a little, not very much. (*to Kate*) You're still shy, aren't you?

Kate stares at her.

ANNA (*cont.*) (*to Deeley*) But when I knew her first she was *so* shy, as shy as a fawn, she really was. When people leaned to speak to her she would fold away from them, so that though she was still standing within their reach she was no longer accessible to them. She folded herself from them, they were no longer able to speak or go through with their touch. I put it down to her upbringing, a parson's daughter, and indeed there was a good deal of Brontë about her.

DEELEY *Was* she a parson's daughter?

ANNA But if I thought Brontë I did not think she was Brontë in passion but only in secrecy, in being so stubbornly private.

Slight pause.

ANNA (*cont.*) I remember her first blush.

DEELEY What? What was it? I mean why was it?

ANNA I had borrowed some of her underwear, to go to a party. Later that night I confessed. It was naughty of me. She stared at me, nonplussed, perhaps, is the word. But I told her that in fact I had been punished for my sin, for a man at the party had spent the whole evening looking up my skirt.

Pause.

DEELEY She blushed at that?

ANNA Deeply.

DEELEY Looking up *your* skirt in *her* underwear. Mmnn.

ANNA But from that night she insisted, from time to time, that I borrow her underwear—she had more of it than I, and a far greater range—and each time she proposed this she would blush, but propose it she did, nevertheless. And when there was anything to tell her, when I got back, anything of interest to tell her, I told her.

DEELEY Did she blush then?

ANNA I could never see then. I would come in late and find her reading under the lamp, and begin to tell her, but she would say no, turn off the light, and I would tell her in the dark. She preferred to be told in the dark. But of course it was never completely dark, what with the light from the gasfire or the light through the curtains, and what she didn't know was that, knowing her preference, I would choose a position in the room from which I could see her face, although she could not see mine. She could hear my voice only. And so she listened and I watched her listening.

DEELEY Sounds a perfect marriage.

ANNA We were great friends.

Pause.

DEELEY You say she was Brontë in secrecy but not in passion. What was she in passion?

ANNA I feel that is your province.

DEELEY You feel it's my province? Well, you're damn right. It is my province. I'm glad someone's showing a bit of taste at last. Of course it's my bloody province. I'm her husband.

Pause.

DEELEY (*cont.*)   I mean I'd like to ask a question. Am I alone in beginning to find all this distasteful?

ANNA   But what can you possibly find distasteful? I've flown from Rome to see my oldest friend, after twenty years, and to meet her husband. What is it that worries you?

DEELEY   What worries me is the thought of your husband rumbling about alone in his enormous villa living hand to mouth on a few hardboiled eggs and unable to speak a damn word of English.

ANNA   I interpret, when necessary.

DEELEY   Yes, but you're here, with us. He's there, alone, lurching up and down the terrace, waiting for a speedboat, waiting for a speedboat to spill out beautiful people, at least. Beautiful Mediterranean people. Waiting for all *that,* a kind of elegance we know nothing about, a slim-bellied Cote d'Azur thing we know absolutely nothing about, a lobster and lobster sauce ideology we know fuck all about, the longest legs in the world, the most phenomenally soft voices. I can hear them now. I mean let's put it on the table, I have my eye on a number of pulses, pulses all round the globe, deprivations and insults, why should I waste valuable space listening to two—

KATE (*swiftly*)   If you don't like it go.

Pause.

DEELEY   Go? Where can I go?

KATE   To China. Or Sicily.

DEELEY   I haven't got a speedboat. I haven't got a white dinner jacket.

KATE   China then.

DEELEY   You know what they'd do to me in China if they found me in a white dinner jacket. They'd bloodywell kill me. You know what they're like over there.

Slight pause.

ANNA   You are welcome to come to Sicily at any time, both of you, and be my guests.

Silence.

Kate and Deeley stare at her.

ANNA (*cont.*) (*to Deeley, quietly*)   I would like you to understand that I came here not to disrupt but to celebrate.

Pause.

ANNA (*cont.*)   To celebrate a very old and treasured friendship, something that was forged between us long before you knew of our existence.

Pause.

ANNA (*cont.*)   I found her. She grew to know wonderful people, through my introduction. I took her to cafés, almost private ones, where artists and writers and sometimes actors collected, and others with dancers, and we sat hardly breathing with our coffee, listening to the life around us. All I wanted for her was her happiness. That is all I want for her still.

Pause.

DEELEY (*to Kate*)   We've met before, you know. Anna and I.

Kate looks at him.

DEELEY (*cont.*)   Yes, we met in The Wayfarers Tavern. In the corner. She took a fancy to me. Of course I was slimhipped in those days. Pretty nifty. A bit squinky, quite honestly. Curly hair. The lot. We had a scene together. She freaked out. She didn't have any bread, so I bought her a drink. She looked at me with big eyes, shy, all that bit. She was pretending to be you at the time. Did it pretty well. Wearing your underwear she was too, at the time. Amiably allowed me a gander. Trueblue generosity. Admirable in a woman. We went to a party. Given by philosophers. Not a bad bunch. Edgware road gang. Nice lot. Haven't seen any of them for years. Old friends. Always thinking. Spoke their thoughts. Those are the people I miss. They're all dead, anyway I've never seen them again. The Maida Vale group. Big Eric and little Tony. They lived somewhere near Paddington library. On the way to the party I took her into a café, bought her a cup of coffee, beards with faces. She thought she was you, said little, so little. Maybe she was you. Maybe it was you, having coffee with me, saying little, so little.

Pause.

KATE   What do you think attracted her to you?

DEELEY   I don't know. What?

KATE   She found your face very sensitive, vulnerable.

DEELEY   Did she?

KATE   She wanted to comfort it, in the way only a woman can.

DEELEY   Did she?

KATE   Oh yes.

DEELEY   She wanted to comfort my face, in the way only a woman can?

KATE   She was prepared to extend herself to you.

DEELEY   I beg your pardon?

KATE   She fell in love with you.

DEELEY   With me?

KATE   You were so unlike the others. We knew men who were brutish, crass.

DEELEY   There really are such men, then? Crass men?

KATE   Quite crass.

DEELEY   But I was crass, wasn't I, looking up her skirt?

KATE   That's not crass.

DEELEY   If it was her skirt. If it was her.

ANNA (*coldly*)   Oh, it was my skirt. It was me. I remember your look . . . very well. I remember you well.

KATE (*to Anna*)   But I remember you. I remember you dead.

Pause.

KATE (*cont.*)   I remember you lying dead. You didn't know I was watching you. I leaned over you. Your face was dirty. You lay dead, your face scrawled with dirt, all kinds of earnest inscriptions, but unblotted, so that they had run, all over your face, down to your throat. Your sheets were immaculate. I was glad. I would have been

316

unhappy if your corpse had lain in an unwholesome sheet. It would have been graceless. I mean as far as I was concerned. As far as my room was concerned. After all, you were dead in my room. When you woke my eyes were above you, staring down at you. You tried to do my little trick, one of my tricks you had borrowed, my little slow smile, my little slow shy smile, my bend of the head, my half closing of the eyes, that we knew so well, but it didn't work, the grin only split the dirt at the sides of your mouth and stuck. You stuck in your grin. I looked for tears but could see none. Your pupils weren't in your eyes. Your bones were breaking through your face. But all was serene. There was no suffering. It had all happened elsewhere. Last rites I did not feel necessary. Or any celebration. I felt the time and season appropriate and that by dying alone and dirty you had acted with proper decorum. It was time for my bath. I had quite a lengthy bath, got out, walked about the room, glistening, drew up a chair, sat naked beside you and watched you.

Pause.

KATE (*cont.*)   When I brought him into the room your body of course had gone. What a relief it was to have a different body in my room, a male body behaving quite differently, doing all those things they do and which they think are good, like sitting with one leg over the arm of an armchair. We had a choice of two beds. Your bed or my bed. To lie in, or on. To grind noses together, in or on. He liked your bed, and thought he was different in it because he was a man. But one night I said let me do something, a little thing, a little trick. He lay there in your bed. He looked up at me with great expectation. He was gratified. He thought I had profited from his teaching. He thought I was going to be sexually forthcoming, that I was about to take a long promised initiative. I dug about in the windowbox, where you had planted our pretty pansies, scooped, filled the bowl, and plastered his face with dirt. He was bemused, aghast, resisted, resisted with force. He would not let me dirty his face, or smudge it, he wouldn't let me. He suggested a wedding instead, and a change of environment.

Slight pause.

KATE (*cont.*)   Neither mattered.

Pause.

317

KATE (*cont.*)   He asked me once, at about that time, who had slept in that bed before him. I told him no one. No one at all.

Long silence.

Anna stands, walks towards the door, stops, her back to them.

Silence.

Deeley starts to sob, very quietly.

Anna stands still.

Anna turns, switches off the lamps, sirs on her divan, and lies down.

The sobbing stops.

Silence.

Deeley stands. He walks a few paces, looks at both divans. He goes to Anna's divan, looks down at her. She is still.

Silence.

Deeley moves towards the door, stops, his back to them.

Silence.

Deeley turns. He goes towards Kate's divan. He sits on her divan, lies across her lap.

Long silence.

Deeley very slowly sits up.

He gets off the divan.

He walks slowly to the armchair.

He sits, slumped.

Silence.

Lights up full sharply. Very bright.

Deeley in armchair.

Anna lying on divan.

Kate sitting on divan.

ONE FOR THE ROAD

One for the Road was first performed at the Lyric Theatre Studio, Hammersmith, on March 13, 1984, with the following cast:

NICOLAS *Mid 40s* Alan Bates
VICTOR *30* Roger Lloyd Pack
GILA *30* Jenny Quayle
NICKY *7* Stephen Kember or Felix Yates

Directed by Harold Pinter

The BBC-TV production, transmitted on July 25, 1985, had the same cast except that Rosie Kerslake played Gila and Paul Adams played Nicky. It was directed by Kenneth Ives.

One for the Road was subsequently presented as part of the triple bill *Other Places* at the Duchess Theatre, London, from March 7 to June 22, 1985, with the following cast:

NICOLAS Colin Blakely
VICTOR Roger Davidson
GILA Rosie Kerslake
NICKY Daniel Kipling or Simon Vyvyan

Directed by Kenneth Ives

One for the Road was also performed in a double bill with *A Kind of Alaska* by the Gate Theatre, Dublin, at the New Ambassadors Theatre, London, July 3–7, 2001, and at Alice Tully Hall as part of the Harold Pinter Festival at the Lincoln Center Festival 2001, New York, July 16–21, 2001. The cast was as follows:

NICOLAS Harold Pinter
VICTOR Lloyd Hutchinson
GILA Indira Varma
NICKY Rory Copus

Directed by Robin Lefèvre

A room. Morning.

NICOLAS *at his desk. He leans forward and speaks into a machine.*

NICOLAS   Bring him in.

He sits back. The door opens. VICTOR *walks in, slowly. His clothes are torn. He is bruised. The door closes behind him.*

NICOLAS (*cont.*)   Hello! Good morning. How are you? Let's not beat about the bush. Anything but that. *D'accord?* You're a civilized man. So am I. Sit down.

Victor slowly sits.

Nicolas stands, walks over to him.

NICOLAS (*cont.*)   What do you think this is? It's my finger. And this is my little finger. I wave my big finger in front of your eyes. Like this. And now I do the same with my little finger. I can also use both . . . at the same time. Like this. I can do absolutely anything I like. Do you think I'm mad? My mother did.

He laughs.

NICOLAS (*cont.*)   Do you think waving fingers in front of people's eyes is silly? I can see your point. You're a man of the highest intelligence. But would you take the same view if it was my boot—or my penis? Why am I so obsessed with eyes? Am I obsessed with eyes? Possibly. Not my eyes. Other people's eyes. The eyes of people who are brought to me here. They're so vulnerable. The soul shines through them. Are you a religious man? I am. Which side do you think God is on? I'm going to have a drink.

He goes to sideboard, pours whiskey.

NICOLAS (*cont.*)   You're probably wondering where your wife is. She's in another room.

He drinks.

NICOLAS (*cont.*)   Good-looking woman.

He drinks.

NICOLAS (*cont.*)   God, that was good.

323

He pours another.

NICOLAS (*cont.*)   Don't worry. I can hold my booze.

He drinks.

NICOLAS (*cont.*)   You may have noticed I'm the chatty type. You probably think I'm part of a predictable, formal, long-established pattern; i.e., I chat away, friendly, insouciant, I open the batting, as it were, in a lighthearted, even carefree manner, while another waits in the wings, silent, introspective, coiled like a puma. No, no. It's not quite like that. I run the place. God speaks through me. I'm referring to the Old Testament God, by the way, although I'm a long way from being Jewish. Everyone respects me here. Including you, I take it? I think that is the correct stance.

Pause.

NICOLAS (*cont.*)   Stand up.

Victor stands.

NICOLAS (*cont.*)   Sit down.

Victor sits.

NICOLAS (*cont.*)   Thank you so much.

Pause.

NICOLAS (*cont.*)   Tell me something. . . .

Silence.

NICOLAS (*cont.*)   What a good-looking woman your wife is. You're a very lucky man. Tell me . . . one for the road, I think. . . .

He pours whiskey.

NICOLAS (*cont.*)   You do respect me, I take it?

He stands in front of Victor and looks down at him. Victor looks up.

NICOLAS (*cont.*)   I would be right in assuming that?

Silence.

VICTOR (*quietly*)   I don't know you.

NICOLAS   But you respect me.

VICTOR   I don't know you.

NICOLAS   Are you saying you don't respect me?

Pause.

NICOLAS (*cont.*)   Are you saying you would respect me if you knew me better? Would you like to know me better?

Pause.

NICOLAS (*cont.*)   Would you like to know me better?

VICTOR   What I would like . . . has no bearing on the matter.

NICOLAS   Oh yes it has.

Pause.

NICOLAS (*cont.*)   I've heard so much about you. I'm terribly pleased to meet you. Well, I'm not sure that *pleased* is the right word. One has to be so scrupulous about language. Intrigued. I'm intrigued. Firstly because I've heard so much about you. Secondly because if you don't respect me you're unique. Everyone else knows the voice of God speaks through me. You're not a religious man, I take it?

Pause.

NICOLAS (*cont.*)   You don't believe in a guiding light?

Pause.

NICOLAS (*cont.*)   What then?

Pause.

NICOLAS (*cont.*)   So . . . morally . . . you flounder in wet shit. You know . . . like when you've eaten a rancid omelet.

Pause.

NICOLAS (*cont.*)   I think I deserve one for the road.

He pours, drinks.

NICOLAS (*cont.*)   Do you drink whiskey?

Pause.

NICOLAS (*cont.*)   I hear you have a lovely house. Lots of books. Someone told me some of my boys kicked it around a bit. Pissed on the rugs, that sort of thing. I wish they wouldn't do that. I do really. But you know what it's like—they have such responsibilities—and they feel them—they are constantly present, day and night, these responsibilities—and so, sometimes, they piss on a few rugs. You understand. You're not a fool.

Pause.

NICOLAS (*cont.*)   Is your son all right?

VICTOR   I don't know.

NICOLAS   Oh, I'm sure he's all right. What age is he . . . seven . . . or thereabouts? Big lad, I'm told. Nevertheless, silly of him to behave as he did. But is he all right?

VICTOR   I don't know.

NICOLAS   Oh, I'm sure he's all right. Anyway, I'll have a word with him later and find out. He's somewhere on the second floor, I believe.

Pause.

NICOLAS (*cont.*)   Well now . . .

Pause.

NICOLAS (*cont.*)   What do you say? Are we friends?

Pause.

NICOLAS (*cont.*)   I'm prepared to be frank, as a true friend should. I love death. What about you?

Pause.

NICOLAS (*cont.*)   What about you? Do you love death? Not necessarily your own. Others. The death of others. Do you love the death of others, or at any rate, do you love the death of others as much as I do?

Pause.

NICOLAS (*cont.*)   Are you always so dull? I understood you enjoyed the cut and thrust of debate.

Pause.

NICOLAS (*cont.*)   Death. Death. Death. Death. As has been noted by the most respected authorities, it is beautiful. The purest, most harmonious thing there is. Sexual intercourse is nothing compared to it.

He drinks.

NICOLAS (*cont.*)   Talking about sexual intercourse . . .

He laughs wildly, stops.

NICOLAS (*cont.*)   Does she . . . fuck? Or does she . . . ? Or does she . . . like . . . you know . . . what? What does she like? I'm talking about your wife. Your *wife*.

Pause.

NICOLAS (*cont.*)   You know the old joke? Does she fuck?

Heavily, in another voice:

NICOLAS (*cont.*)   Does she fuck!

He laughs.

NICOLAS (*cont.*)   It's ambiguous, of course. It could mean she fucks like a rabbit or she fucks not at all.

Pause.

NICOLAS (*cont.*)   Well, we're all God's creatures. Even your wife.

Pause.

NICOLAS (*cont.*)   There is only one obligation. *To be honest*. You have no other obligation. Weigh that. In your mind. Do you know the man who runs this country? No? Well, he's a very nice chap. He took me aside the other day—last Wednesday, I think it was—he took me aside at a reception, visiting dignitaries, he took *me* aside, *me,* and he said to me, he said, in what I can only describe as a hoarse whisper, Nic, he said, Nic (that's my name), Nic, if you ever come across anyone whom you have good reason to believe is getting on my tits, tell them one thing, tell them honesty is the best policy. The cheese was superb. Goat. One for the road.

He pours.

NICOLAS (*cont.*)   Your wife and I had a very nice chat, but I couldn't help noticing she didn't look her best. She's probably menstruating. Women do that.

Pause.

NICOLAS (*cont.*)   You know, old chap, I do love other things, apart from death. So many things. Nature. Trees, things like that. A nice blue sky. Blossoms.

Pause.

NICOLAS (*cont.*)   Tell me . . . truly . . . are you beginning to love me?

Pause.

NICOLAS (*cont.*)   I think your wife is. Beginning. She is beginning to fall in love with me. On the brink . . . of doing so. The trouble is, I have rivals. Because everyone here has fallen in love with your wife. It's her eyes have beguiled them. What's her name? Gila . . . or something?

Pause.

NICOLAS (*cont.*)   Who would you prefer to be? You or me?

Pause.

NICOLAS (*cont.*)   I'd go for me if I were you. The trouble about you, although I grant your merits, is that you're on a losing wicket, while I can't put a foot wrong. Do you take my point? Ah, God, let me confess, let me make a confession to you. I have never been more moved, in the whole of my life, as when—only the other day, last Friday, I believe—the man who runs this country announced to the country: We are all patriots, we are as one, we all share a common heritage. Except you, apparently.

Pause.

NICOLAS (*cont.*)   I feel a link, you see, a bond. I share a commonwealth of interest. I am not alone. I am not alone!

Silence.

VICTOR   Kill me.

NICOLAS   What?

VICTOR Kill me.

Nicolas goes to him, puts his arm around him.

NICOLAS What's the matter?

Pause.

NICOLAS (*cont.*) What in heaven's name is the matter?

Pause.

NICOLAS (*cont.*) Mmmnnn?

Pause.

NICOLAS (*cont.*) You're probably just hungry. Or thirsty. Let me tell you something. I hate despair. I find it intolerable. The stink of it gets up my nose. It's a blemish. Despair, old fruit, is a cancer. It should be castrated. Indeed I've often found that that works. Chop the balls off and despair goes out the window. You're left with a happy man. Or a happy woman. Look at me.

Victor does so.

NICOLAS (*cont.*) Your soul shines out of your eyes.

Blackout.

LIGHTS UP. AFTERNOON.

Nicolas standing with a small boy.

NICOLAS What is your name?

NICKY Nicky.

NICOLAS Really? How odd.

Pause.

NICOLAS (*cont.*) Do you like cowboys and Indians?

NICKY Yes. A bit.

NICOLAS What do you really like?

NICKY I like airplanes.

NICOLAS   Real ones or toy ones?

NICKY   I like both kinds of ones.

NICOLAS   Do you?

Pause.

NICOLAS *(cont.)*   Why do you like airplanes?

Pause.

NICKY   Well . . . because they go so fast. Through the air. The real ones do.

NICOLAS   And the toy ones?

NICKY   I pretend they go as fast as the real ones do.

Pause.

NICOLAS   Do you like your mummy and daddy?

Pause.

NICOLAS *(cont.)*   Do you like your mummy and daddy?

NICKY   Yes.

NICOLAS   Why?

Pause.

NICOLAS *(cont.)*   Why?

Pause.

NICOLAS *(cont.)*   Do you find that a hard question to answer?

Pause.

NICKY   Where's Mummy?

NICOLAS   You don't like your mummy and daddy?

NICKY   Yes. I do.

NICOLAS   Why?

Pause.

NICOLAS *(cont.)*   Would you like to be a soldier when you grow up?

NICKY   I don't mind.

NICOLAS   You don't? Good. You like soldiers. Good. But you spat at my soldiers and you kicked them. You attacked them.

NICKY   Were they your soldiers?

NICOLAS   They are your country's soldiers.

NICKY   I didn't like those soldiers.

NICOLAS   They don't like you either, my darling.

Blackout.

LIGHTS UP. NIGHT.

Nicolas sitting. GILA *standing. Her clothes are torn. She is bruised.*

NICOLAS   When did you meet your husband?

GILA   When I was eighteen.

NICOLAS   Why?

GILA   Why?

NICOLAS   Why?

GILA   I just met him.

NICOLAS   Why?

GILA   I didn't plan it.

NICOLAS   Why not?

GILA   I didn't know him.

NICOLAS   Why not?

Pause.

NICOLAS (*cont.*)   Why not?

GILA   I didn't know him.

NICOLAS   Why not?

GILA   I met him.

NICOLAS When?

GILA When I was eighteen.

NICOLAS Why?

GILA He was in the room.

NICOLAS Room?

Pause.

NICOLAS (*cont.*) Room?

GILA The same room.

NICOLAS As what?

GILA As I was.

NICOLAS As I was?

GILA (*screaming*) As I was!

Pause.

NICOLAS Room? What room?

GILA A room.

NICOLAS What room?

GILA My father's room.

NICOLAS Your father? What's your father got to do with it?

Pause.

NICOLAS (*cont.*) Your *father*? How dare you? Fuckpig.

Pause.

NICOLAS (*cont.*) Your father was a wonderful man. His country is proud of him. He's dead. He was a man of honor. He's dead. Are you prepared to insult the memory of your father?

Pause.

NICOLAS (*cont.*) Are you prepared to defame, to debase, the memory of your father? Your father fought for his country. I knew him. I revered him. Everyone did. He believed in God. He didn't *think,* like you shitbags. He *lived.* He lived. He was iron and gold. He would die, he would die, he would die, for his country, for his God. And he did die, he died, he died, for his God. You turd. To spawn such a daughter. What a fate. Oh, poor, perturbed spirit, to be haunted forever by such scum and spittle. How do you dare speak of your father to me? I loved him, as if he were my own father.

Silence.

NICOLAS *(cont.)* Where did you meet your husband?

GILA In a street.

NICOLAS What were you doing there?

GILA Walking.

NICOLAS What was he doing?

GILA Walking.

Pause.

GILA *(cont.)* I dropped something. He picked it up.

NICOLAS What did you drop?

GILA The evening paper.

NICOLAS You were drunk.

Pause.

NICOLAS *(cont.)* You were drugged.

Pause.

NICOLAS *(cont.)* You had absconded from your hospital.

GILA I was not in a hospital.

NICOLAS Where are you now?

Pause.

NICOLAS *(cont.)* Where are you now? Do you think you are in a hospital?

Pause.

NICOLAS (*cont.*)   Do you think we have nuns upstairs?

Pause.

NICOLAS (*cont.*)   What do we have upstairs?

GILA   No nuns.

NICOLAS   What do we have?

GILA   Men.

NICOLAS   Have they been raping you?

She stares at him.

NICOLAS (*cont.*)   How many times?

Pause.

NICOLAS (*cont.*)   How many times have you been raped?

Pause.

NICOLAS (*cont.*)   How many times?

He stands, goes to her, lifts his finger.

NICOLAS (*cont.*)   This is my big finger. And this is my little finger. Look. I wave them in front of your eyes. Like this. How many times have you been raped?

GILA   I don't know.

NICOLAS   And you consider yourself a reliable witness?

He goes to sideboard, pours drink, sits, drinks.

NICOLAS (*cont.*)   You're a lovely woman. Well, you were.

He leans back, drinks, sighs.

NICOLAS (*cont.*)   Your son is . . . seven. He's a little prick. You made him so. You have taught him to be so. You had a choice. You could have encouraged him to be a good person. Instead, you encouraged him to be a little prick. You encouraged him to spit, to strike at soldiers of honor, soldiers of God.

Pause.

NICOLAS (*cont.*)   Oh well . . . in one way I suppose it's academic.

Pause.

NICOLAS (*cont.*)   You're of no interest to me. I might even let you out of here, in due course. But I should think you might entertain us all a little more before you go.

Blackout.

LIGHTS UP. NIGHT.

Nicolas standing.

Victor sitting. Victor is tidily dressed.

NICOLAS   How have you been? Surviving?

VICTOR   Yes.

NICOLAS   Yes?

VICTOR   Yes. Yes.

NICOLAS   Really? How?

VICTOR   Oh . . .

Pause.

NICOLAS   I can't hear you.

VICTOR   It's my mouth.

NICOLAS   Mouth?

VICTOR   Tongue.

NICOLAS   What's the matter with it?

Pause.

NICOLAS (*cont.*)   What about a drink? One for the road. What do you say to a drink?

He goes to the bottle, pours two glasses, gives a glass to Victor.

335

NICOLAS (*cont.*)   Drink up. It'll put lead in your pencil. And then we'll find someone to take it out.

He laughs.

NICOLAS (*cont.*)   We can do that, you know. We have a first-class brothel upstairs, on the sixth floor, chandeliers, the lot. They'll suck you in and blow you out in little bubbles. All volunteers. Their daddies are in our business. Which is, I remind you, to keep the world clean for God. Get me? Drink up. Drink up. Are you refusing to drink with me?

Victor drinks. His head falls back.

NICOLAS (*cont.*)   Cheers.

Nicolas drinks.

NICOLAS (*cont.*)   You can go.

Pause.

NICOLAS (*cont.*)   You can leave. We'll meet again, I hope. I trust we will always remain friends. Go out. Enjoy life. Be good. Love your wife. She'll be joining you in about a week, by the way. If she feels up to it. Yes. I feel we've both benefited from our discussions.

Victor mutters.

NICOLAS (*cont.*)   What?

Victor mutters.

NICOLAS (*cont.*)   What?

VICTOR   My son.

NICOLAS   Your son? Oh, don't worry about him. He was a little prick.

Victor straightens and stares at Nicolas.

Silence.

Blackout.

MOUNTAIN LANGUAGE

Mountain Language was first performed at the National Theatre in London on October 20, 1988. The cast was as follows:

YOUNG WOMAN   Miranda Richardson
ELDERLY WOMAN   Eileen Atkins
SERGEANT   Michael Gambon
OFFICER   Julian Wadham
GUARD   George Harris
PRISONER   Tony Haygarth
HOODED MAN   Alex Hardy
SECOND GUARD   Douglas McFerran

Directed by Harold Pinter

Mountain Language received its American premiere in a double bill with *The Birthday Party* by the Classic Stage Company at CSC Repertory Theatre, New York, on October 31, 1989, with the following cast:

ELDERLY WOMAN   Jean Stapleton
YOUNG WOMAN   Wendy Makkena
SERGEANT   Richard Riehle
OFFICER   David Strathairn
PRISONER   Peter Riegert
GUARD   Miguel Perez
HOODED MAN   David Strathairn
SECOND GUARD   Thomas Delling
WOMEN IN LINE   Katie Cohen, Ellie Hannibal, Mary Beth Kilkelly, Gwynne Rivers

Directed by Carey Perloff

I

A PRISON WALL

A line of women. An ELDERLY WOMAN, *cradling her hand.*

A basket at her feet.

A YOUNG WOMAN *with her arm around the Woman's shoulders.*

A SERGEANT *enters, followed by an* OFFICER. *The Sergeant points to the Young Woman.*

SERGEANT Name?

YOUNG WOMAN We've given our names.

SERGEANT Name?

YOUNG WOMAN We've given our names.

SERGEANT Name?

OFFICER (*to Sergeant*) Stop this shit. (*to Young Woman*) Any complaints?

YOUNG WOMAN She's been bitten.

OFFICER Who?

Pause.

OFFICER (*cont.*) Who? Who's been bitten?

YOUNG WOMAN She has. She has a torn hand. Look. Her hand has been bitten. This is blood.

SERGEANT (*to Young Woman*) What is your name?

OFFICER Shut up.

He walks over to Elderly Woman.

OFFICER (*cont.*) What's happened to your hand? Has someone bitten your hand?

The Woman slowly lifts her hand. He peers at it.

OFFICER (*cont.*) Who did this? Who bit you?

YOUNG WOMAN A Doberman pinscher.

OFFICER Which one?

Pause.

OFFICER (*cont.*) Which one?

Pause.

OFFICER (*cont.*) Sergeant!

Sergeant steps forward.

SERGEANT Sir!

OFFICER Look at this woman's hand. I think the thumb is going to come off. (*to Elderly Woman*) Who did this?

She stares at him.

OFFICER (*cont.*) Who did this?

YOUNG WOMAN A big dog.

OFFICER What was his name?

Pause.

OFFICER (*cont.*) What was his *name*?

Pause.

OFFICER (*cont.*) Every dog has a *name*! They answer to their name. They are given a name by their parents and that is their name, that is their *name*! Before they bite, they *state* their name. It's a formal procedure. They state their name and then they bite. What was his name? If you tell me one of our dogs bit this woman without giving his name I will have that dog shot!

Silence.

OFFICER (*cont.*) Now—attention! Silence and attention! Sergeant!

SERGEANT Sir?

OFFICER Take any complaints.

SERGEANT Any complaints? Has anyone got any complaints?

YOUNG WOMAN We were told to be here at nine o'clock this morning.

SERGEANT Right. Quite right. Nine o'clock this morning. Absolutely right. What's your complaint?

YOUNG WOMAN We were here at nine o'clock this morning. It's now five o'clock. We have been standing here for eight hours. In the snow. Your men let Doberman pinschers frighten us. One bit this woman's hand.

OFFICER What was the name of this dog?

She looks at him.

YOUNG WOMAN I don't know his name.

SERGEANT With permission, sir?

OFFICER Go ahead.

SERGEANT Your husbands, your sons, your fathers, these men you have been waiting to see, are shithouses. They are enemies of the State. They are shithouses.

The Officer steps towards the Women.

OFFICER Now hear this. You are mountain people. You hear me? Your language is dead. It is forbidden. It is not permitted to speak your mountain language in this place. You cannot speak your language to your men. It is not permitted. Do you understand? You may not speak it. It is outlawed. You may only speak the language of the capital. That is the only language permitted in this place. You will be badly punished if you attempt to speak your mountain language in this place. This is a military decree. It is the law. Your language is forbidden. It is dead. No one is allowed to speak your language. Your language no longer exists. Any questions?

YOUNG WOMAN I do not speak the mountain language.

Silence. The Officer and Sergeant slowly circle her. The Sergeant puts his hand on her bottom.

SERGEANT What language do you speak? What language do you speak with your arse?

OFFICER   These women, Sergeant, have as yet committed no crime. Remember that.

SERGEANT   Sir! But you're not saying they're without sin?

OFFICER   Oh, no. Oh, no, I'm not saying that.

SERGEANT   This one's full of it. She bounces with it.

OFFICER   She doesn't speak the mountain language.

The Woman moves away from the Sergeant's hand and turns to face the two men.

YOUNG WOMAN   My name is Sara Johnson. I have come to see my husband. It is my right. Where is he?

OFFICER   Show me your papers.

She gives him a piece of paper. He examines it, turns to Sergeant.

OFFICER (*cont.*)   He doesn't come from the mountains. He's in the wrong batch.

SERGEANT   So is she. She looks like a fucking intellectual to me.

OFFICER   But you said her arse wobbled.

SERGEANT   Intellectual arses wobble the best.

Blackout.

2
VISITORS ROOM

A PRISONER *sitting. The Elderly Woman sitting, with basket. A* GUARD *standing behind her.*

The Prisoner and the Woman speak in a strong rural accent.

Silence.

ELDERLY WOMAN   I have bread—

The Guard jabs her with a stick.

GUARD   Forbidden. Language forbidden.

She looks at him. He jabs her.

GUARD (*cont.*)   It's forbidden. (*to Prisoner*) Tell her to speak the language of the capital.

PRISONER   She can't speak it.

Silence.

PRISONER (*cont.*)   She doesn't speak it.

Silence.

ELDERLY WOMAN   I have apples—

The Guard jabs her and shouts.

GUARD   Forbidden! Forbidden forbidden forbidden! Jesus Christ! (*to Prisoner*) Does she understand what I'm saying?

PRISONER   No.

GUARD   Doesn't she?

He bends over her.

GUARD (*cont.*)   Don't you?

She stares up at him.

PRISONER   She's old. She doesn't understand.

GUARD   Whose fault is that?

He laughs.

GUARD (*cont.*)   Not mine, I can tell you. And I'll tell you another thing. I've got a wife and three kids. And you're all a pile of shit.

Silence.

PRISONER   I've got a wife and three kids.

GUARD   You've what?

Silence.

GUARD (*cont.*)   You've got what?

Silence.

GUARD (*cont.*)   What did you say to me? You've got what?

Silence.

GUARD (*cont.*)   You've got *what*?

He picks up the telephone and dials one digit.

GUARD (*cont.*)   Sergeant? I'm in the Blue Room . . . yes . . . I thought I should report, Sergeant . . . I think I've got a joker in here.

Lights to half. The figures are still.

Voices over:

ELDERLY WOMAN'S VOICE   The baby is waiting for you.

PRISONER'S VOICE   Your hand has been bitten.

ELDERLY WOMAN'S VOICE   They are all waiting for you.

PRISONER'S VOICE   They have bitten my mother's hand.

ELDERLY WOMAN'S VOICE   When you come home there will be such a welcome for you. Everyone is waiting for you. They're all waiting for you. They're all waiting to see you.

Lights up. The Sergeant comes in.

SERGEANT   What joker?

Blackout.

3
VOICE IN THE DARKNESS

SERGEANT'S VOICE   Who's that fucking woman? What's that fucking woman doing here? Who let that fucking woman through that fucking door?

SECOND GUARD'S VOICE   She's his wife.

Lights up.

A corridor.

A HOODED MAN *held up by the Guard and the Sergeant. The Young Woman at a distance from them, staring at them.*

SERGEANT   What is this, a reception for Lady Duck Muck? Where's the bloody Babycham? Who's got the bloody Babycham for Lady Duck Muck?

He goes to the Young Woman.

SERGEANT (*cont.*)   Hello, miss. Sorry. A bit of a breakdown in administration, I'm afraid. They've sent you through the wrong door. Unbelievable. Someone'll be done for this. Anyway, in the meantime, what can I do for you, dear lady, as they used to say in the movies?

Lights to half. The figures are still.

Voices over:

MAN'S VOICE   I watch you sleep. And then your eyes open. You look up at me above you and smile.

YOUNG WOMAN'S VOICE   You smile. When my eyes open I see you above me and smile.

MAN'S VOICE   We are out on a lake.

YOUNG WOMAN'S VOICE   It is spring.

MAN'S VOICE   I hold you. I warm you.

YOUNG WOMAN'S VOICE   When my eyes open I see you above me and smile.

Lights up. The Hooded Man collapses. The Young Woman screams.

YOUNG WOMAN Charley!

The Sergeant clicks his fingers. The Guard drags the Man off.

SERGEANT Yes, you've come in the wrong door. It must be the computer. The computer's got a double hernia. But I'll tell you what—if you want any information on any aspect of life in this place, we've got a bloke comes into the office every Tuesday week, except when it rains. He's right on top of his chosen subject. Give him a tinkle one of these days and he'll see you all right. His name is Dokes. Joseph Dokes.

YOUNG WOMAN Can I fuck him? If I fuck him, will everything be all right?

SERGEANT Sure. No problem.

YOUNG WOMAN Thank you.

Blackout.

4
VISITORS ROOM

GUARD *Elderly Woman. Prisoner.*

Silence.

The Prisoner has blood on his face. He sits trembling. The Woman is still. The Guard is looking out of a window. He turns to look at them both.

GUARD Oh, I forgot to tell you. They've changed the rules. She can speak. She can speak in her own language. Until further notice.

PRISONER She can speak?

GUARD Yes. Until further notice. New rules.

Pause.

PRISONER Mother, you can speak.

Pause.

PRISONER (*cont.*) Mother, I'm speaking to you. You see? We can speak. You can speak to me in our own language.

She is still.

PRISONER (*cont.*) You can speak.

Pause.

PRISONER (*cont.*) Mother. Can you hear me? I am speaking to you in our own language.

Pause.

PRISONER (*cont.*) Do you hear me?

Pause.

PRISONER (*cont.*) It's our language.

Pause.

PRISONER (*cont.*) Can't you hear me? Do you hear me?

She does not respond.

PRISONER (*cont.*) Mother?

GUARD Tell her she can speak in her own language. New rules. Until further notice.

PRISONER Mother?

She does not respond. She sits still.

The Prisoner's trembling grows. He falls from the chair onto his knees, begins to gasp and shake violently.

The Sergeant walks into the room and studies the Prisoner shaking on the floor.

SERGEANT (*to Guard*) Look at this. You go out of your way to give them a helping hand and they fuck it up.

Blackout.

CELEBRATION

CHARACTERS

LAMBERT
JULIE
MATT
PRUE

all in their forties

RUSSELL, a man in his thirties
SUKI, a woman of twenty-eight
RICHARD, a man in his fifties
WAITER, a man of twenty-five
SONIA, a woman in her thirties

Celebration was first presented in a double bill with *The Room,* by the Almeida Theatre Company at the Almeida Theatre, London, on March 16, 2000. The cast was as follows:

LAMBERT   Keith Allen
JULIE   Susan Wooldridge
MATT   Andy de la Tour
PRUE   Lindsay Duncan
RUSSELL   Stephen Pacey
SUKI   Lia Williams
RICHARD   Thomas Wheatley
WAITER   Danny Dyer
SONIA   Indira Varma
WAITRESS 1   Nina Raine
WAITRESS 2   Katherine Tozer

Directed by Harold Pinter

Celebration received its American premiere by the American Conservatory Theater (ACT) in a double bill with *The Room* at the Geary Theatre, San Francisco, from September 13 to October 14, 2001. The cast was as follows:

LAMBERT   Peter Riegert
JULIE   Joan McMurtrey
MATT   Marco Barricelli
PRUE   Diane Venora
RUSSELL   James Butler Harner
SUKI   René Augesen
RICHARD   Anthony Fusco
WAITER   Gregory Wallace
SONIA   Melissa Smith
SERVER   Arosa Babaoff
SERVER   Tommy A. Gomez

Directed by Carey Perloff

SCENE: A *restaurant. Two curved banquettes.* LAMBERT, JULIE, MATT, *and* PRUE *sit at one banquette,* RUSSELL *and* SUKI *at the other.*

TABLE ONE

WAITER   Who's having the duck?

LAMBERT   The duck's for me.

JULIE   No it isn't.

LAMBERT   No it isn't. Who's it for?

JULIE   Me.

LAMBERT   What am I having? I thought I was having the duck?

JULIE (*to Waiter*)   The duck's for me.

MATT (*to Waiter*)   Chicken for my wife, steak for me.

WAITER   Chicken for the lady.

PRUE   Thank you so much.

WAITER   And who's having the steak?

MATT   Me. (*He picks up a wine bottle and pours.*) Here we are. Frascati for the ladies. And Valpolicella for me.

LAMBERT   And for me. I mean, what about me? What did I order? I haven't the faintest idea. What did I order?

JULIE   Who cares?

LAMBERT   Who cares? I bloody care.

PRUE   Osso buco.

LAMBERT   Osso what?

PRUE   Buco.

MATT   It's an old Italian dish.

LAMBERT   Well, I knew *osso* was Italian but I know bugger all about *buco*.

355

MATT   I didn't know arsehole was Italian.

LAMBERT   Yes, but on the other hand what's the Italian for arsehole?

PRUE   Julie, Lambert. Happy anniversary.

MATT   Cheers.

They lift their glasses and drink.

TABLE TWO

RUSSELL   They believe in me.

SUKI   Who do?

RUSSELL   They do. What do you mean, who do? They do.

SUKI   Oh, do they?

RUSSELL   Yes, they believe in me. They reckon me. They're investing in me. In my *nous*. They believe in me.

SUKI   Listen. I believe you. Honestly. I do. No really, honestly. I'm sure they believe in you. And they're right to believe in you. I mean, listen, I want you to be rich, believe me, I want you to be rich so that you can buy me houses and panties and I'll know that you really love me.

They drink.

RUSSELL   Listen, she was just a secretary. That's all. No more.

SUKI   Like me.

RUSSELL   What do you mean like you? She was nothing like you.

SUKI   I was a secretary once.

RUSSELL   She was a scrubber. A tart. They're all the same, these secretaries, these scrubbers. They're like politicians. They love power. They've got a bit of power, they use it. They go home, they get on the phone, they tell their girlfriends, they have a good laugh. Listen to me. I'm being honest. You won't find many like me. I fell for it. I've admitted it. She just twisted me round her little finger.

SUKI That's funny. I thought she twisted you round *your* little finger.

Pause.

RUSSELL You don't know what these girls are like. These secretaries.

SUKI Oh I think I do.

RUSSELL You don't.

SUKI Oh I do.

RUSSELL What do you mean, you do?

SUKI I've been behind a few filing cabinets.

RUSSELL What?

SUKI In my time. When I was a plump young secretary. I know what the back of a filing cabinet looks like.

RUSSELL Oh, do you?

SUKI Oh yes. Listen. I would invest in you myself if I had any money. Do you know why? Because I believe in you.

RUSSELL What's all this about filing cabinets?

SUKI Oh, that was when I was a plump young secretary. I would never do all those things now. Never. Out of the question. You see, the trouble was I was so excitable, their excitement made me so excited, but I would never do all those things now I'm a grown-up woman and not a silly young thing, a silly and dizzy young girl, such a naughty, saucy, flirty, giggly young thing; sometimes I could hardly walk from one filing cabinet to another I was so excited, I was so plump and wobbly it was terrible, men simply couldn't keep their hands off me, their demands were outrageous but coming back to more important things, they're right to believe in you; why shouldn't they believe in you?

TABLE ONE

JULIE I've always told him. Always. But he doesn't listen. I tell him all the time. But he doesn't listen.

PRUE   You mean he just doesn't listen?

JULIE   I tell him all the time.

PRUE (*to Lambert*)   Why don't you listen to your wife? She stands by you through thick and thin. You've got a loyal wife there and never forget it.

LAMBERT   I've got a loyal wife where?

PRUE   Here! At this table.

LAMBERT   I've got one under the table, take my tip. (*He looks under the table.*) Christ. She's really loyal under the table. Always has been. You wouldn't believe it.

JULIE   Why don't you go and buy a new car and drive it into a brick wall?

LAMBERT   She loves me.

MATT   No, she loves new cars.

LAMBERT   With soft leather seats.

MATT   There was a song once.

LAMBERT   How did it go?

MATT   "Ain't she neat?
Ain't she neat?
As she's walking up the street.
She's got a lovely bubbly pair of tits
And a soft leather seat."

LAMBERT   That's a really beautiful song.

MATT   I've always admired that song. You know what it is? It's a traditional folk song.

LAMBERT   It's got class.

MATT   It's got tradition and class.

LAMBERT   They don't grow on trees.

MATT   Too bloody right.

LAMBERT Hey, Matt!

MATT What?

Lambert picks up the bottle of Valpolicella. It is empty.

LAMBERT There's something wrong with this bottle.

Matt turns and calls.

MATT Waiter!

TABLE TWO

RUSSELL All right. Tell me. Do you think I have a nice character?

SUKI Yes, I think you do. I think you do. I mean I think you do. Well . . . I mean . . . I think you could have quite a nice character but the trouble is that when you come down to it you haven't actually got any character to begin with—I mean as such, that's the thing.

RUSSELL As such?

SUKI Yes, the thing is you haven't really got any character at all, have you? As such. *Au fond.* But I wouldn't worry about it. For example look at me. I don't have any character either. I'm just a reed. I'm just a reed in the wind. Aren't I? You know I am. I'm just a reed in the wind.

RUSSELL You're a whore.

SUKI A whore in the wind.

RUSSELL With the wind blowing up your skirt.

SUKI That's right. How did you know? How did you know the sensation? I didn't know that men could possibly know about that kind of thing. I mean men don't wear skirts. So I didn't think men could possibly know what it was like when the wind blows up a girl's skirt. Because men don't wear skirts.

RUSSELL You're a prick.

SUKI Not quite.

RUSSELL   You're a prick.

SUKI   Good gracious. Am I really?

RUSSELL   Yes. That's what you are really.

SUKI   Am I really?

RUSSELL   Yes. That's what you are really.

TABLE ONE

LAMBERT   What's that other song you know? The one you said was a classic.

MATT   "Wash me in the water where you washed your dirty daughter."

LAMBERT   That's it. (*to Julie*) Know that one?

JULIE   It's not in my repertoire, darling.

LAMBERT   This is the best restaurant in town. That's what they say.

MATT   That's what they say.

LAMBERT   This is a piss-up dinner. Do you know how much money I made last year?

MATT   I know this is a piss-up dinner.

LAMBERT   It is a piss-up dinner.

PRUE   (*to Julie*)   His mother always hated me. The first time she saw me she hated me. She never gave me one present in the whole of her life. Nothing. She wouldn't give me the drippings off her nose.

JULIE   I know.

PRUE   The drippings off her nose. Honestly.

JULIE   All mothers-in-law are like that. They love their sons. They love their boys. They don't want their sons to be fucked by other girls. Isn't that right?

PRUE   Absolutely. All mothers want their sons to be fucked by themselves.

JULIE   By their mothers.

PRUE   All mothers—

LAMBERT   All mothers want to be fucked by their mothers.

MATT   Or by themselves.

PRUE   No, you've got it the wrong way round.

LAMBERT   How's that?

MATT   All mothers want to be fucked by their sons.

LAMBERT   Now wait a minute—

MATT   My point is—

LAMBERT   No, my point is—how old do you have to be?

JULIE   To be what?

LAMBERT   To be fucked by your mother.

MATT   Any age, mate. Any age.

They all drink.

LAMBERT   How did you enjoy your dinner, darling?

JULIE   I wasn't impressed.

LAMBERT   You weren't impressed?

JULIE   No.

LAMBERT   I bring her to the best caff in town—spending a fortune— and she's not impressed.

MATT   Don't forget this is your anniversary. That's why we're here.

LAMBERT   What anniversary?

PRUE   It's your wedding anniversary.

LAMBERT   All I know is this is the most expensive fucking restaurant in town and she's not impressed.

RICHARD *comes to the table.*

RICHARD   Good evening.

MATT   Good evening.

PRUE   Good evening.

JULIE   Good evening.

LAMBERT   Good evening, Richard. How you been?

RICHARD   Very very well. Been to a play?

MATT   No. The ballet.

RICHARD   Oh, the ballet? What was it?

LAMBERT   That's a fucking good question.

MATT   It's unanswerable.

RICHARD   Good, was it?

LAMBERT   Unbelievable.

JULIE   What ballet?

MATT   None of them could reach the top notes. Could they?

RICHARD   Good dinner?

MATT   Fantastic.

LAMBERT   Top-notch. Gold-plated.

PRUE   Delicious.

LAMBERT   My wife wasn't impressed.

RICHARD   Oh, really?

JULIE   I liked the waiter.

RICHARD   Which one?

JULIE   The one with the fur-lined jockstrap.

LAMBERT   He takes it off for breakfast.

JULIE   Which is more than you do.

RICHARD   Well, how nice to see you all.

PRUE   She wasn't impressed with her food. It's true. She said so. She thought it was dry as dust. She said—what did you say, darling?—she's my sister—she said she could cook better than that with one hand stuffed between her legs; she said—no, honestly—she said she could make a better sauce than the one on that plate if she pissed into it. Don't think she was joking—she's my sister, I've known her all my life, all my life, since we were little innocent girls, all our lives, when we were babies, when we used to lie in the nursery and hear Mummy beating the shit out of Daddy. We saw the blood on the sheets the next day—when Nanny was in the pantry—my sister and me—and Nanny was in the pantry—and the pantry maid was in the larder and the parlor maid was in the laundry-room washing the blood out of the sheets. That's how my little sister and I were brought up and she could make a better sauce than yours if she pissed into it.

MATT   Well, it's lovely to be here, I'll say that.

LAMBERT   Lovely to be here.

JULIE   Lovely. Lovely.

MATT   Really lovely.

RICHARD   Thank you.

Prue stands and goes to Richard.

PRUE   Can I thank you? Can I thank you personally? I'd like to thank you myself, in my own way.

RICHARD   Well, thank you.

PRUE   No, no, I'd really like to thank you in a very personal way.

JULIE   She'd like to give you her personal thanks.

PRUE   Will you let me kiss you? I'd like to kiss you on the mouth.

JULIE   That's funny. I'd like to kiss him on the mouth too.

She stands and goes to him.

JULIE (*cont.*)   Because I've been maligned, I've been misrepresented. I never said I didn't like your sauce. I love your sauce.

PRUE   We can't both kiss him on the mouth at the same time.

LAMBERT   You could tickle his arse with a feather.

RICHARD Well, I'm so glad. I'm really glad. See you later I hope.

Richard goes. Prue and Julie sit.

Silence.

MATT Charming man.

LAMBERT That's why this is the best and most expensive restaurant in the whole of Europe—because he *insists* upon proper standards, he *insists* that standards are maintained with the utmost rigour, you get me? That standards are maintained up to the highest standards, up to the very highest fucking standards—

MATT He doesn't jib.

LAMBERT Jib? Of course he doesn't jib—it would be more than his life was worth. He jibs at nothing!

PRUE I knew him in the old days.

MATT What do you mean?

PRUE When he was a chef.

Lambert's mobile phone rings.

LAMBERT Who the fuck's this?

He switches it on.

LAMBERT (*cont.*) Yes? What? (*He listens briefly.*) I said no calls! It's my fucking wedding anniversary!

He switches it off.

LAMBERT (*cont.*) Cunt.

TABLE TWO

SUKI I'm so proud of you.

RUSSELL Yes?

SUKI And I know these people are good people. These people who believe in you. They're good people. Aren't they?

RUSSELL Very good people.

SUKI   And when I meet them, when you introduce me to them, they'll treat me with respect, won't they? They won't want to fuck me behind a filing cabinet?

SONIA *comes to the table.*

SONIA   Good evening.

RUSSELL   Good evening.

SUKI   Good evening.

SONIA   Everything all right?

RUSSELL   Wonderful.

SONIA   No complaints?

RUSSELL   Absolutely no complaints whatsoever. Absolutely numero uno all along the line.

SONIA   What a lovely compliment.

RUSSELL   Heartfelt.

SONIA   Been to the theatre?

SUKI   The opera.

SONIA   Oh, really, what was it?

SUKI   Well. . . . there was a lot going on. A lot of singing. A great deal, as a matter of fact. They never stopped. Did they?

RUSSELL *(to Sonia)*   Listen, let me ask you something.

SONIA   You can ask me absolutely anything you like.

RUSSELL   What was your upbringing?

SONIA   That's funny. Everybody asks me that. Everybody seems to find that an interesting subject. I don't know why. Isn't it funny? So many people express curiosity about my upbringing. I've no idea why. What you really mean of course is how did I arrive at the position I hold now—*maîtresse d'hôtel*—isn't that right? Isn't that your question? Well, I was born in Bethnal Green. My mother was a chiropodist. I had no father.

RUSSELL Fantastic.

SONIA Are you going to try our bread-and-butter pudding?

RUSSELL In spades.

Sonia smiles and goes.

RUSSELL Did I ever tell you about my mother's bread-and-butter pudding?

SUKI You never have. Please tell me.

RUSSELL You really want me to tell you? You're not being insincere?

SUKI Darling. Give me your hand. There. I have your hand. I'm holding your hand. Now please tell me. Please tell me about your mother's bread-and-butter pudding. What was it like?

RUSSELL It was like drowning in an ocean of richness.

SUKI How beautiful. You're a poet.

RUSSELL I wanted to be a poet once. But I got no encouragement from my dad. He thought I was an arsehole.

SUKI He was jealous of you, that's all. He saw you as a threat. He thought you wanted to steal his wife.

RUSSELL His wife?

SUKI Well, you know what they say.

RUSSELL What?

SUKI Oh, you know what they say.

The Waiter comes to the table and pours wine.

WAITER Do you mind if I interject?

RUSSELL Eh?

WAITER I say, do you mind if I make an interjection?

SUKI We'd welcome it.

WAITER It's just that I heard you talking about T. S. Eliot a little bit earlier this evening.

SUKI Oh, you heard that, did you?

WAITER I did. And I thought you might be interested to know that my grandfather knew T. S. Eliot quite well.

SUKI Really?

WAITER I'm not claiming that he was a close friend of his. But he was a damn sight more than a nodding acquaintance. He knew them all, in fact, Ezra Pound, W. H. Auden, C. Day-Lewis, Louis MacNeice, Stephen Spender, George Barker, Dylan Thomas, and if you go back a few years he was a bit of a drinking companion of D. H. Lawrence, Joseph Conrad, Ford Madox Ford, W. B. Yeats, Aldous Huxley, Virginia Woolf, and Thomas Hardy in his dotage. My grandfather was carving out a niche for himself in politics at the time. Some saw him as a future Chancellor of the Exchequer or at least First Lord of the Admiralty but he decided instead to command a battalion in the Spanish Civil War but as things turned out he spent most of his spare time in the United States where he was a very close pal of Ernest Hemingway—they used to play gin rummy together until the cows came home. But he was also boon compatriots with William Faulkner, Scott Fitzgerald, Upton Sinclair, John Dos Passos—you know, that whole vivid Chicago gang—not to mention John Steinbeck, Erskine Caldwell, Carson McCullers, and other members of the old Deep South conglomerate. I mean— what I'm trying to say is—that as a man my grandfather was just about as all-round as you can get. He was never without his pocket Bible and he was a dab hand at pocket billiards. He stood four-square in the centre of the intellectual and literary life of the tens, twenties, and thirties. He was James Joyce's godmother.

Silence.

RUSSELL Have you been working here long?

WAITER Years.

RUSSELL You going to stay until it changes hands?

WAITER Are you suggesting that I'm about to get the boot?

SUKI They wouldn't do that to a nice lad like you.

WAITER To be brutally honest, I don't think I'd recover if they did a thing like that. This place is like a womb to me. I prefer to stay in my womb. I strongly prefer that to being born.

RUSSELL I don't blame you. Listen, next time we're talking about T. S Eliot I'll drop you a card.

WAITER You would make me a very happy man. Thank you. Thank you. You are incredibly gracious people.

SUKI How sweet of you.

WAITER Gracious and graceful.

He goes.

SUKI What a nice young man.

TABLE ONE

LAMBERT You won't believe this. You're not going to believe this—and I'm only saying this because I'm among friends—and I know I'm well liked because I trust my family and my friends—because I know they like me fundamentally—you know, deep down they trust me, deep down they respect me—otherwise I wouldn't say this. I wouldn't take you all into my confidence if I thought you all hated my guts—I couldn't be open and honest with you if I thought you thought I was a pile of shit. If I thought you would like to see me hung, drawn and fucking quartered—I could never be frank and honest with you if that was the truth—never. . . .

Silence.

LAMBERT (*cont.*) But as I was about to say, you won't believe this. I fell in love once and this girl I fell in love with loved me back. I know she did.

Pause.

JULIE Wasn't that me, darling?

LAMBERT Who?

MATT   Her.

LAMBERT   Her? No, not her. A girl. I used to take her for walks along the river.

JULIE   Lambert fell in love with me on the top of a bus. It was a short journey. Fulham Broadway to Shepherd's Bush, but it was enough. He was trembling all over. I remember. (*to Prue*) When I got home I came and sat on your bed, didn't I?

LAMBERT   I used to take this girl for walks along the river. I was young; I wasn't much more than a nipper.

MATT   That's funny. I never knew anything about that. And I knew you quite well, didn't I?

LAMBERT   What do you mean you knew me quite well? You knew nothing about me. You know nothing about me. Who the fuck are you anyway?

MATT   I'm your big brother.

LAMBERT   I'm talking about love, mate. You know, real fucking love, walking along the banks of a river holding hands.

MATT   I saw him the day he was born. You know what he looked like? An alcoholic. Pissed as a newt. He could hardly stand.

JULIE   He was trembling like a leaf on top of that bus. I'll never forget it.

PRUE   I was there when you came home. I remember what you said. You came into my room. You sat down on my bed.

MATT   What did she say?

PRUE   I mean we were sisters, weren't we?

MATT   Well, what did she say?

PRUE   I'll never forget what you said. You sat on my bed. Didn't you? Do you remember?

LAMBERT   This girl was in love with me—I'm trying to tell you.

PRUE   Do you remember what you said?

Table Two

Richard comes to the table.

RICHARD Good evening.

RUSSELL Good evening.

SUKI Good evening.

RICHARD Everything in order?

RUSSELL First class.

RICHARD I'm so glad.

SUKI Can I say something?

RICHARD But indeed—

SUKI Everyone is so happy in your restaurant. I mean women *and* men. You make people so happy.

RICHARD Well, we do like to feel that it's a happy restaurant.

RUSSELL It is a happy restaurant. For example, look at me. Look at me. I'm basically a totally disordered personality; some people would describe me as a psychopath. (*to Suki*) Am I right?

SUKI Yes.

RUSSELL But when I'm sitting in this restaurant I suddenly find I have no psychopathic tendencies at all. I don't feel like killing everyone in sight, I don't feel like putting a bomb under everyone's arse. I feel something quite different, I have a sense of equilibrium, of harmony, I love my fellow diners. Now this is very unusual for me. Normally I feel—as I've just said—absolute malice and hatred towards everyone within spitting distance—but here I feel love. How do you explain it?

SUKI It's the ambience.

RICHARD Yes, I think ambience is that intangible thing that cannot be defined.

RUSSELL Quite right.

SUKI It is intangible. You're absolutely right.

RUSSELL Absolutely.

RICHARD   That is absolutely right. But it does—I would freely admit—exist. It's something you find you are part of. Without knowing exactly what it is.

RUSSELL   Yes. I had an old schoolmaster once who used to say that ambience surrounds you. He never stopped saying that. He lived in a little house in a nice little village but none of us boys were ever invited to tea.

RICHARD   Yes, it's funny you should say that. I was brought up in a little village myself.

SUKI   No? Were you?

RICHARD   Yes, isn't it odd? In a little village in the country.

RUSSELL   What, right in the country?

RICHARD   Oh, absolutely. And my father once took me to our village pub. I was only that high. Too young to join him for his pint, of course. But I did look in. Black beams.

RUSSELL   On the roof?

RICHARD   Well, holding the ceiling up in fact. Old men smoking pipes, no music of course, cheese rolls, gherkins, happiness. I think this restaurant—which you so kindly patronise—was inspired by that pub in my childhood. I do hope you noticed that you have complimentary gherkins as soon as you take your seat.

SUKI   That was you! That was your idea!

RICHARD   I believe the concept of this restaurant rests in that public house of my childhood.

SUKI   I find that incredibly moving.

TABLE ONE

LAMBERT   I'd like to raise my glass.

MATT   What to?

LAMBERT   To my wife. To our anniversary.

JULIE   Oh, darling! You remembered!

LAMBERT I'd like to raise my glass. I ask you to raise your glasses to my wife.

JULIE I'm so touched by this, honestly. I mean, I have to say—

LAMBERT Raise your fucking glass and shut up!

JULIE But darling, that's naked aggression. He doesn't normally go in for naked aggression. He usually disguises it under honeyed words. What is it, sweetie? He's got a cold in the nose, that's what it is.

LAMBERT I want us to drink to our anniversary. We've been married for more bloody years than I can remember and it don't seem a day too long.

PRUE Cheers.

MATT Cheers.

JULIE It's funny our children aren't here. When they were young we spent so much time with them, the little things, looking after them.

PRUE I know.

JULIE Playing with them.

PRUE Feeding them.

JULIE Being their mothers.

PRUE They always loved me much more than they loved him.

JULIE Me too. They loved me to distraction. I was their mother.

PRUE Yes, I was too. I was my children's mother.

MATT They have no memory.

LAMBERT Who?

MATT Children. They have no memory. They remember nothing. They don't remember who their father was or who their mother was. It's all a hole in the wall for them. They don't remember their own life.

Sonia comes to the table.

SONIA Everything all right?

JULIE   Perfect.

SONIA   Were you at the opera this evening?

JULIE   No.

PRUE   No.

SONIA   Theatre?

PRUE   No.

JULIE   No.

MATT   This is a celebration.

SONIA   Oh my goodness! A birthday?

MATT   Anniversary.

PRUE   My sister and her husband. Anniversary of their marriage. I was her leading bridesmaid.

MATT   I was his best man.

LAMBERT   I was just about to fuck her at the altar when somebody stopped me.

SONIA   Really?

MATT   I stopped him. His zip went down and I kicked him up the arse. It would have been a scandal. The world's press was on the doorstep.

JULIE   He was always impetuous.

SONIA   We get so many different kinds of people in here, people from all walks of life.

PRUE   Do you really?

SONIA   Oh yes. People from all walks of life. People from different countries. I've often said, "You don't have to speak English to enjoy good food." I've often said that. Or even understand English. It's like sex, isn't it? You don't have to be English to enjoy sex. You don't have to speak English to enjoy sex. Lots of people enjoy sex without being English. I've known one or two Belgian people, for example, who love sex and they don't speak a word of English. The same applies to Hungarians.

LAMBERT   Yes. I met a chap who was born in Venezuela once and he didn't speak a fucking word of English.

MATT   Did he enjoy sex?

LAMBERT   Sex?

SONIA   Yes, it's funny you should say that. I met a man from Morocco once and he was very interested in sex.

JULIE   What happened to him?

SONIA   Now you've upset me. I think I'm going to cry.

PRUE   Oh, poor dear. Did he let you down?

SONIA   He's dead. He died in another woman's arms. He was on the job. Can you see how tragic my life has been?

Pause.

MATT   Well, I can. I don't know about the others.

JULIE   I can too.

PRUE   So can I.

SONIA   Have a happy night.

She goes.

LAMBERT   Lovely woman.

The Waiter comes to the table and pours wine into their glasses.

WAITER   Do you mind if I interject?

MATT   What?

WAITER   Do you mind if I make an interjection?

MATT   Help yourself.

WAITER   It's just that a little bit earlier I heard you saying something about the Hollywood studio system in the thirties.

PRUE   Oh, you heard that?

WAITER   Yes. And I thought you might be interested to know that my grandfather was very familiar with a lot of the old Hollywood film stars back in those days. He used to knock about with Clark Gable and Elisha Cook, Jr. and he was one of the very few native-born Englishmen to have had it off with Hedy Lamarr.

JULIE No!

LAMBERT What was she like in the sack?

WAITER He said she was really tasty.

JULIE I'll bet she was.

WAITER Of course there was a very well-established Irish Mafia in Hollywood in those days. And there was a very close connection between some of the famous Irish film stars and some of the famous Irish gangsters in Chicago. Al Capone and Victor Mature, for example. They were both Irish. Then there was John Dillinger, the celebrated gangster, and Gary Cooper, the celebrated film star. They were Jewish.

Silence.

JULIE It makes you think, doesn't it?

PRUE It does make you think.

LAMBERT You see the girl at that table? I know her. I fucked her when she was eighteen.

JULIE What, by the banks of the river?

Lambert waves at Suki. Suki waves back. Suki whispers to Russell, gets up and goes to Lambert's table, followed by Russell.

SUKI Lambert! It's you!

LAMBERT Suki! You remember me!

SUKI Do you remember me?

LAMBERT Do I remember you? *Do* I remember you!

SUKI This is my husband, Russell.

LAMBERT Hello, Russell.

RUSSELL Hello, Lambert.

LAMBERT   This is my wife, Julie.

JULIE   Hello, Suki.

SUKI   Hello, Julie.

RUSSELL   Hello, Julie.

JULIE   Hello, Russell.

LAMBERT   And this is my brother, Matt.

MATT   Hello, Suki, hello, Russell.

SUKI   Hello, Matt.

RUSSELL   Hello, Matt.

LAMBERT   And this is his wife, Prue. She's Julie's sister.

SUKI   She's not!

PRUE   Yes, we're sisters and they're brothers.

SUKI   They're not!

RUSSELL   Hello, Prue.

PRUE   Hello, Russell.

SUKI   Hello, Prue.

PRUE   Hello, Suki.

LAMBERT   Sit down. Squeeze in. Have a drink.

They sit.

LAMBERT (*cont.*)   What'll you have?

RUSSELL   A drop of that red wine would work wonders.

LAMBERT   Suki?

RUSSELL   She'll have the same.

SUKI (*to Lambert*)   Are you still obsessed with gardening?

LAMBERT   Me?

SUKI (*to Julie*)   When I knew him he was absolutely obsessed with gardening.

LAMBERT   Yes, well, I would say I'm still moderately obsessed with gardening.

JULIE   He likes grass.

LAMBERT   It's true. I love grass.

JULIE   Green grass.

SUKI   You used to love flowers, didn't you? Do you still love flowers?

JULIE   He adores flowers. The other day I saw him emptying a piss pot into a bowl of lilies.

RUSSELL   My dad was a gardener.

MATT   Not your grandad?

RUSSELL   No, my dad.

SUKI   That's right, he was. He was always walking about with a lawn-mower.

LAMBERT   What, even in the Old Kent Road?

RUSSELL   He was a man of the soil.

MATT   How about your grandad?

RUSSELL   I never had one.

JULIE   Funny that when you knew my husband you thought he was obsessed with gardening. I always thought he was obsessed with girls' bums.

SUKI   Really?

PRUE   Oh, yes, he was always a keen wobbler.

MATT   What do you mean? How do you know?

PRUE   Oh, don't get excited. It's all in the past.

MATT   What is?

SUKI   I sometimes feel that the past is never past.

RUSSELL   What do you mean?

JULIE   You mean that yesterday is today?

SUKI That's right. You feel the same, do you?

JULIE I do.

MATT Bollocks.

JULIE I wouldn't like to live again though, would you? Once is more than enough.

LAMBERT I'd like to live again. In fact I'm going to make it my job to live again. I'm going to come back as a better person, a more civilized person, a gentler person, a nicer person.

JULIE Impossible.

Pause.

PRUE I wonder where these two met? I mean Lambert and Suki.

RUSSELL Behind a filing cabinet.

Silence.

JULIE What is a filing cabinet?

RUSSELL It's a thing you get behind.

Pause.

LAMBERT No, not me, mate. You've got the wrong bloke. I agree with my wife. I don't even know what a filing cabinet looks like. I wouldn't know a filing cabinet if I met one coming round the corner.

Pause.

JULIE So what's your job now then, Suki?

SUKI Oh, I'm a schoolteacher now. I teach infants.

PRUE What, little boys and little girls?

SUKI What about you?

PRUE Oh, Julie and me—we run charities. We do charities.

RUSSELL Must be pretty demanding work.

JULIE Yes, we're at it day and night, aren't we?

PRUE Well, there are so many worthy causes.

MATT (*to Russell*)   You're a banker? Right?

RUSSELL   That's right.

MATT (*to Lambert*)   He's a banker,

LAMBERT   With a big future before him.

MATT   Well, that's what he reckons.

LAMBERT   I want to ask you a question. How did you know he was a banker?

MATT   Well, it's the way he holds himself, isn't it?

LAMBERT   Oh yes.

SUKI   What about you two?

LAMBERT   Us two?

SUKI   Yes.

LAMBERT   Well, we're consultants, Matt and me. Strategy consultants.

MATT   Strategy consultants.

LAMBERT   It means we don't carry guns.

Matt and Lambert laugh.

LAMBERT (*cont.*)   We don't have to!

MATT   We're peaceful strategy consultants.

LAMBERT   Worldwide. Keeping the peace.

RUSSELL   Wonderful.

LAMBERT   Eh?

RUSSELL   Really impressive. We need a few more of you about.

Pause.

RUSSELL (*cont.*)   We need more people like you. Taking responsibility. Taking charge. Keeping the peace. Enforcing the peace. Enforcing peace. We need more like you. I think I'll have a word with my bank. I'm moving any minute to a more substantial bank. I'll have a word with them. I'll suggest lunch. In the City. I know the ideal restaurant. All the waitresses have big tits.

SUKI Aren't you pushing the tits bit a bit far?

RUSSELL Me? I thought you did that.

Pause.

LAMBERT Be careful. You're talking to your wife.

MATT Have some respect, mate.

LAMBERT Have respect. That's all we ask.

MATT It's not much to ask.

LAMBERT But it's crucial.

Pause.

RUSSELL So how is the strategic consultancy business these days?

LAMBERT Very good, old boy. Very good.

MATT Very good. We're at the receiving end of some of the best tea in China.

Richard and Sonia come to the table with a magnum of champagne, the Waiter with a tray of glasses. Everyone gasps.

RICHARD To celebrate a treasured wedding anniversary.

Matt looks at the label on the bottle.

MATT That's the best of the best.

The bottle opens. Richard pours.

LAMBERT And may the best man win!

JULIE The woman always wins.

PRUE Always.

SUKI That's really good news.

PRUE The woman always wins.

Richard and Sonia raise their glasses.

RICHARD To the happy couple. God bless. God bless you all.

EVERYONE   Cheers. Cheers . . .

MATT   What a wonderful restaurant this is.

SONIA   Well, we do care. I will say that. We care. That's the point. Don't we?

RICHARD   Yes. We do care. We care about the welfare of our clientele. I will say that.

Lambert stands and goes to them.

LAMBERT   What you say means so much to me. Let me give you a cuddle. (*He cuddles Richard.*) And let me give you a cuddle. (*He cuddles Sonia.*) This is so totally rare, you see. None of this normally happens. People normally—you know—people normally are so distant from each other. That's what I've found. Take a given bloke—this given bloke doesn't know that another given bloke exists. It goes down through history, doesn't it?

MATT   It does.

LAMBERT   One bloke doesn't know that another bloke exists. Generally speaking. I've often noticed.

SONIA (*to Julie and Prue*)   I'm so touched that you're sisters. I had a sister. But she married a foreigner and I haven't seen her since.

PRUE   Some foreigners are all right.

SONIA   Oh, I think foreigners are charming. Most people in this restaurant tonight are foreigners. My sister's husband had a lot of charm but he also had an enormous mustache. I had to kiss him at the wedding. I can't describe how awful it was. I've got such soft skin, you see.

WAITER   Do you mind if I interject?

RICHARD   I'm sorry?

WAITER   Do you mind if I make an interjection?

RICHARD   What on earth do you mean?

WAITER   Well, it's just that I heard all these people talking about the Austro-Hungarian Empire a little while ago and I wondered if they'd ever heard about my grandfather. He was an incredibly close friend of the Archduke himself and he once had a cup of tea with Benito Mussolini. They all played poker together, Winston Churchill included. The funny thing about my grandfather was that the palms of his hands always seemed to be burning. But his eyes were elsewhere. He had a really strange life. He was in love, he told me once, with the woman who turned out to be my grandmother, but he lost her somewhere. She disappeared, I think, in a sandstorm. In the desert. My grandfather was everything men aspired to be in those days. He was tall, dark and handsome. He was full of goodwill. He'd even give a cripple with no legs crawling on his belly through the slush and mud of a country lane a helping hand. He'd lift him up, he'd show him his way, he'd point him in the right direction. He was like Jesus Christ in that respect. And he was gregarious. He loved the society of his fellows, W. B. Yeats, T. S. Eliot, Igor Stravinsky, Picasso, Ezra Pound, Bertolt Brecht, Don Bradman, the Beverley Sisters, the Ink Spots, Franz Kafka, and the Three Stooges. He knew these people where they were isolated, where they were alone, where they fought against savage and pitiless odds, where they suffered vast wounds to their bodies, their bellies, their legs, their trunks, their eyes, their throats, their breasts, their balls—

LAMBERT (*standing*) Well, Richard—what a great dinner!

RICHARD I'm so glad.

Lambert opens his wallet and unpeels fifty-pound notes. He gives two to Richard.

LAMBERT This is for you.

RICHARD No, no really—

LAMBERT No, no, this is for you. (*to Sonia*) And this is for you.

SONIA Oh, no, please—

Lambert dangles the notes in front of her cleavage.

LAMBERT Shall I put them down here? (*Sonia giggles.*) No, I'll tell you what—you wearing suspenders? (*Sonia giggles.*) Stick them in your suspenders. (*to Waiter*) Here you are, son. Mind how you go. (*puts a note into his pocket*) Great dinner. Great restaurant. Best in the country.

MATT   Best in the world, I'd say.

LAMBERT   Exactly. (*to Richard*) I'm taking their bill.

RUSSELL   No, no, you can't—

LAMBERT   It's my wedding anniversary! Right? (*to Richard*) Send me their bill.

JULIE   And his.

LAMBERT   Send me both bills. Anyway . . . (*He embraces Suki.*) It's for old time's sake as well, right?

SUKI   Right.

RICHARD   See you again soon?

MATT   Absolutely.

SONIA   See you again soon.

PRUE   Absolutely.

SONIA   Next celebration?

JULIE   Absolutely.

LAMBERT   Plenty of celebrations to come. Rest assured.

MATT   Plenty to celebrate.

LAMBERT   Dead right.

Matt slaps his thighs.

MATT   Like—who's in front? Who's in front?

Lambert joins in the song, slapping his thighs in time with Matt.

LAMBERT and **MATT**   Who's in front? Who's in front?

LAMBERT   Get out the bloody way
    You silly old cunt!

Lambert and Matt laugh.

Suki and Russell go to their table to collect handbag and jacket, etc.

SUKI   Sweet of him to take the bill, wasn't it?

RUSSELL   He must have been very fond of you.

SUKI   Oh, he wasn't all that fond of me really. He just liked my . . . oh, you know . . .

RUSSELL   Your what?

SUKI   Oh, my . . . you know . . .

LAMBERT   Fabulous evening.

JULIE   Fabulous.

RICHARD   See you soon then.

SONIA   See you soon.

MATT   I'll be here for breakfast tomorrow morning.

SONIA   Excellent!

PRUE   See you soon.

SONIA   See you soon.

JULIE   Lovely to see you.

SONIA   See you soon, I hope.

RUSSELL   See you soon.

SUKI   See you soon.

They drift off.

JULIE'S VOICE   So lovely to meet you.

SUKI'S VOICE   Lovely to meet you.

Silence.

The Waiter stands alone.

WAITER   When I was a boy my grandfather used to take me to the edge of the cliffs and we'd look out to sea. He bought me a telescope. I don't think they have telescopes any more. I used to look through this telescope and sometimes I'd see a boat. The boat would grow bigger through the telescopic lens. Sometimes I'd see people on the boat. A man, sometimes, and a woman, or sometimes two men. The sea glistened.

My grandfather introduced me to the mystery of life and I'm still in the middle of it. I can't find the door to get out. My grandfather got out of it. He got right out of it. He left it behind him and he didn't look back.

He got that absolutely right.

And I'd like to make one further interjection.

He stands still.

Slow fade.

PRESS CONFERENCE

Press Conference was first presented as part of an evening of sketches on February 8 and 11, 2002, at the Royal National Theatre, London. The cast was as follows:

MINISTER Harold Pinter
PRESS Members of the Company

The company included Linda Bassett, Danny Dyer, Douglas Hodge, Patrick Marber, Kika Markham, Catherine McCormack, Corin Redgrave, Samantha Robson, Gary Shelford, Andy de la Tour, Frances de la Tour, Penelope Wilton, Susan Wooldridge, Henry Woolf

Directed by Gari Jones

Press Conference received its American premiere in a triple bill with *One for the Road* and Edward Albee's *The American Dream* by the Potomac Theatre Project at the Mulitz-Gudelski Theatre Lab of the Olney Theatre Center for the Arts as part of the Potomac Theatre Festival 2005, Olney, Maryland, from July 14 to August 7, 2005. The cast was:

MINISTER Richard Pilcher
PRESS Members of the Company

The company included Daniel di Tomasso, Rachel Dunlap, Valerie Leonard, Rebecca Martin, Julia Proctor, Nigel Reed, Vivienne Shub

Directed by Richard Romagnoli

PRESS Sir, before you became Minister of Culture I believe you were the head of the Secret Police.

MINISTER That is correct.

PRESS Do you find any contradiction between those two roles?

MINISTER None whatsoever. As head of Secret Police it was my responsibility, specifically, to protect and to safeguard our cultural inheritance against forces which were intent upon subverting it. We were defending ourselves against the worm. And we still are.

PRESS The worm?

MINISTER The worm.

PRESS As head of the Secret Police what was your policy towards children?

MINISTER We saw children as a threat if—that is—they were the children of subversive families.

PRESS So how did you employ your policy towards them?

MINISTER We abducted them and brought them up properly or we killed them.

PRESS How did you kill them? What was the method adopted?

MINISTER We broke their necks.

PRESS And women?

MINISTER We raped them. It was all part of an educational process, you see. A cultural process.

PRESS What was the nature of the culture you were proposing?

MINISTER A culture based on respect and the rule of law.

PRESS How do you understand your present role as Minister of Culture?

MINISTER The Ministry of Culture holds to the same principles as the guardians of National Security. We believe in a healthy, muscular, and tender understanding of our cultural heritage and our cultural obligations. These obligations naturally include loyalty to the free market.

PRESS How about cultural diversity?

MINISTER We subscribe to cultural diversity; we have faith in a flexible and vigorous exchange of views; we believe in fecundity.

PRESS And critical dissent?

MINISTER Critical dissent is acceptable—if it is left at home. My advice is—leave it at home. Keep it under the bed. With the piss pot.

He laughs.

MINISTER (*cont.*) Where it belongs.

PRESS Did you say *in* the piss pot?

MINISTER I'll put your head in the piss pot if you're not careful.

He laughs. They laugh.

MINISTER (*cont.*) Let me make myself quite clear. We need critical dissent because it keeps us on our toes. But we don't want to see it in the marketplace or on the avenues and piazzas of our great cities. We don't want to see it manifested in the houses of any of our great institutions. We are happy for it to remain at home, which means we can pop in at any time and read what is kept under the bed, discuss it with the writer, pat him on the head, shake him by his hand, give him perhaps a minor kick up the arse or in the balls, and set fire to the whole shebang. By this method we keep our society free from infection. There is of course, however, always room for confession, retraction, and redemption.

PRESS So you see your role as Minister of Culture as vital and fruitful?

MINISTER Immensely fruitful. We believe in the innate goodness of your ordinary Jack and your ordinary Jill. This is what we seek to protect. We seek to protect the essential goodness of your ordinary Jack and your ordinary Jill. We understand that as a moral obligation. We are determined to protect them from corruption and subversion with all the means at our disposal.

PRESS   Minister, thank you for your frank words.

MINISTER   It has been my pleasure. Can I say one thing more?

PRESS (*various*)   Please. Yes. Yes please. Please do. Yes!

MINISTER   Under our philosophy . . . he that is lost is found. Thank you!

Applause. The Minister waves and exits.

Blackout.

PARIS

The curtain white in folds,
She walks two steps and turns,
The curtain still, the light
Staggers in her eyes.

The lamps are golden.
Afternoon leans, silently.
She dances in my life.
The white day burns.

1975

IT IS HERE
(for A)

What sound was that?

I turn away, into the shaking room.

What was that sound that came in on the dark?
What is this maze of light it leaves us in?
What is this stance we take,
To turn away and then turn back?
What did we hear?

It was the breath we took when we first met.

Listen. It is here.

1990

JOSEPH BREARLEY 1909–1977
(Teacher of English)

Dear Joe, I'd like to walk with you
From Clapton Pond to Stamford Hill
And on,
Through Manor House to Finsbury Park,
And back,
On the dead 653 trolleybus,
To Clapton Pond,
And walk across the shadows on to Hackney Downs,
And stop by the old bandstand,
You tall in moonlight,
And the quickness in which it all happened,
And the quick shadow in which it persists.

You're gone. I'm at your side,
Walking with you from Clapton Pond to Finsbury Park,
And on, and on.

1977

MESSAGE

Jill. Fred phoned. He can't make tonight.
He said he'd call again, as soon as poss.
I said (on your behalf) OK, no sweat.
He said to tell you he was fine,
Only the crap, he said, you know, it sticks,
The crap you have to fight.
You're sometimes nothing but a walking shithouse.

I was well acquainted with the pong myself,
I told him, and I counselled calm.
Don't let the fuckers get you down,
Take the lid off the kettle a couple of minutes,
Go on the town, burn someone to death,
Find another tart, give her some hammer,
Live while you're young, until it palls,
Kick the first blind man you meet in the balls.

Anyway he'll call again.

I'll be back in time for tea.

Your loving mother.

1977

AMERICAN FOOTBALL
A reflection upon the Gulf War

Hallelujah!
It works.
We blew the shit out of them.

We blew the shit right back up their own ass
And out their fucking ears.

It works.
We blew the shit out of them.
They suffocated in their own shit!

Hallelujah.
Praise the Lord for all good things.

We blew them into fucking shit.
They are eating it.

Praise the Lord for all good things.

We blew their balls into shards of dust,
Into shards of fucking dust.

We did it.

Now I want you to come over here and kiss me
on the mouth.

August 1991

THE BOMBS

There are no more words to be said
All we have left are the bombs
Which burst out of our head
All that is left are the bombs
Which suck out the last of our blood
All we have left are the bombs
Which polish the skulls of the dead

February 2003

DEMOCRACY

There's no escape.
The big pricks are out.
They'll fuck everything in sight.
Watch your back.

March 2003

CANCER CELLS

"Cancer cells are those which have forgotten how to die."
(Nurse, Royal Marsden Hospital)

They have forgotten how to die
And so extend their killing life.

I and my tumour dearly fight.
Let's hope a double death is out.

I need to see my tumour dead
A tumour which forgets to die
But plans to murder me instead.

But I remember how to die
Though all my witnesses are dead.
But I remember what they said
Of tumours which would render them
As blind and dumb as they had been
Before the birth of that disease
Which brought the tumour into play.

The black cells will dry up and die
Or sing with joy and have their way.
They breed so quietly night and day,
You never know, they never say.

March 2002

DEATH MAY BE AGEING

Death may be ageing
But he still has clout

But death disarms you
With his limpid light

And he's so crafty
That you don't know at all

Where he awaits you
To seduce your will
And to strip you naked
As you dress to kill

But death permits you
To arrange your hours

While he sucks the honey
From your lovely flowers

April 2005

DEATH

(Births and Deaths Registration Act 1953)

Where was the dead body found?
Who found the dead body?
Was the dead body dead when found?
How was the dead body found?

Who was the dead body?

Who was the father or daughter or brother
Or uncle or sister or mother or son
Of the dead and abandoned body?

Was the body dead when abandoned?
Was the body abandoned?
By whom had it been abandoned?

Was the dead body naked or dressed for a journey?

What made you declare the dead body dead?
Did you declare the dead body dead?
How well did you know the dead body?
How did you know the dead body was dead?

Did you wash the dead body
Did you close both its eyes
Did you bury the body
Did you leave it abandoned
Did you kiss the dead body

1997